Whiteness at the End of the World

RECENT TITLES

Fareed Ben-Youssef, *No Jurisdiction*

Tony Tracy, *White Cottage, White House*

Tom Conley, *Action, Action, Action*

Lindsay Coleman and Roberto Schaefer, editors, *The Cinematographer's Voice*

Nolwenn Mingant, *Hollywood Films in North Africa and the Middle East*

†Charles Warren, edited by William Rothman and Joshua Schulze, *Writ on Water*

Jason Sperb, *The Hard Sell of Paradise*

William Rothman, *The Holiday in His Eye*

Brendan Hennessey, *Luchino Visconti and the Alchemy of Adaptation*

Alexander Sergeant, *Encountering the Impossible*

Erica Stein, *Seeing Symphonically*

George Toles, *Curtains of Light*

Neil Badmington, *Perpetual Movement*

Merrill Schleier, editor, *Race and the Suburbs in American Film*

Matthew Leggatt, editor, *Was It Yesterday?*

Homer B. Pettey, editor, *Mind Reeling*

Alexia Kannas, *Giallo!*

Bill Krohn, *Letters from Hollywood*

Alex Clayton, *Funny How?*

Niels Niessen, *Miraculous Realism*

A complete listing of books in this series can be found online at www.sunypress.edu

Whiteness at the End of the World

Race in Post-Apocalyptic Cinema

David Venditto

Published by State University of New York Press, Albany

Printed in the United States of America

For information, contact State University of New York Press, Albany, NY
www.sunypress.edu

Library of Congress Cataloging-in-Publication Data

Name: Venditto, David, 1978– author.
Title: Whiteness at the end of the world : race in post-apocalyptic cinema / David Venditto.
Description: Albany : State University of New York Press, [2022] | Series: SUNY series, horizons of cinema | Includes bibliographical references and index.
Identifiers: LCCN 2022005649 | ISBN 9781438489438 (hardcover : alk. paper) | ISBN 9781438489452 (ebook)
Subjects: LCSH: Apocalyptic films—History and criticism. | White people in motion pictures. | Race in motion pictures. | Race relations in motion pictures. | Motion pictures—Social aspects—United States—History—21st century. | Motion pictures—Political aspects—United States—History—21st century. | Motion pictures—United States—History—21st century.
Classification: LCC PN1995.9.A64 V43 2022 | DDC 791.43/615—dc23
LC record available at https://lccn.loc.gov/2022005649

10 9 8 7 6 5 4 3 2 1

For Arya, my little lady;
and for Tenn, my fuzzy orange spirit animal

Contents

Introduction

> For reasons long forgotten two mighty warrior tribes went to war and touched off a blaze which engulfed them all. Without fuel they were nothing. They'd built a house of straw. The thundering machines sputtered and stopped. Their leaders talked and talked and talked, but nothing could stem the avalanche. Their world crumbled. Cities exploded—a whirlwind of looting, a firestorm of fear.
>
> —*The Road Warrior*

As far removed as we are from the beginning of apocalyptic myths, we still cling to these same myths, as evidenced in innumerable films and books containing apocalyptic themes. As Susan Sontag once noted in "The Imagination of Disaster," many sci-fi films seem preoccupied with depicting mass destruction, becoming apocalyptic or postapocalyptic in nature. In fact, the majority of the general public still believes in these myths, as seen in a survey of religious beliefs done in 1996, in which 42 percent of the American respondents answered in the affirmative when asked if "the world will end in a battle in Armageddon between Jesus and the Antichrist" (Boyer 315). Perhaps a little less surprising is the large number of Southern Baptist Convention ministers that subscribe to these end-time beliefs, at 63 percent (Boyer 315). With millions upon millions of people still believing, these myths have an incredible staying power. But why? Many theorists have speculated about what makes these myths endure, even though there's hardly any consensus—just as there are a multitude of ways to define "apocalypse."

Apocalyptic texts, despite religious themes that followers often cling to, have deep political meaning, revealing certain aspects of a respective society's social groups and their relation to one another. It is not just Christian myths that function this way, but virtually all end-time myths in all cultures throughout history.[1] However, the texts need to be viewed in their historical context in order to produce an exegesis that identifies the political forces at work and provides an explanation for their purpose in a given society. Viewed historically, apocalyptic texts are often used by oppressed groups as a response to their own oppression, in an attempt to comfort the adherents and possibly even restructure a hierarchy supporting the subjugation of certain groups. Apocalyptic myths today, however, are used by the dominant culture, as a way of reestablishing dominance in an era of increasing minority rights.

What Is the Apocalypse?

The term *eschatology* is often used to describe apocalypticism, though the two terms are actually distinct. Eschatology is defined by Bernard McGinn as "any form of belief about the nature of history that interprets historical process in the light of final events." Apocalyptic eschatology refers to a specific pattern in end-time beliefs, a pattern that usually follows a "crisis-judgment-reward" pattern that is revealed in a sacred book like the Bible (McGinn 13). Thus, the apocalypse refers to a pattern and not simply the mass destruction of society, which is but one part of the overarching template. Of the "crisis-judgment-reward" facets of apocalypse, the "crisis" is often the main focus in popular culture, evidenced in both secular and religious works of fiction.

After the "crisis," judgment comes and brings even more death, as the evil forces are finally extirpated. In most Christian myths, after a large portion of humanity has been eradicated, the Messiah returns to Earth. In addition, most of these myths reserve salvation for only a select few, and thus "planetary cataclysm only ever has a positive net value from the point of view of the small minority who are saved. And

1. Some Hindu texts like the *Bhagavata Purana*, for example, describe the disintegration of the caste system in the Age of Kali as a harbinger of the end times.

salvation, moreover, always comes at a price, that price often involving terror and destruction" (McGinn 10). In many secular versions of the apocalypse, "crisis" and "judgment" are conflated without any explicit spiritual judgment raining down from God and Christ. Visited upon the world are a variety of afflictions and disasters, from nuclear fallout to virulent diseases that affect most of the populace. After the "terror and destruction" have subsided, a reward is experienced by the handful of people that emerge unscathed, often coming in the form of a revelation. In religious depictions of the end times, Christ seems to reward the faithful with an effulgent new kingdom. In the more secular renderings, which are the focus of this book, the reward comes in the form of a changed understanding about the surrounding world.

A changed perspective is, of course, understood to be part of the "revelation," which is an integral part of any apocalyptic myth. James Berger explains that

> apocalypse thus, finally, has an interpretive, explanatory function, which is, of course, its etymological sense: as revelation, unveiling, uncovering. The apocalyptic event, in order to be properly apocalyptic, must in its destructive moment clarify and illuminate the true nature of what has been brought to an end. (Berger 5)

Postapocalyptic media often has a revelation that functions in the sense that Berger outlines. For instance, the moment in *Planet of the Apes* (1968) when the remnants of the Statue of Liberty come into view is a succinct encapsulation of a revelation that occurs in a "destructive moment"—so called because it is unclear until that very moment that the monuments of mankind's reign over the Earth had been largely wiped out. The Statue of Liberty, as an object, becomes an emblem for the whole of the dominant culture and the revelation is, beyond the obvious, that society was perhaps never quite as evolved as we thought.

Though films like *Planet of the Apes* are Anglocentric, the myths embodied in the films parallel those found across continents and time periods. There is a great similarity in these myths, including a belief in history as a "divinely predetermined totality." Furthermore, the present day is viewed in a negative light, while hope is held for a coming judgment to punish the wicked and reward the faithful. The reward can be a literal, physical reward, or "other-worldly, individual or collective, temporary or definitive, or a combination of some or all of these elements" (McGinn

10). As McGinn points out, the "reward" can take many forms, comprising a revelation about the world or an actual concrete remuneration.

The reward for believers in Christian myths is sometimes a reshaping of society to allow disenfranchised classes a voice and a way to shape the hierarchies that define human relations. In the world of the myths themselves, the faithful are rewarded with a world without the pain that has characterized their lives. The Bible explicitly promotes the idea that the poor and destitute are to be lifted up, while the rich and powerful are brought down. Much has been written about the New Testament's attitudes toward the rich and powerful. Luke 18:25 notes that "it is easier for a camel to go through the eye of a needle than for a rich person to enter the kingdom of God." Furthermore, Christ is quoted as saying, "Blessed are you who are poor, for yours is the kingdom of God. . . . Blessed are you who are hungry now, for you shall be satisfied. . . . Blessed are you who weep now, for you shall laugh" (Luke 6:20–21). The Gospel of James uses even stronger language, warning:

> You rich, weep and howl for the miseries that are coming upon you. Your riches have rotted and your garments are moth-eaten. Your gold and silver have corroded, and their corrosion will be evidence against you and will eat your flesh like fire. You have laid up treasure in the last days. Behold, the wages of the laborers who mowed your fields, which you kept back by fraud, are crying out against you, and the cries of the harvesters have reached the ears of the Lord of hosts. You have lived on the earth in luxury and in self-indulgence. You have fattened your hearts in a day of slaughter. (James 5:1–6)

While these texts are not explicitly apocalyptic, they *do* couch these scenarios in apocalyptic terms, warning of an end-time scenario where power and wealth evaporate, and God finally creates a dramatic reversal for the "laborers," upon whose backs the victories of the dominant culture have been built. This suggests a complete alteration of the hegemonic system, allowing power to be reappropriated by those who have been previously beholden to the desires of a dominant culture often controlled by a select few. Beyond the actual text, the people actually reading these myths may be given hope that their lack of power will not be eternal—that those at the bottom will soon rise as God's chosen people. Fuller, quoting David Hellholm, notes that "apocalyptic thought is 'intended for a group in crisis with the purpose of exhortation and/or consolation by means of divine authority.' " This "divine authority" edifies the faithful, who are asked to view history in a larger, almost transcendental context, where ultimately the poor and meek inherit the Earth. In this "mythic context," "a victorious outcome is assured" (Fuller 21).

The Apocalyptic Genre

Apocalyptic media, including the films and books discussed in this book, use myths that were part of the apocalyptic genre from its inception. As a genre, apocalyptic writings include mostly early Jewish and Christian texts, the earliest being the Astronomical Book, part of the Book of Enoch, dated to the late third or early second century BCE. Among contemporary scholars, the list of apocalyptic works usually includes the Christian Book of Revelation, and several Jewish works: Daniel, 1 Enoch, 4 Ezra, and 2 Baruch (J. Collins 3). These texts are generally agreed upon as demonstrating the characteristics of the genre, though other works are sometimes included (parts of the Synoptic Gospels, for instance). In keeping with the original Greek meaning of the word, this type of literature involves a prophet's encounter with an otherworldly intermediary that reveals "a transcendent reality which is both temporal, insofar as it envisages eschatological salvation, and spatial, insofar as it involves another, supernatural world" (A. Collins 62). Apocalyptic texts have certain generally consistent characteristics. Specifically, they contain a Last Judgment and the ultimate destruction of the world, in addition to astrophysical marvels, a heavenly temple, and the punishment of the wicked as the faithful are rewarded. The Book of Daniel was originally assumed to be the oldest example of apocalyptic literature, but several fragments of the Dead Sea Scrolls were published in the 1970s, containing original Aramaic manuscripts of 1 Enoch. Himmelfarb notes that "the manuscripts from the Scrolls make it clear that two of the apocalypses included in 1 Enoch, the Astronomical Book (1 Enoch 72–82) and the Book of the Watchers (1 Enoch 1–36), pre-date Daniel" (2).

These Jewish and Christian apocalypses can be broken down into categories based on the nature of the revelation. There were those texts that involve a revelatory vision and those that take the prophet on a mystical journey (A. Collins 62). Within the "revelatory vision" category, Jacob's Ladder contains a review of history, while Revelation, the Apocalypse of St. John the Theologian, the Apocalypse of Peter, the Shepherd of Hermas, and the Testament of the Lord contain visions of cosmic destruction. Of these, only Revelation and the Apocalypse of St. John the Theologian illustrate any kind of cosmic renewal after the destruction of the world. Within the category of apocalyptic texts that contain an "otherworldly journey," some include images of cosmic destruction, including the Ascension of Isaiah, the Apocalypse of Esdras, and the Apocalypse or Vision of the Virgin Mary. Only one mystical journey shows both the destruction of the world and its renewal: the Apocalypse of Paul (J. Collins 22–23).

Beyond Christian and Jewish texts,[2] there are Greek and Latin texts that display some characteristics of the genre, from the first three centuries of the Roman Empire (founded in 27 BCE). These texts were clearly not as old as 1 Enoch, but they were contemporary to several Christian apocalyptic works and "like their Jewish and Christian counterparts, these texts are narratives of alleged revelatory experiences which disclose a transcendent world and proclaim eschatological doctrine" (Attridge 159). The Hermetica were Egyptian-Greek texts written in the second and third centuries CE. Of these, several display characteristics of the genre, including the Poimandres, which details the vision of an unnamed prophet who is guided in his desire to understand the world by Poinmandres, his mystic guide. The prophet is shown "the process of creation . . . accompanied by an explanation of the vision by Poimandres." After a discussion of "creation and [the] nature of man," there is an "eschatological section which expresses the ultimate aim of Hermetic gnosis as the divinization of the essential element in the human soul." The text concludes with an exhortation for mankind to awaken from metaphorical dormancy (Attridge 161). In addition to Egyptian-Greek works like Poimandres, there are Persian texts that display characteristics of the Christian and Jewish apocalyptic works, but it has been very difficult to date these. These scriptures were transcribed oral accounts written somewhere between 250 BCE and 250 CE, yet were not compiled until 221–642

2. The Sibylline Oracles also had a massive influence on Christian apocalyptic imagery. The Sibylline Oracles, written in Greek hexameters, comprise fourteen books, the fourth of which contains many apocalyptic themes and images. Preserved at Rome, the Sibyllines were supposedly the inspired words of prophetesses, originating in Asia Minor's Greek colonies between the second and sixth century CE (McGinn 19). Norman Cohn further notes that "indeed save for the Bible and the works of the Fathers they were probably the most influential writings known to medieval Europe. They often dictated the pronouncements of dominant figures in the Church" (Cohn 33).

CE during the Sasanian Empire. Some of the writings supposedly came from Zarathustra himself, while others can't be accurately dated (J. Collins 207). The most important collection of these Persian religious texts is the Avesta, which does not itself directly discuss the end of the world. Apocalyptic imagery only explicitly appears in the Zand, an exegetical commentary on the Avesta. Zands were commentaries, paraphrases, and glosses that sometimes accompanied the actual texts in the Avesta. The Zand, so called because it is the only one to survive intact, illustrates elements of the apocalyptic genre. Zarathustra is granted a vision by Ahura Mazda (the supreme God of the Persians), and sees a tree with four branches, each representing four kingdoms, the fourth being the Greeks. The fourth kingdom, according to the vision, will come "when thy tenth century will be at an end." Zarathustra asks about the signs of the end in the tenth century BCE and is told by Ahura Mazda to expect:

> A long series of upheavals and disturbances, both political and cosmic. Chapters 7–9 prophesy what will happen "when the Zarathustian millenium will end and Aûsîtar's will begin" (8^8). Then "near the end of the millenium PêsyÔtan son of Vistâsp will appear" as a savior figure who will destroy the divs. The millennium of Aûsîtarmâh follows, when men will not even die because they "will be so versed in medicine" (9:12). Then at the end of this millennium "Sôsîyôs will make the creatures pure again and resurrection and the final most material existence will occur" (9:23). (J. Collins 209)

The influence of this text on the images in Revelation is apparent, illustrating the profound influence of Zoroastrianism on religions in that part of the world.

Contemporary Apocalypticism

Contemporary American apocalyptic myths can be broken into two categories: those that show the apocalyptic event and those that begin postapocalypse and do not flash back to significant portrayals of the event. The majority of apocalyptic films and books do not show the apocalyptic event, and if they do, it's shown merely in passing. *The Road Warrior*, for example, mentions a nuclear war in the first few moments of the film, but this is merely a few seconds in a ninety-five-minute film. Films that take place in a world *after* the apocalypse include *Children of Men* (2006), *The Book of Eli* (2010), all of the *Mad Max* films, *The Road* (2009), *Waterworld* (1995), *WALL-E* (2008), *The Quiet Earth* (1985), *Stalker* (1979), *Escape from New York* (1981), *The Planet of the Apes* (1968), and *Oblivion* (2013). In *Children of Men*, the end of the world was precipitated by an infertility crisis that seemed to culminate in a calamitous war between countries, from which only England survived relatively unscathed. Others of these films make no mention of the apocalyptic event at all, like *The Book of Eli*.

Films that actually show the apocalyptic event include *Invasion of the Body Snatchers* (1956), *12 Monkeys* (1995), *Melancholia* (2011), *Dr. Strangelove* (1964), *The Day after Tomorrow* (2004), and *2012* (2009). These films have plots that mainly revolve around the events leading up to the annihilation of the world, and attempts to thwart this destruction. Parts of the apocalyptic event(s) are shown in all of these films, but the only one to truly end with complete obliteration is *Melancholia*; the final image of the film depicts a planet crashing into the Earth. No one is saved, and the screen goes black after the Earth is shattered into pieces. All of the other postapocalyptic films mentioned show parts of the world that have managed to survive catastrophe.

Books that take place in a world *after* the apocalypse include *The Handmaid's Tale*, *Riddley Walker*, *I Am Legend*, *1984*, *The Postman*, *Brave New World*, *The Chrysalids*, and *Fahrenheit 451*. The destructive events vary from virulent epidemics to nuclear war, and in all cases there is some push or a desire to revert back to the world before the apocalypse. The protagonist in *The Postman*, for instance, is quite literally a symbol of the fallen world. What he symbolizes brings hope to the people he encounters, with the promise of civilization embodied in his uniform and in the notion of an organized communication system via the USPS. Not all of these books present the preapocalyptic world as desirable, however. Some of these touch on our longing for this world, while also highlighting its capacity for destruction and oppression of minorities. *Riddley Walker*, for instance, shows a primitive postapocalyptic world on the brink of discovering gunpowder, while illuminating the cataclysmic potential of this discovery. *Riddley Walker*, the main character, realizes this and tries to thwart the attempts at creating a substance that will likely be the foundation for yet another apocalyptic event.

Books that actually show the apocalyptic event or deal with the events leading up to it include *Oryx and Crake*, *On the Beach*, *A Canticle for Leibowitz*, *The War of the Worlds*, *Lucifer's Hammer*, *Alas, Babylon*, and *The Stand*. Of these, only *On the Beach* never actually shows the world after the worldwide catastrophe: in this case a radiation cloud that envelops the whole planet—the aftermath of nuclear war. *On the Beach* romanticizes the world before the apocalypse, focusing on mundane day-to-day relationships with others. The author seems to be using the threat of apocalypse to call attention to things we perhaps take for granted. The nuclear family and the institution of marriage are important in the novel; it's clearly meant to be tragic that these things will inevitably be lost. *Oryx and Crake* and *A Canticle for Leibowitz* are more critical of society's institutions, implying that the flaws in human society are the problem, *not* the answer to the apocalyptic tragedy.

None of these films and books show the better, more perfect world described in the Bible. Revelation describes a beautiful, amazing world during the thousand-year reign of Christ, before Satan is thrown into the Lake of Fire and devout followers of Christ are brought to heaven. In the majority of contemporary apocalyptic media, the world after the cataclysm is worse—an empty wasteland. It's a place filled with possibility and hope in most cases, but it's hardly the place of splendor and incandescence that Revelation outlines in detail. The focus in contemporary media is either on stopping the apocalypse or, in the case of those narratives that begin after the apocalypse, on bringing back the civilizations and institutions of the old world. In this way, modern apocalyptic media focuses on moving to the world of the past, instead of the perfect future world in the Bible. In addition, modern myths have no explicit revelation, wherein the protagonist learns something pivotal about human history or man's relation to the cosmos. Instead, we see the idealization of human civilization before the apocalypse, the capitalist world of white male hegemony that must be reestablished to bring the world back from the brink. God can't save us, but the education, government, and marriage institutions of the preapocalyptic world can.

History and Origins of the Christian Myths

The main apocalyptic texts in the Bible are found in Daniel and, of course, Revelation. Most scholars believe that both books were heavily influenced by events happening at the time in which they were written. Daniel, for instance, was influenced by the tyrannical reign of Antiochus IV, whose policies prohibited a number of Jewish practices. At the time of its inception, in the second century BCE, the Jews had been involved in an extended conflict with the king of Syria, Antiochus IV. The trouble began when, in order to fund a war with Egypt, Antiochus IV had plundered the temple in Jerusalem, and gave one of his own appointed priests authority over the temple. This incited a number of riots among the Jews, though Antiochus IV's punishment for their insubordination went well beyond just plundering their temple. Issuing a number of edicts, he launched an assault on many Jewish practices, forbidding worship on the Sabbath and circumcision. In addition, the sacrifice of lambs, normally done on their own Jewish shrines, was to be replaced with the sacrifice of pigs on the non-Jewish shrines built throughout Judea. Within the context of all these troubling events, the author of Daniel is believed to have written this highly influential apocalyptic text, inspiring followers to join in a literal and spiritual battle with the Antichrist. At the time, Antiochus IV filled the role of Antichrist and inspired a powerful opposition among the Jewish community, though the text would later become of great importance to Christians, even to this day (Fuller 22). Scholars believe now that he is the "ten headed beast" in Daniel, though since his reign, many others have been substituted for Antiochus IV. Indeed, for many centuries, the Papacy was thought to be linked to the "ten headed beast," as the Pope himself occupied the role of "Antichrist." In the twentieth century, many others have claimed the dubious distinction of being the Antichrist, including Henry Kissinger, Communists, and workers' unions. In essence, the goal is to create "religious commitment and strident opposition" to perceived threats to the status quo.

The other great Christian apocalypse—dated toward the end of the first century CE—is Revelation, written by someone named "John," about whom is known very little, only that he is not the same author of the "Gospel of John" or the "Epistles of John." Revelation is believed to reference Nero, whose Antichristian policies marked him as a major enemy to Christians everywhere. Nero placed the blame for the Great Fire of Rome in 64 CE on Christians to deflect blame from himself, as many came to believe that he had started the conflagration. Roman historian Tacitus noted that to absolve himself from blame, "Nero falsely blamed the people, detested for their abominable crimes, who were called Christians by the populace and inflicted exquisite tortures on them" (Green 50). In the aftermath of Nero's scapegoating of Christians, they were crucified, while "the name of Christian was vilified, associated with secret abominations, and non-Christian Jews were more likely than ever to distance themselves from a hated and alien group" (Green 52). It's no wonder that John of Patmos cast him as a beast in Revelation then, as Nero made quite a spectacle of persecuting Christians at the time. The beast in Revelation, inspired by Nero and later used to represent other enemies of Christianity, is often conflated with the beast in Daniel to create the figure of the Antichrist.

Since the writing of these books, many events transpired to further alter the myths and the fervor with which they are followed; consequently, there have been varying degrees of interest in the Christian apocalypse over the years. The Crusades increased apocalyptic speculation, as did certain religious figures, such as Joachim of Fiore. The Christian world became mired in apocalyptic interest after the Muslim occupation of Jerusalem and when Christian pilgrims began to be oppressed and mistreated in the eleventh century. Jerusalem, previously controlled by the Egyptian Fatimids, passed into the hands of the Seljuk Turks—a genuine and nefarious threat to Byzantium. This only increased the Christian fascination with the end of the world. This, of course, all became most salient during the first Crusade, from 1095 to 1099. The purpose of the Crusade, as decreed by Pope Urban II, was to reclaim the Holy Land. The rhetoric associated with the Crusades was rife with apocalyptic imagery "interpreting the protection, or recovery, of Jerusalem from the Muslims as essential to the fulfillment of the Bible's end-time prophecies." Joachim of Fiore, a Calabrian monk known as a "medieval prophecy expositor" in the twelfth century, "was much influenced by . . . Muslim leader and warrior Saladin, who recaptured Jerusalem in 1187." Using the Book of Revelation, Joachim asserted that the fourth head of the seven-headed dragon, outlined within chapters 12 and 17, represented Muhammad. The Muslim leader Saladin was presented as the sixth head of the dragon, directly adjacent to the head of the Antichrist (Boyer 320). In the case of Revelation, apocalyptic imagery was used to vilify perceived threats and create a situation in which good must triumph over evil. The enemy becomes not simply another country or culture; the enemy is an agent of evil that must be destroyed at any cost. The lower classes, in a "Peoples' Crusade" with more than three hundred thousand participants, were caught up in the religious, apocalyptic fanaticism purveyed by the likes of Walter the Penniless and Peter the Hermit (a prominent priest from Amiens), and sought to extirpate the evil army of Muslims occupying the Holy Land. In this way, the lower classes became involved because of apocalyptic rhetoric and ideologies, and without proper training and equipment they were ultimately massacred by the Turks (Child et al. 16). While the nobility was also very deeply religious, illustrating how Christianity occupied a position of power at the time, the vast majority of Christians at the time were oppressed in a feudal system that perpetuated harsh living conditions and poor life expectancy. In addition, many of their church leaders found that these apocalyptic myths contained "millenarian expectations that 'respectable' members of the clergy must have found distasteful or dangerous in their more extreme manifestations" (Whalen 64). Thus, these myths were not being directly promoted by the people at the top of the hierarchy; they were predominantly used by the oppressed. Apocalyptic rhetoric clearly had an affirmative effect on these impoverished crusaders, who hoped the retaking of Jerusalem would foment the end times, which would ultimately end in rewards for the destitute faithful.

Current apocalyptic myths bear only some semblance of their ancient antecedents. The end of the world is sometimes presented as a vision or otherworldly journey, but more often the audience arrives *after* the apocalypse, seeing the aftermath of a cataclysmic event. Unlike older apocalyptic myths, there is no overt judgment and reward. In addition, the world after the apocalypse is still the world of human inhabitants; there are no angels and religious figures that remake the world into an ethereal paradise. On the contrary, the world is barren and mostly lifeless, and the protagonist is often a catalyst for bringing back the preapocalyptic world, resurrecting institutions like government, marriage, and education. The postapocalyptic world does not mirror the beauty of God's kingdom as it might in traditional Christian myths but instead most closely resembles the American frontier. In adapting the Christian and Jewish myths, American culture has molded the imagery to mimic something uniquely American, a frontier myth wherein an empty world becomes a place of possibility and renewal—a place where raw individuality claims an uncultivated space in the name of civilization. Beyond frontier mythology, there is, of course, a true Christian influence on American culture, as Oldring notes:

> In contemporary America, apocalypse is part of a spectrum of religious beliefs ingrained into the American Way of life. Commercial America has resurrected the apocalypse myth as spectacle commodity. Apocalyptic media today reflect current values of the American hegemon in globalization, and are portrayed as particularly real in order to be effective. (Oldring 8)

The use of religion "by those seeking to maintain White, male, heteronormative hegemony" has a long history in the United States, one that will be discussed more fully in the first chapter (Oldring 11). In essence, religious myths can be used to disseminate patriarchal ideologies through the media. Apocalyptic myths also connect with the American public when they are "portrayed as particularly real"—when the disaster shown is something distinctly possible: nuclear fallout, global warming, and overpopulation, for instance. The forces behind the adaptation of apocalyptic myths in American society are the corporations and institutions that can maintain power by the proliferation of these myths. These myths are "mediums for hegemony . . . their highest concern is to suppress individual experiences by supplanting them with archetypes of behavior and systems of meaning-making derived from and maintained in civil society" (Oldring 9–10). The capitalist system has assimilated all institutions, bringing religion under its control—yet another instrument to maintain power.

The Science Fiction Genre

Contemporary apocalyptic media is often considered a subgenre of science fiction. There have been a number of different definitions of science fiction as a genre, making it difficult to write a singular one. Margaret Atwood defines science fiction as "fiction in which things happen that are not possible today—that depend, for instance, on advanced space travel, time travel, the discovery of green monsters on other planets or galaxies, or that contain various technologies we have not yet developed" (Atwood 92). However, simply focusing on iconography like spaceships and time machines doesn't adequately define sci-fi, since these objects and devices can be used in other genres. Spaceships, for instance, could be used in a comedy, or a time machine could find its way into a detective story. A story in which "things happen that are not possible today" could describe any genre. By that definition, *Hot Tub Time Machine* (2010) would be categorized as science fiction. A more apt definition of sci-fi can be found when Judith Merril, in 1966, wrote that the objective of sci-fi was "to explore, to discover, to *learn* . . . something about the nature of the universe, of man, or 'reality' ":

> [The genre uses] the traditional "scientific method" (observation, hypothesis, experiment) to examine some postulated approximation of reality, by introducing a given set of changes—imaginary or inventive—into the common background of "known facts," creating an environment in which the responses and perceptions of the characters will reveal something about the inventions, the characters, or both. (Merril 27)

Science fiction takes existing science and inventions and extrapolates these to create a revelatory future, which, as Merril notes, "reveal[s] something about the inventions, the characters, or both." By examining broad questions "about the nature of the universe, or man, or 'reality,'" sci-fi has philosophical concerns that aren't explicitly a part of other genres. Vivian Sobchack, in comparing sci-fi to horror films, notes that "the horror film is primarily concerned with the individual in conflict with society or with some extension of himself, the SF film with society and its institutions in conflict with each other or with some alien other" (Sobchack 29–30). For this reason, Sobchack argues, horror films often take place in small towns or an old castle, while sci-fi films involve large cities or the entire planet. The difference between sci-fi and other genres is often a matter of scale; sci-fi goes beyond individual struggles to explore conflicts that affect the entire planet or universe. A film like *The Day the Earth Stood Still* (1951), for instance, has much larger stakes than a film like *A Nightmare on Elm Street* (1984). The latter focuses on a group of teenagers in one suburban town, while the former deals with the fate of the planet. This difference in scale is what separates a film like *Gravity* (2013) from *Moon* (2009). *Gravity* would not qualify as sci-fi since the focus is on Sandra Bullock's emotional pain and eventual catharsis. *Moon*, however, deals with broader philosophical issues about the nature of identity and the moral quandaries associated with cloning. Sobchack's definition of sci-fi parallels James Gunn's, as he writes that "it usually involves matters whose importance is greater than the individual or the community; often civilization or the race itself is in danger" (6).

Another key feature of science fiction is the explicit and overt use of defamiliarization, something implied when Judith Merril writes that sci-fi "examine[s] some postulated approximation of reality, by introducing a given set of changes—imaginary or inventive—into the common background of 'known facts'" (27). Sci-fi takes a familiar object or idea and changes it in such a way that it becomes foreign and difficult to fully comprehend. Defamiliarization, as it pertains to art, is a way to break up our unconscious ways of perceiving the world—a way to make us examine things that would normally dissolve in the periphery of our experiences. The problem, according to Viktor Shklovsky, is that "perception becomes habitual, it becomes automatic. Thus, for example, all of our habits retreat into the area of the unconscious automatic." The way art functions is to make "an object 'unfamiliar,' to make forms difficult, to increase the difficulty and length of perception because the process of perception is an aesthetic end in itself and must be prolonged" (Shklovsky 778). This is achieved in a variety of ways, each medium having its own readily available tools. The iconography of Westerns, for instance, is easily recognizable—rugged terrain surrounding a small frontier town with a train passing through. Science fiction, on the other hand, uses the iconography of other genres, with subtle differences. For instance, it is possible to have a space Western, and indeed many of those exist, for example *Outland* (1981) and *Serenity* (2005). However, each familiar icon is used in a way that renders it slightly off-kilter. The rocky terrain of the American Southwest is replaced by unexplored planets—a frontier to be explored. The reluctant hero, so common in Westerns like *Shane* (1953), is still present. However, instead of being a former gunslinger in bars with desperadoes, someone like Han Solo spends time in a cantina with an assortment of alien races. For science fiction, then, defamiliarization is key, as creatures enhanced by radiation and aliens are a combination of familiar and unusual body structures and features. Some of the defamiliarization is simply part of the medium of film, as film allows for an altered perception of the world around us via close-ups, dissolves, and other techniques. Walter Benjamin, of the cinema, writes:

> By focusing on hidden details of familiar objects, by exploring commonplace milieus under the ingenious guidance of the camera, the film . . . extends our comprehension of the necessities which rule our lives; it reveals entirely new structural formations of the subject. (1105)

Defamiliarization is also more generally an inherent part of the way objects are depicted within the diegetic world of film. Our gaze is often held because of the way it is shown, not necessarily because of what it is. There is a potential to create practically limitless new connotations, all contingent on things like context and film techniques like close-ups, lighting, and even the way the object is constructed. Science fiction seems particularly dependent on defamiliarization in the sense that unknown objects and alien creatures often possess uncanny similarities with something the audience actually recognizes. Godzilla does call to mind pet lizards; spaceships look an awful lot like hubcaps (and sometimes are); the androids in *Blade Runner* (1982) appear to be human. Fredric Jameson notes that the purpose of "SF . . . [is] not to give us 'images' of the future . . . but rather to defamiliarize and restructure our experience of our own *present*, and to do so in specific ways distinct from all other forms of defamiliarization" (216). The subgenre of postapocalyptic films seems especially reliant on defamiliarization, since it's predicated on the assumption that people will compare this "post" world with the one before it, looking for changes in familiar places and things. *The Road Warrior* (1981), for instance, illustrates the extreme, ultimate conclusion to a very familiar issue—a scarcity of fuel. A film like *Planet of the Apes* (1968) depends on such comparisons to achieve the dramatic realization at the end—that we were indeed on Earth all along.

Postapocalyptic film can be categorized as a subgenre of science fiction—including its large-scale events and focus on defamiliarization—displaying many of the same characteristics, including the large scale in which the events take place and the heavy focus on defamiliarization. In addition, sci-fi often uses Christian symbols and ideas, and so the use of the apocalypse in sci-fi film is part of a pattern. Robert Torry writes that "to be at all familiar with science fiction cinema is to observe how commonly the genre rehearses traditional religious themes and motifs," using "what is perhaps the most common religious motif in science fiction film: that of apocalypse" (7). The use of religious symbols, Torry argues, is seen throughout sci-fi film, from E.T. as a Christ figure to the Christ-like alien in *Starman* (1984) (7). The use of the Judeo-Christian apocalypse in sci-fi film is often tied to events transpiring at the time of the film's production. Some of the more obvious examples of this are films produced in the wake of the atomic bomb. After the demonstrations of the destructive power of the bomb in 1944, "Science fiction films quite often deplored the world threatening capacities unleashed by modern science" (Torry 7). In the 1950s, many of the monsters in the ubiquitous "creature features" were the result of atomic radiation that caused horrible mutations: the ants in *Them!* (1954), for instance. Similarly, the 1954 version of *Godzilla* is believed by film scholars to depict either the physical manifestation of the nuclear bombs dropped on Hiroshima and Nagasaki, or retribution for nuclear proliferation.[3] Since then, films have depicted many other sources of apocalyptic destruction, touching on both environmental issues and advances in computer technology.

3. For instance, Jason Jones, writing in *The Atomic Bomb in Japanese Cinema*, notes that "Godzilla's presence serv[es] as punishment against human transgression in the form of testing and proliferation of nuclear weapons" (36). See Jason Jones, "Japan Removed: Godzilla Adaptations and Erasure of the Politics of Nuclear Experience," *The Atomic Bomb in Japanese Cinema: Critical Essays*, edited by Matthew Edwards (Jefferson, NC: McFarland, 2015), 34–54.

The American Frontier and Apocalypticism

The similarities between frontier and apocalyptic myths are striking. They are, first of all, visually quite similar, and "frontier ideology, which has been a part of American world-views since colonization, has found a fertile ground for dissemination in apocalyptic cinema. Most of us recognize the frontier in the image of the Wild West." The visual images of apocalyptic films—an untamed, wide-open expanse—"promise . . . *rebirth* and *renewal*, the chance to start over, and to do things right" (Oldring 11). The frontier myths and those of the apocalypse provide a new beginning, free from a troubled history of oppressing native peoples, in essence rewriting America. America was treated as though it were a blank slate in the frontier myths, despite the Native Americans that had been living on the land long before American settlers. Contemporary history makes it clear that the American West was fraught with conflict between white settlers and indigenous peoples, often because the settlers wished to take land from the native inhabitants.[4] Similarly the contemporary apocalyptic myths wipe out everything, allowing for the white male to emerge from the rubble and rebuild civilization, free from the hindrance of a growing minority population. All of the dominant culture's symbols of oppression "such as the West's long history of oppression, slavery, and colonialism, and the general malaise of rigid socioeconomic class divisions are simply erased." Large-scale catastrophes create a blank slate, as the West is freed from "social burdens and responsibilities." Social hierarchies are "symbolically exalted," and restored to the level of prominence they had before the apocalypse. This ensures the continuation of a "class based society . . . by disseminating the frontier myth without requiring the ruling class to relinquish any real power" (Oldring 15–16). Beyond erasing a troubled past, the apocalypse allows the dominant white male to create physical space in a world that has none; the frontier had closed long ago, and the world had been not only completely inhabited but overpopulated. There is nothing left to colonize and dominate, but the apocalypse wipes the land clean, as "unpopulated space can only be achieved by destroying what already exists beyond memory or reparation. . . . An apocalypse equates to agentless global destruction, which provides a guilt-free void

4. Between 1850 and 1890, there were 21,586 casualties in the Indian Wars, 14,990 (69 percent) of which were Native Americans (Michno 353). See Gregory Michno, *Encyclopedia of Indian Wars: Western Battles and Skirmishes, 1850–1890* (Missoula: Mountain Press, 2003).

enabling ideological expansion anywhere" (Oldring 12). The world of *The Road Warrior* (1981), for instance, is mostly an empty void, but this creates an opportunity for Max, the white male, to have a fresh start, as he makes the decision to help the virtuous settlers clad in white. His troubled past haunts him, but the postapocalyptic landscape allows for renewal and redemption; he can help guide the "good guys" to safety and be an important catalyst for the rebirth of order and stability.

The Purpose of These Myths

The fact that these myths still endure speaks to their ability to adapt and take on various other texts as influences, in addition to being pliable enough to be applied to whatever enemy is believed most nefarious. Frank Kermode also speaks to this adaptability, noting how "apocalypse can be disconfirmed without being discredited. This is part of its extraordinary resilience. It can also absorb changing interests, rival apocalypses, such as the Sibylline writings. It is patient of change and of historiographical sophistications" (Kermode 8–9). However, beyond demonizing enemies, the myths perform several functions within Christian-influenced culture. Generalizations can be made because, apparently, a certain amount of uniformity exists in patterns of apocalyptic beliefs. Speaking of apocalypticism in the Middle Ages, Norman Cohn discusses how "a bird's-eye view suggests that the social situations in which outbreaks of revolutionary millenarianism occurred were in fact remarkably uniform." The ancient end-time prophecies became prevalent in areas that were experiencing issues with overpopulation and dramatic economic changes, essentially creating a class of disenfranchised, impressionable people. For those in the midst of these changes, "life came to differ vastly from the settled agricultural life which was the norm throughout the thousand-year span of the Middle Ages" (Cohn 53–54). Cohn argues that awareness of income disparity facilitated belief in Christian end-time myths, and this awareness was most pronounced in burgeoning urban centers. In this sense, these myths are palliative, a form of consolation for groups that have been financially (or otherwise) mistreated. Fuller further corroborates this, sharing that "apocalyptic thought is 'intended for a group in crisis with the purpose of exhortation and/or consolation by means of divine authority.' Sociological studies indicate that apocalyptic writing commonly originates during times of crisis and tension." It was a reaction to any number of things, including a threat to a group's well-being, extreme persecution, diminished interest in religious ideas, or cognizance of the growing split between "eschatological expectations and current sociopolitical realities." The comfort in apocalyptic thought is that victory is guaranteed if a religious follower reframes their conflicts within the context of the mythic battle between good and evil (Fuller 21). The "severe persecution" of which Fuller speaks becomes somewhat loosely interpreted in the twentieth and twenty-first centuries, where persecution can be something as simple as living in a society with disparate opinions, where communists are terrifying simply because they're different. But this idea, that apocalyptic myths are linked to a feeling of persecution, seems fairly consistent across time.

Hofstadter and Current Political Myths

Another reason for the endurance of these myths, one that more explicitly ties in with their political underpinnings, connects with Richard Hofstadter's discussion of paranoia in American politics. Richard Hofstadter, writing about the culture of American politics, points out that

> history *is* a conspiracy, set in motion by demonic forces of almost transcendent power, and what is felt to be needed to defeat it is not the usual methods of political give-and-take, but an all-out crusade. The paranoid spokesman sees the fate of this conspiracy in apocalyptic terms—he traffics in the birth and death of whole worlds, whole political orders, whole systems of human values.

The political pundits using paranoid rhetoric see themselves as "manning the barricades of civilization" and much "like religious millenarians," articulate the "anxiety of those who are living through the last days" (Hofstadter 29–30). The accusations against Communism, Islam, and countless other factions, reach a kind of fever pitch, invoking the language of "religious millenarians." Public leaders, including media figures and presidents, even use apocalyptic terminology to describe the struggles against evil forces—Reagan's use of the term "evil empire," for example.

There are many postapocalyptic films that illustrate this anxiety, some of them overtly political. A contemporary film like *The Purge: Election Year* (2016) is rife with paranoia about classism and extremist political ideologies, showing upper-class depravity that literally results in mass murder. "The Purge" is the name of a twelve-hour period in which all crimes are legal, intended as a solution to high crime rates and strife between social classes. The "purge" itself is meant to act as a safety valve, releasing aggression and violence all in a twelve-hour period in order to curb people's violent tendencies for the rest of the year. In this particular film, the third in the series, an antipurge group is running for election, prompting pushback from the New Founding Fathers of America (NFFA). What follows is a civil war of sorts between two extremist groups: one far-right group and one far-left group. The NFFA is meant to be a far-right conservative group, intent on maintaining class division. Jay Dyer, author of the book *Esoteric Hollywood: Sex, Cults and Symbols in Film*, notes that "there's no doubt . . . [the NFFA] represents a right-wing political faction on the surface" (Dyer). However, the would-be liberators, the antipurge group, also employ violent methods to achieve revolution. After joining forces with an African American gang, specifically the Crips, the rebels "resemble an amalgam of the George Soros funded *Black Lives Matter* 'movement,' as well as other 1960's radical militant organizations" (Dyer). Dyer's comment is rife with the repugnant anti-Semitism of various right-wing pundits, who use George Soros as the shadowy figurehead behind perceived left-wing extremism. His comment does, however, serve to highlight the contradictions of the film, which is ostensibly arguing against antiminority violence, while at the same time "explicitly link[ing] immigrants to crime and homicide. Furthermore, it glorifies excessive forms of aestheticized violence, while explicitly denouncing them" (Khader). If nothing else, the extremism in the film is a satirical representation of the rampant partisanship in America, not only in Congress but also among American citizens. It's a paranoid scenario where partisanship leads to massacres and literal warfare. The decay and chaos of this postapocalyptic world is a direct result of extremist ideologies, and the film uses "the Purge" as a symbol of lower-class oppression. While *The Purge* might not be explicitly characterized as a science fiction film, most modern apocalyptic films and books fall under the umbrella of sci-fi.

A Contemporary, Perpetual Apocalypse

Environmental issues, as they became a pressing concern in the 1970s, increasingly were described in apocalyptic terms. The images of destruction so vividly evoked in the Bible were thought to be presently developing, as rivers became more toxic, air more polluted, and the ozone more fragile.

In an effort to perhaps render such widespread earthly corruption comprehensible, certain authors and pundits began framing these problems, once again, in large-scale, biblical terms. Global warming, holes in the ozone layer, genetic experiments, the bizarre weather caused by El Niño, acid rain, and other horrible environmental anomalies were described in tandem with the "darkening sun, rivers of blood, horrible sores and monstrous insects of the *Book of Revelation*." The line between religious and secular renderings of the apocalypse became ill-defined, illustrated in Hal Lindsey's *Planet Earth—2000 A.D.* (1994), as he writes, "'The physical tribulations of the Earth and its environment have been one of the most significant developments—prophetically speaking—since I authored *the Late Great Planet Earth* 25 years ago" (Boyer 325). These concerns with environmental apocalypse continue today, evidenced in such films as *The Day after Tomorrow* (2004), a film very clearly concerned with global warming. While such films as this are often secular in tone, the more religious evocations of the Bible still remain.

Book Overview

Early Christians used apocalyptic myths as a way to deal with contemporary issues of the time; however, the early Christians were a genuinely oppressed group, writing about issues with violent despots. In the late twentieth century, the dominant groups—typically white, heterosexual males—used these apocalyptic myths. They used a *perceived* sense of persecution to frame themselves as victims of changes in America, often having to do with immigrants, women, and sexual preferences. In reality, the Christian-influenced dominant class enjoys a privileged status, compared to other groups in the United States. Apocalyptic myths used by this large demographic illustrate anxiety over changing demographics and provide reassurance that the American patriarchy—of which Christianity is a part—will prevail and bring back an older, more vibrant America. Anxiety about changing demographics is quite obvious in the current American political climate, where large portions of the country voted for Donald Trump, whose slogan "Make America Great Again" implied that an older, better America had transformed into something inferior. Hazleton, Pennsylvania, a former coal-mining town that serves as a microcosm of working-class America, has experienced dramatic demographic changes. Over a span of sixteen years, Latinos went from 5 percent of the total population to 52 percent of the population of Hazleton. This is but one, albeit extreme, example of the seismic shifts in American demographics.

The loss of white majority status in Hazleton, and the imminent loss of majority status in the rest of the country, have led to anxiety among some whites. One resident of Hazleton, when asked about her vote for Trump, noted that "we have one of us in that White House. . . . We are going to make America great again. . . . The 'we' are the Caucasians that built this country." These whites feel "that their story, their traditions, their tastes, and their cultural aesthetic were . . . quintessentially American," and "react anxiously and angrily to a sense that their way of life is under threat" (Norris). This feeling of persecution by a dominant white culture is seen clearly in the use of postapocalyptic myths, which usually end with preapocalyptic institutions reestablished, after a white male emerges victorious from a conflict instigated by outgroups or a government tainted by minority influence.

Beyond merely elucidating the anxieties of white Christian America, apocalyptic myths function as a form of cognitive mapping, used to help alleviate these same anxieties by attempting to make sense of an increasingly complex world fraught with geopolitical alliances, global economies, environmental disasters, and protean racial and ethnic populations. Postapocalyptic media not only depict the reclaiming of the world by heroic white males but also provide a framework through which the world begins to make sense. These myths offer "believers with an already determined structure of meaning within which they can deal with the crises, the evil, and the absence of meaning they encounter in the world around them" (McGinn 16). In this way, Christian apocalypticism and frontier myths are utilized to create an effective tool through which to reify dominant ideologies, while at the same time providing solace in the creation of a cognitive map that makes sense of an inscrutable world.

The struggle to reestablish dominance can be seen on a much smaller scale as well, through the use of objects. A clear, almost obsessive focus on objects can be seen in most apocalyptic media, including video games, TV shows, movies, and books. This characteristic is even seen historically and cross-culturally—for instance, the tree in Ragnarok,[5] the Temple of Jerusalem in Christianity, or the "coarse grains"[6] in the Age of

5. After the apocalypse in Norse mythology, Yggdrasil—an immense tree that connects all nine realms of existence—helps regenerate a new world.

6. In the Age of Kali in Hinduism, there is a mass exodus toward countries with wheat and barley, which suddenly become valuable commodities after a series of apocalyptic events (Wilson 624). Horace Hayman Wilson, ed., *The Vishṅu Puráṅa: A System of Hindu Mythology and Tradition*, vol. 52 (London, J. Murray, 1840).

Kali. Contemporary American apocalyptic media focus on objects after an apocalyptic scenario and how these objects change in use and connotation. In *Mad Max*, for instance, the titular character's car represents the police force, and the law and order that entails, before the apocalyptic event. After the apocalypse, his car becomes a symbol of survival. Even video games like *Fallout 4* have this preoccupation with objects, forcing players to collect "junk" and reappropriate it for the purposes of enhancing weapons and armor. Apocalyptic myths themselves are political, and one way to explicitly analyze the politics involved is through these objects. Not only are they of central importance to most types of apocalyptic media, but objects themselves are an extension of our late capitalist culture. In this way, any subjugation of minority groups would be found therein, along with any attempt at rebellion. Dick Hebdige wrote extensively about the ideologies hidden in these objects and how any changes in the normal ideologies of the dominant culture can be profoundly disruptive. He notes:

> Any elision, truncation or convergence of prevailing linguistic and ideological categories can have profoundly disorienting effects. These deviations briefly expose the arbitrary nature of the codes which underlie and shape all forms of discourse . . . Predictably then, violations of the authorized codes through which the social world is organized and experienced have considerable power to provoke and disturb. (90–91)

When an object is used in entirely new ways, it can be an attempt to assert power or aggressively subvert the undesirable forces of the dominant culture. As Hebdige indicates, it can be something as simple as a safety pin being conspicuously displayed on one's clothing. In apocalyptic film and literature, doll heads are used as necklaces, and engine grease as a type of tribal war paint (*Fury Road*). In all of these cases, the power to imbue objects with ideas and value is being disputed—indicating a struggle to adjust, reify, or abolish the hegemonic structure of society.

Chapter Overview

The quote at the beginning of this introduction comes from the opening monologue of *The Road Warrior* (1981), and aptly touches on the undercurrent of fear and paranoia seen in the reactions of the dominant class to growing minority rights. The quotes in all of the chapter titles are taken from Trump's inaugural address, illustrating the close link between apocalyptic myths and politics and the continued relevance of these myths. The examples used in the chapters come from both text and film, illustrating the ubiquity of these myths in major media forms. The film examples in every chapter are from the late twentieth century, in an attempt to elucidate the prominent place the apocalypse has in an era of sexual discrimination laws and civil rights legislation, among many other policies aimed at helping marginalized groups.

The order of the chapters is intended to first establish that the dominant culture because of anxiety over the increasing rights of minorities, uses apocalyptic myths to paint themselves an oppressed minority that must take a stand against a nefarious "Other." Subsequently, I illustrate why these myths resonate and are used ad nauseam by the dominant culture, owing chiefly to ways we identify as Americans—the American frontier and Christianity. The book then attempts to illustrate how these myths play out on both a macro and micro level, first looking at the use of apocalypse to simplify complex issues and make it easier to scapegoat minority groups, reestablishing white male superiority. Afterward, I examine the obsessive focus on objects, which indicates how these apocalyptic themes play out at the most fundamental level—the level of objects and words. White anxiety—the thread that runs throughout this work—can be seen at an almost molecular level, illustrating the fervent preoccupation of the dominant group with reifying their own power to allay anxieties.

Chapter 1—"The Ravages of Other Countries": Loss of White America

Chapter 1 looks at how early Christians were oppressed in a variety of ways by various Roman emperors. The apocalyptic myths they used were meant to have a palliative effect, assuring Christian followers that the hardship they endured was only temporary and that further down the line they would be rewarded, while their oppressors would be punished. The movement from feudalism to capitalism allowed the apocalyptic genre to be co-opted by the dominant culture to reify a power structure that kept white males at the top of the hierarchy. Religion in the twentieth century was used by corporations and the government to maintain power, as Christianity became the unofficial national religion. Maintaining power, however, became problematic as minorities and women gained more power. Consequently, Christian apocalyptic myths were used to paint a portrait of white males being oppressed, and the apocalyptic media used often ended with the white male emerging victorious—an event usually shown in a positive light.

This chapter argues that apocalyptic myths have gone from being used by genuinely disenfranchised groups to being used by a dominant white male culture in America. Contemporary white anxiety over growing minority rights manifests itself in postapocalyptic media, specifically literature and film. In most cases, a threatening group of outsiders must be defeated in order for the white male to bring back preapocalyptic institutions, such as family, marriage, and Christianity.

Chapter 2—"Unite the Civilized World": Frontier Eschatology

Chapter 2 looks at the reasons why these apocalyptic myths are used and seen to be effective, which lies in their conflation with American frontier iconography. The American frontier is an integral part of American identity, embodying many traits considered to be quintessentially American—rugged individualism, men standing up against less civilized peoples, open spaces with endless potential, etc. The Western myth itself was created by the likes of Teddy Roosevelt, Frederick Jackson Turner, and Buffalo Bill Cody and found its way into a variety of media, most explicitly in the Western genre. As the twentieth century wore on, the Western adapted to each period, reflecting the concerns and anxieties of the culture at the time. Apocalyptic films and books began to bear striking similarities with frontier myths, using the same landscapes and iconography of Westerns. And like Westerns, the ideologies therein mostly promoted a status quo that centers on white male dominance. The dominant culture thus began using a readily available frontier iconography with Christian myths, increasing the effectiveness of the conservative message by using two things that resonate with American audiences—the frontier and postapocalyptic myths.

This chapter argues that apocalyptic myths in film and literature are used to bring back an older, idealized America, closely linked to conceptions of the American frontier. The frontier, like contemporary apocalyptic media, allows the white "frontiersman" to emerge a conquering hero, holding back throngs of threatening outgroups.

Chapter 3—"The Red Blood of Patriots": Paranoia and Scapegoating

The third chapter looks at specific film and book examples of white male paranoia and the attempt to frame an increasingly inscrutable global economy and culture in simple terms by reducing everything to a conflict between white men and minority groups. The dominant white male culture uses media to present itself as an oppressed minority that must stand against threatening outside forces. Conspiracy theory is a type of cognitive mapping that appears in many films, including postapocalyptic ones. Conspiracy theory can sometimes show minorities as a threatening Other attempting to infiltrate the government and bring about the collapse of a status quo that allows for white male dominance. In other cases, the minorities are made into literal monsters that bring about an apocalyptic event or scenario, and such a scenario lays the blame for any number of complicated social or environmental issues at the feet of these monsters. In this sense, complicated world issues are reduced to a simplistic battle between a threatening Other and white male heroes, once again illustrating white anxiety and paranoia that an ideal America has been lost.

This chapter argues that postapocalyptic media is used by the dominant culture to simplify complex issues, facilitating easy scapegoating of minority groups. These minority groups, in film and literature, are often depicted as robots, androids, and monsters, figures that are blamed for a variety of apocalyptic scenarios.

Chapter 4—"New Roads, and Highways, and Bridges, and Airports, and Tunnels": Apocalyptic Objects

The fourth and final chapter examines objects in the context of material culture that embodies ideologies promoting a capitalist hierarchy essential for white male dominance. The white male anxiety of postapocalyptic films and books manifests itself through a preoccupation with objects and their changed meanings after an apocalyptic event. After the apocalypse, objects no longer mean what they did before, creating an anxiety that a more perfect world has been lost. There is an effort in postapocalyptic media to either preserve these objects or to imbue them with meaning once again, reestablishing a referent that has disappeared after the apocalypse. This obsessive focus on objects and the anxiety over their changes in meaning fit with a larger notion that a better world has been lost. In some cases, like in the book *Roadside Picnic*, objects with no clear referent *are* linked to an Other embodied by aliens or monsters. Objects with clear meanings are replaced by objects that are utterly inscrutable.

This chapter argues that a close examination of objects in postapocalyptic media reveals anxieties over a loss of meaning in contemporary society, where an older, idealized America has been lost. Objects have a long history of being used to signify status, and there is a general thrust toward restoring this signifying power in order to concretize boundaries between the dominant group and minorities.

1

"The Ravages of Other Countries"

Loss of White America

A Boy and His Dog (1975), a postapocalyptic film, ends with a disturbingly misogynist display, as the main character and his canine companion consume a female love interest. The film plays with the audience's expectations, as it's strongly implied that the dog will be eaten—a dog capable of telepathically communicating with the protagonist. The film ends with a discussion of the now deceased woman:

> Blood (the dog): But after we walk all day, you'll probably have to cook up what's left.
>
> Vic: She said she loved me. Oh, hell. It wasn't my fault she picked me to get all wet-brained over.

Subsequently, we hear the narration of the dog, explaining that the love between a boy and a dog is paramount. Relationships with women in the film are decidedly negative, as the main group of women in the film imprison him and attempt to use his sperm to repopulate the Earth. In this sense, the film prioritizes the male component of reproduction over that of women. The film, in this way, not only ends with a reaffirmation of the patriarchy but also illustrates a world where even female reproductive power is subsumed. This type of postapocalyptic film, where male power is positively affirmed and bolstered, is extremely common, though perhaps not as conspicuous as in *A Boy and His Dog*. It's part of a larger trend in the latter half of the twentieth century, where the anxiety about increasing rights of minorities to the perceived detriment of white male power manifests itself in various media. The postapocalyptic genre works especially well as a means of reestablishing white male dominance, and the audience can see that the coming destruction can be ameliorated if we can just put the white male back in charge. In addition, following the template of apocalyptic writing is in keeping with the Christian traditions of phallocentric culture.

Postapocalyptic media clearly illustrate white male anxiety and the desire to maintain power, with a structure that identifies a disaster inflicted by minorities that must be corrected by the white male protagonist. Apocalyptic myths have moved from providing solace to genuinely oppressed people to reestablishing the power of the dominant group—an almost total reversal.

Anxiety Over the Loss of White Male Dominance

The anxiety over the perceived loss of white dominance in America can be seen throughout contemporary postapocalyptic media, including films like *World War Z* (2013) and the *Planet of the Apes* (1968) films. In cases like these, the fear is that a foreign entity will assume a position of dominance, relegating the white male to a subordinate role. *World War Z* follows the protagonist, Gerry, as he attempts to find a cure for a virus that turns people into zombies. Gerry is a white male, with a traditional nuclear family—a wife and two children. Throughout the course of the film, it's clear that being reunited with his family is a primary motivation for solving the epidemic. Much has been written about the use of zombies as representative of race or minority status[1] in the United States, since "cultural representations of the zombie in the United States have thus been intimately linked with cultural ideas regarding African Americans and other people of color, southern and eastern European immigrants, and 'modern' women." These groups are "considered potentially dangerous to white, middle-class society in the early twentieth-century," much like the

1. This will be explored more fully in subsequent chapters.

zombies that represent them in film (Kordas 16). The fear, in *World War Z*, is that these animalistic creatures will replace the dominant culture via consumption. Gerry sees people devouring each other in the middle of a city, for instance, as he tries to carry his family to safety. Normal commuters in traffic eat each other, transmitting the disease quickly. We later see pedestrians in Jerusalem break out in panic as zombies climb over a protective wall, and soon people consume one another in a chaotic display of savagery. Ultimately, however, the film shows a white male performing acts of heroism, after a zombie threat has led to the breakup of the nuclear family and the disintegration of society. His heroic journey is completed at the end, when he reunites with his family and has produced a viable solution to the epidemic. The nuclear family emerges unscathed, and the white male saves the world from ubiquitous hordes of zombies. Zombie films have become extremely popular, evidenced in the string of films produced over the last two decades: *Zombieland* (2009), *28 Days Later* (2002), *Resident Evil* (2002), *Day of the Dead* (2008), *I Am Legend* (2007), and many others. This indicates that these film scenarios, wherein a malevolent outgroup threatens society and the white male must save the day, resonate with the American public. For a significant portion of the American patriarchy, this fear seems very real—the fear of being supplanted by minority groups.

The *Planet of the Apes* has been revived in a new series of films, the last of which came out in 2017. The original film and the more recent prequels illustrate the same anxieties as zombie films, in the sense that there is a fear of the white male losing a place of prominence in society. Taylor, the white male hero of the original film, finds himself on an unknown planet, after being stuck in hibernation for over two thousand years on his spaceship. The planet is dominated by intelligent apes that communicate, use tools, and have a system of governance. The humans in the film, with the exception of Taylor and his two fellow astronauts, are mute, feral, atavistic beings that are hunted like vermin by the apes. At the end, when Taylor realizes he had been on Earth all along, we see that the dominant society of humans has been replaced, and made subservient to animals, typically thought of as inferior to human beings. The apes that replace humans in the film call to mind historic, racist parallels drawn between apes and Black people, and "while crude historical depictions of African Americans as ape-like may have disappeared from mainstream US culture, research suggests that many Americans subconsciously associate blacks with apes" (Sani 62). Writing of the original 1968 film, Susan McHugh, in the *South Atlantic Review*, notes that the film

> visualizes race in terms of species difference. . . . From the perspective of Taylor, the film imagines a radical reordering of sociality on a global scale: apes have taken the role of speaking, tool-using culture-bearers while humans have become their mute, animal counterparts, at best the apes' pets and at worst their research-subject vermin. Encountering this ape society, racially stratified according to species differences, the same features that secured for Taylor the privilege of social invisibility, namely his whiteness, maleness, and American-ness, mark him instead as a member of an inferior species. (McHugh 40)

In one scene, an ape named Julius takes away one of the mute, primitive humans—a white woman—and Taylor responds, "Take your hands off her, you black monster!" (*Planet of the Apes*). This speaks to the undercurrent of anxiety over an Other—in this case a "black" male—taking white women away from Caucasians. Later in the film, Dr. Zaius literally discusses a surgical procedure he wishes to perform on Taylor that ends in "emasculation" (his exact word). The fact that the film has been revived and made into a new trilogy over the past decade illustrates that the anxiety of the film—the fear of white males becoming a "member of an inferior species"—is still widespread enough that the three newer films made over five hundred million dollars at the box office. Between zombie films, *Planet of the Apes* films, and a whole host of films about alien outsiders destroying the planet, it's clear that anxiety of being made into an "inferior species" is very much on the minds of large swaths of white Americans.

A recent ABC news report that interviewed Trump supporters revealed the common anxiety felt by white males. The man interviewed, a machinist named Brian Keith Patterson, says:

> I'm not afraid to say that I'm in fear for the white man. I'm in fear. . . . What I'm afraid of seeing is the reverse role—a white man is taking on the position of being the minority. A white man might have a difficult time finding a job because companies need this balancing act, need to have more Hispanics, more African-Americans working. (Smith)

This sentiment is typical among working-class individuals on the right of the political spectrum. With affirmative action, quotas, and legislation like Title IX and the Dream Act, there is a fear that the power of the patriarchy is slipping away. The belief is that a profound legacy will be lost. Robert Jones, in *The End of White Christian America*, explains that

> among WCA's [White Christian America] many notable achievements was its service to the nation as a cultural touchstone during most of its life. It provided a shared aesthetic, a historical framework, and a moral vocabulary. During its long life, WCA also produced a dizzying array of institutions, from churches to hospitals, social service organizations, and civic organizations. (Jones 2)

It might seem like the author Robert Jones is a fringe figure, but studies show that this is not the case. Jones and men like Brian Keith Patterson are ubiquitous in American culture and played a key role in the election of Donald Trump. A study of 594 American citizens showed that "as White Americans' numerical majority shrinks and they increasingly feel that their group's status is threatened, White identity will become increasingly salient and central to White Americans" (Major et al. 8). In other words, the white majority was not as cognizant of whiteness as part of their identity, specifically because they were a majority, enjoying what is termed "white privilege." However, the threat to this power has created an anxiety that makes the patriarchy more aware of "whiteness." In the study, the more a white person was preoccupied with their own race, the more they leaned toward Trump as their candidate of choice. The study notes that

> consistent with our theorizing, among Whites high in ethnic identification, the racial shift message indirectly predicted increased support for Trump and anti-immigrant policies, increased opposition to political correctness norms, and decreased support for Sanders via increased group status threat. (Major et al. 7)

This preoccupation with the perceived threat to white dominance permeates many facets of American culture, illustrating the close link between white hegemony and the capitalist system. Culture itself is used to reify the capitalist system and, as a corollary, a white, patriarchal hierarchy. In this sense, postapocalyptic media is but one facet of a cultural output that vehemently attempts to maintain the power of the American white male. A cursory examination of education reveals the same anxieties, as policies favorable to minorities are lamented, including widespread change in academic reading lists. Minority and women writers are being included in curricula that, in the past, had been dominated by white male writers. Affirmative action, changes in the curriculum, and even changes in campus design are among the events that lead Dinesh d'Souza in *Illiberal Education* to ask, "When America loses her predominantly white stamp, what impact will that have on her Western cultural traditions? . . . How should society cope with the agenda of increasingly powerful minority groups?" (13–14). Throughout the book, d'Souza shares the fear that the increasing influence of minorities is an affront to Western civilization, as academia becomes diluted by minority inclusion alongside the likes of Shakespeare and Aristotle. The stance that d'Souza takes is not unusual. Many conservative pundits have expressed frustration at an academic culture that has focused on seemingly insignificant matters, with the advent of safe spaces and trigger warnings. Certainly, there is validity to some of the arguments against these, but ultimately, the arguments ignore very important questions: why were things like safe spaces created in the first place? What cultural conditions resulted in their creation? The end result—safe spaces and trigger spaces—may be ineffectual and antithetical to the ideological challenges that academia is supposed to engender, but does the central argument make sense—that minorities of all kinds are underrepresented and marginalized? There is a mountain of evidence in the affirmative, and it's hard to believe that only white males wrote worthy, historically significant literature. Rather than focus on how better to deal with perceived marginalization, d'Souza and others merely decry policies as promoting "snowflake" culture, where students want to live in an ideological bubble in which their notions of the world are never challenged. While this point of their argument has weight, their anxiety seems more directed toward the diminution of Western culture. Authors and pundits like d'Souza read these activities as deeply threatening to Western culture, a culture comprising mostly white males. "When America loses her predominantly white stamp, what impact will that have on her Western cultural traditions?" d'Souza asks, and then he wonders how to cope with the increasing powers of minorities. In this way, there is little difference in the anxiety of d'Souza and the Trump voters mentioned in the study.

Demographic changes, occurring most dramatically in the twentieth century, have created the perception that there is a coming "white minority," which is supported by census statistics. Americans classified as racial minorities comprised one-eighth of the population in the 1960s, but by 1990, this group had doubled in size. Knowledge of these changing demographics is widespread and "has created a deluge of proclamations from all walks of political life, nervously or excitedly anticipating what [author and academic] Dale Maharidge calls "the coming white minority" (Hill 49). The growth of the nonwhite population has been substantial, going from 9.6 million in 1970 to 40 million only 30 years later. By 2065, the Pew Research Center projects that 88 percent of America's population growth will come from immigrants and their progeny. Causes range from globalization and a decrease in the family size of the native population, to the usual and continual flow of immigrants into the country (Gest 6). Michael Kimmel, in *Angry White Men: American Masculinity and the End of an Era*, discusses the swell of indignation among the dominant class, which rose during the latter half of the twentieth century. For most of America's history, white, male, heterosexual Christians occupied most positions of authority, in government, in business, and in various aspects of culture. As access to this type of financial, cultural, and governmental power has become more egalitarian, these dominant males are experiencing what author Michael Kimmel has called "aggrieved entitlement"—a sense that the power they are entitled to has begun to elude their grasp. Women and minority groups of all types, for the most part, have enjoyed an increase in the rights afforded them. White males, however, feel that these gains for minorities are at their own expense:

> At the same time as white American men cling ever more tenaciously to old ideals, women and minorities have entered those formerly all-male bastions of untrammeled masculinity. Gender and racial equality feels like a loss to white men: if "they" gain, "we" lose. In the zero-sum game, these gains have all been at white men's expense. (Kimmel 59)

These feelings of loss manifest themselves in all forms of media. Talk radio is one such outlet for white male rage, including notorious political agitator, Rush Limbaugh. Limbaugh, despite a dip in popularity, still enjoyed thirteen million listeners a week prior to his death. When Sotomayor was appointed the new Supreme Court justice, the reaction on the part of Limbaugh and many of his fans was anger, indignation, and a feeling that they were being oppressed. Limbaugh, in an unfiltered rant on May 29, 2009, asked the question:

> How do you get promoted in a Barack Obama administration? By hating white people—or even saying you do, or that they're not good or put 'em down, whatever. Make white people the new oppressed minority, and they're going right along about it 'cause they're shutting up. They're moving to the back of the bus. They're saying, "I can't use that drinking fountain? Okay! I can't use that restroom? Okay!" That's the modern day Republican Party, the equivalent of the Old South: the new oppressed minority. Whatever happened to the content of one's character as the basis of judging people? ("America's Piñata Strikes Back")

This diatribe is emblematic of the general sentiment in large portions of the once unilaterally powerful white male population. On the surface, Limbaugh's argument is utterly absurd, implying that there were a series of Jim Crow–style laws against white men. Since this Limbaugh broadcast in 2009, Donald Trump has been elected president, with support from huge numbers of the very sort of people that Limbaugh appeals to, illustrating this feeling that the white, male, hetero Christian is the new oppressed minority. It is for this reason that apocalyptic myths have become a tool of this demographic, even though they are not as explicitly oppressed as their antecedents. Thus, a postapocalyptic film like *A Boy and His Dog* ends with the main male character eating his female companion, while keeping his canine cohort, after escaping an all-female enclave that sought to imprison and control men. Almost any apocalyptic story that ends with the traditions of the dominant white male culture being reified is presented as a "happy ending."

Part of what has enabled these apocalyptic ideas to be readily accessible is late capitalism, which has managed to co-opt all forms of expression and subculture, using it to maintain an oppressive hierarchical system. In Fredric Jameson's overview of "late capitalism," he claims that the term originated with the Frankfurt School, with the likes of Adorno and Horkheimer, who stressed the powerful link between government and big business amid a growing web of bureaucracies. Economic changes after World War II included the growth of transnational business, "computers and automation, the flight of production to advanced Third World areas, along with all the more familiar social consequences, including the crisis of traditional labor, the emergence of yuppies, and gentrification on a now-global scale" (Jameson xviii). I employ Jameson's use of "late capitalism" to demarcate the economic and cultural changes that followed in post–World War II America. Unlike previous systems, late capitalism infiltrated every aspect of people's lives, through extensive control over all types of media. Ernest Mandel, discussing late capitalism, notes how the influence of this economic system suffuses every aspect of culture, including music, art, and the film industry. Everything is "subordinated to the laws of the market," and " 'every-day experience' reinforces and internalizes the neo-fatalist ideology of the immutable nature of the late capitalist social order" (Mandel 502). All forms of expression—in addition to all attempts at protest—are subsumed and controlled by the far-reaching grasp of the system. While previous systems may not have controlled recreation and allowed a certain amount of personal autonomy, there is virtually nothing that falls outside of the umbrella of late capitalism. What is believed to be personal choice takes place within "a real network or infrastructure of new kinds of commercial and economic institutions" (Hall and Jefferson 187). Everything becomes a form of consumption, and personal choice is limited to choices between prepackaged products. The consequence of this is that apocalyptic myths are now used in the same way most other myths and ideas are used in contemporary society—to reify the power of the group at the top of the hierarchy. Instead of the "beast" in Revelation representing the unilateral power of an emperor, it becomes emblematic of "outsiders" (African Americans, Latinos, homosexuals, etc.) who appear to be far less threatening than Nero and Domitian but are presented as insidious enemies of the dominant culture. The dominant group, Hofstadter notes, perceives threats "in apocalyptic terms—he traffics in the birth and death of whole worlds, whole political orders, whole systems of human values" (Hofstadter 29–30).

Apocalyptic myths have always been political; however, the group using these myths has gone from a class of disenfranchised minorities to a dominant culture using these myths in response to perceived threats to its unilateral power. What has prompted this change has been the economic system within which these myths proliferate. One need only look at the way corporate interests and Christianity merged in the 1930s to see this. The movement from the feudal system to the current system of late capitalism has seen these myths fall into the hands of a dominant culture that has managed to absorb and nullify any attempts at subversion. Threatened by the growth of nonwhite, nonheteronormative, non-Christian, and culturally divergent groups of people, the dominant class paints a picture in which they are the group threatened with catastrophe, the minority[2] who must pull the world out of the wreckage to start again. Thus, when apocalyptic films and books end with the reestablishment of the nuclear family and the hierarchies concomitant with capitalism, the audience is meant to celebrate this return to "civilization."

Early Christians

The perceived persecution of the white male Christian pales in comparison to the experiences of early Christians and illustrates the change in usage of apocalyptic myths. Even before the Diocletianic Persecution, Christians had been subject to sporadic persecution in various parts of the Roman Empire. Their social class made them easy scapegoats in many cases, the *Cambridge History of Christianity* noting that the

> early Christian community of Rome drew its membership from the artisans and freedmen living in large tenement blocks (*insulae*), and from freedmen and slaves working in the imperial household, particularly in the time of Commodus, Septimius Severus and their successors. . . . The Latin-speaking Christians of late second-century Rome were African provincials. The low social status of Christians led to their victimization in periodic persecutions designed to rid the urban centre of 'bad people' (*mali homines*)—individuals and groups who flouted the social norms, and abhorred public entertainments and religious festivals. (Trombley 310)

In addition to social class, Christians were subject to oppression because of xenophobic tendencies, wherein any religion without a long, storied history was a threatening enigma. The Christians of that period "had

2. The label "minority" is not simply predicated on a number but is a fairly complex concept. There are, in fact, a "variety of ways in which an ethnic group can be dominant: demographic, cultural, political, and economic" and scholars such as Ashley Doane identify "politico-economic hegemony as the metre of dominant ethnicity" (Kaufman 2). Thus, the peasants during the time of the Crusades were numerically and culturally dominant yet were a political and economic minority, having very little control over laws and their own standard of living. Conversely, the contemporary white patriarch has enjoyed a "majority" status in every sense: sheer numbers of people, and in a cultural, political, and economic capacity.

no ancient tradition, no national identity, and no homeland or religious center besides those of the Jews" (Collins 85). In the second century, Christianity was grouped with other religions that Rome regarded with distrust—those who worshipped Dionysus, for instance, and had a variety of accusations leveled against it. Arson and incest were among the charges. For instance, after the infamous fire during the reign of Nero, Roman historian Tacitus explains that Nero himself directed public anger toward Christians "because there was already a widespread animosity against them," as "many Romans and provincials hated Christians for a variety of reasons" (Collins 87).

Despite these very common instances of vitriol toward Christians, it wasn't until a succession of emperors issued edicts beginning in 303 CE that an official policy of oppression became the norm. The destruction of churches, burning of scriptures, and forbidding of Christian religious practice began with the first edict. Subsequent edicts ordered the arrest of Christian religious figureheads, and "the handing over and public burning of its texts—was deemed by the emperor as crucial to the demolition of this cult as the razing of churches and civil disenfranchisement of its leaders" (Mitchell 177). Around 311 CE, the official policies of persecution were ended, and two years later, Emperor Constantine issued the Edict of Milan, which decreed that Christians be treated benevolently within the Roman Empire.

Revelation is thought to have been written by John of Patmos, an island in the Aegean Sea close to Asia Minor. At that point, Asia Minor had a number of Christian churches, many of which had been addressed by the apostle Paul in his letters. It is generally believed that John of Patmos is not the apostle John, given the many differences in style and content between Revelation and the Gospel of John. He had been exiled to Patmos by Emperor Domitian for engaging in Christian missionary work, though the exact date of this and the subsequent text he produced remains unclear. It's believed to have been written in the latter half of the first century CE, given the allusions to Rome, referred to as "Babylon" after the destruction of the temple in Jerusalem, an event that happened after 70 CE. Also used to date the text is a reference to Emperor Nero returning from the dead, his death having occurred in 68 CE. Ultimately, it is believed to have been written during the reign of Emperor Domitian, who ruled from 92–96 CE. The latter portion of Domitian's reign created a crisis for Christians, as he demanded to be worshipped as a God. Defined by Roman historians as a horrific despot, Domitian's "reign provides a plausible social, political setting of the Book of Revelation" (Thompson 14, 17). While Domitian's reign was hardly as oppressive as the edicts issued two centuries later, it was marked by conflict that directly affected the Christian community at that time.

At their inception, Christian apocalyptic myths were the domain of actual minorities facing various forms of oppression, in some cases encountering violent confrontation.[3] Sometimes, the oppression took the form of restrictive laws of worship that forced Christians to relinquish certain religious practices but embrace others. Roman historians Tacitus and Pliny the Younger—and later the Roman senator, Dio Chrysostom—almost unequivocally describe Emperor Domitian as a horrible tyrant. Speaking of Domitian, Pliny describes his palace as a

> place where . . . that fearful monster built his defences with untold terrors, where lurking in his den he licked up the blood of his murdered relatives or emerged to plot the massacre and destruction of his most distinguished subjects. Menaces and horror were the sentinels at his doors . . . always he sought darkness and mystery, and only emerged from the desert of his solitude to create another. (Pan. 48.3–5)

The empire was supposedly replete with informers looking to charge people with treason for fairly innocuous transgressions, thus creating a constant fear of reprisal. Economically, his excess expenditures on his clothing and various entertainments created dire financial situations for the empire, which was often forced to plunder provinces for financial assets (Thompson 101). Some modern historians, however, call this vivid portrait of a tyrant into question, noting the unavoidable bias of these ancient figures reporting on Domitian. Despite whatever faults he may have had, it seems likely that the actual Domitian, while certainly oppressive, was not necessarily the unadulterated beast he was made out to be. For the Book of Revelation, however, the culturally produced image of Domitian is more important than the actual man. Early Christians, like John of Patmos, were responding to this image of Domitian, the nefarious and despotic philanderer.

3. Thompson writes, "Early Christians are characterized demographically as an oppressed minority who belong to the powerless poor. . . . The civic and imperial machinery in the province of Asia works to persecute those Christians, bringing them into the circuses and games to fight with wild animals and skilled gladiators" (7).

Revelation is, in essence, an allegory referring to the perceived enemies of Christianity, including Nero, whose Antichristian policies marked him as a major enemy of Christians everywhere. Most of the symbolism that John used in Revelation refers to various aspects of the Roman Empire, including Roman currency. The image of the current ruler was obviously displayed on Roman coins, making the use of this money problematic, John having warned against using anything bearing the "mark of the beast." Revelation 12:15–18 says:

> And the second beast required all people small and great, rich and poor, free and slave, to receive a mark on their right hand or on their forehead, so that no one could buy or sell unless he had the mark—the name of the beast or the number of its name. This calls for wisdom. Let the person who has insight calculate the number of the beast, for it is the number of a man. That number is 666. (Revelation 13:15–18)

Some scholars infer that John's reference to having this mark on one's forehead or hand is possibly an allusion to the Jewish use of phylacteries on these same respective parts of the body. Phylacteries were small leather boxes containing Hebrew texts on vellum, used during morning prayer. The number 666, in this same passage, was thought to be "a punning device drawn from the practice of using both Greek and Hebrew letters as numerals. John apparently translated Nero Caesar into Greek, Neron Kaisar, and then transliterated the result into a Hebrew form whose numerical value was 666." However, the symbols used throughout Revelation have, since their inception, been couched in so much mystery that they are still of great interest to soothsayers two thousand years later (Fuller 29). The allusions in Revelation are vague enough that they have inspired innumerable interpretations that continue to this day.

Modern-Day Christians

The circumstances in which more contemporary American Christians live differ quite dramatically. Over the last hundred years, Christianity managed to become the unofficial national religion with a pervasive influence perhaps most poignantly felt during the Eisenhower administration, as author Kevin Kruse argues in *One Nation Under God: How Corporate America Invented Christian America*. The merging of corporate interests and Christian ideologies was the primary catalyst for this, exemplified in the bestseller *The Man Nobody Knows* (1925), in which "liberal Protestant Bruce Barton cast Jesus as a brawny, efficient, pioneering entrepreneur and 'the founder of modern business'" (Grem 18). This fusion of conservative politics and religion, facilitated by the direct involvement of corporations, gained momentum in the 1930s. Corporations found that they could widely disseminate conservative ideologies to the masses through religious messages and figureheads. These ideologies were meant to counteract Roosevelt's progressive policies, which many corporate leaders were strongly opposed to. Kruse argues that

> the postwar revolution in America's religious identity had its roots not in the foreign policy panic of the 1950s but rather in the domestic politics of the 1930s and early 1940s. Decades before Eisenhower's inaugural prayers, corporate titans enlisted conservative clergymen in an effort to promote new political arguments embodied in the phrase "freedom under God." As the private correspondence and public claims of the men leading this charge make clear, this new ideology was designed to defeat the state power its architects feared most—not the Soviet regime in Moscow, but Franklin D. Roosevelt's New Deal administration in Washington. (Kruse 14–15)

Corporations sought to counter New Deal policies through programs like the Christian Business Men's Committee, International (CBMCI), which "had marshaled the resources of and relationships between businessmen . . . to increase Christian influence in the public square." This mixture of Christianity, politics, and corporate interests not only promoted free enterprise and the end of the welfare state but also further bolstered the ideologies of the patriarchy. In tune with many businessmen of the time, "the CBMCI assumed white privilege and male leadership were divine sanctions and confirmed by their authority as the heads of large corporations" (Grem 13–14).

The union of religion, politics, and corporate interests reached its apex during the Eisenhower administration, during which the president read an inauguration prayer, began the now annual Dedicatory Prayer Breakfast, and facilitated the addition of "under God" to the Pledge of Allegiance, among other things. Men from General Motors, Chase Bank, and other major corporate powers were part of Eisenhower's cabinet, which was an integral part of a presidency that "succeeded in sacralizing the state, swiftly implementing a host of religious ceremonies and symbols and thereby inscribing . . . an apparently permanent public religion on the institutions of American government" (Kruse 102). In 1954, during the drama of the McCarthy era and the landmark *Brown v. Board of Education* case, a subcommittee of the Judiciary Committee deliberated on an amendment to the Constitution that would have stated, "This Nation devoutly recognizes the authority and law of Jesus Christ, Saviour and Ruler of nations through whom are bestowed the blessings of Almighty God" (108). This illustrates the extent to which religion became entrenched in American politics, albeit through the powerful backing of corporations. Companies within the capitalist system co-opted religious myths that were once the tools of oppressed Christians, claiming these myths as their own.

Over the last hundred years, many different groups have been scapegoated as the Antichrist. The United States, for instance, has a long history of singling out ideological groups like Unionists and Communists, who were thought by the dominant culture to be obvious precursors to the Antichrist's rule. It was believed, in fact, that the words "union made" on labels were equivalent to the "mark of the Beast," without which buying and selling are impossible (Fuller 151). Post-WWII, contemporary events dramatically affected which groups were given the dubious pleasure of being part of an apocalyptic scenario. Boyer writes the following:

> From the end of the Second World War through the 1980s, the years of the Cold War and the nuclear arms race, popularizers of pre-millennial dispensationalism promulgated a scenario of Last-days events adapted to the global realities of these years. (324)

This explains the preoccupation with nuclear catastrophes in films and books, including Hal Lindsey's *The Late Great Planet Earth*, which focuses on a massive war between nuclear-capable countries, obviously a manifestation of fear about Russian military might. In Lindsey's book, the Russians invade Jerusalem, and a new world order is established, comprising diabolical organizations paving the way for the Antichrist's rule (Boyer 324). This, coupled with myriad environmental catastrophes, at least partially explains the copious apocalyptic films and books that have been developed over the last half century.

Communists have been very famously scapegoated, most notoriously during the McCarthy era. Some of the inflammatory rhetoric used against Communists became apocalyptic in nature. A major reason became its association with the USSR, which had become the primary adversary of the United States. Countries have always tended to vilify enemies through the use of apocalyptic imagery. In the United States, threats have very commonly been symbolized via apocalyptic imagery, for instance in the case of the thinkers behind the French Revolution, King George of England, or Catholic France. Thus, declaring the Soviet Union as Gog or the Antichrist fit in with a long history of disparaging perceived threats. Many Americans, with Ronald Reagan perhaps leading the charge, believed the USSR to be the "evil empire." Consequently, acts of aggression against the USSR were believed to be fully justified (Fuller 158). In addition, there were many characteristics of Communism that easily allowed for this portrayal, including its atheistic tendencies. Gerald Winrod once noted that "communist Russia, inspired by 'Jewish hatred for Christianity,' had emerged with the sole intention of wiping the Christian faith off the face of the earth" (Fuller 156). Portraying the USSR in this way allowed the United States to take drastic measures against Communism, justifying each action in the name of saving Christians across the country. Christians were almost presented as an oppressed minority group, struggling against a tide of evil coming from Eastern Europe. Threats to the established order in America are quite frequently hyperbolic, for example during the McCarthy era, where the "communist threat" was grossly exaggerated. The Communist Party of the United States had only seventy thousand members in the 1930s, and in 1950 the number of Communists was even lower. McCarthy, however, portrayed the threat as biblical in proportion:

> Today we can almost physically hear the mutterings and rumblings of an invigorated god of war. . . . The one encouraging thing is that the "mad moment" has not yet arrived for the firing of the gun or the exploding of the bomb which will set civilization about the final task of destroying itself. . . . We are now engaged in a show-down fight . . . not the usual war between nations for land areas or other material gains, but a war between two diametrically opposed ideologies. The great difference between our western Christian world and the atheistic Communist world is not political, gentlemen, it is moral. . . . Today we are engaged in a final, all-out battle between communistic atheism and Christianity. (McCarthy, "Enemies from Within")

The rhetoric here indicates a clearly delineated battle between good and evil, with the fate of the world in the balance. He freely admits the religious nature of his ideology and worldview, framing the conflict as an "all-out battle" between the "Western Christian world" and the "atheistic Communist world."

Not only have countries and entire groups been labeled "the Antichrist," but individuals have also obviously had that dubious distinction. Henry Kissinger occupied this role for a time, likely for a variety of reasons. He was Jewish, and he was also a driving force behind the tenuous truce that eventually took root between the United States and the USSR. Given the huge stakes of the war against Communism, any conciliatory approach would have been seen as almost succumbing to evil. Therefore, Kissinger's willingness to negotiate was seen as a failure or, worse, an evil conspiracy. Fuller, in describing Kissinger's portrayal as Antichrist, continues by describing how "his name in Hebrew was said to add up to 111, which when multiplied by 6 surely designated him as the feared beast. Kissinger's role as a peacemaker in Middle East diplomacy also fit the Antichrist tradition, as, of course, did his Jewish heritage" (Fuller 157). Kissinger was obviously not the last person to be given this moniker.

Political figures have used apocalyptic imagery as a way to elicit unilateral support for actions against perceived enemies,[4] perhaps most famously with President Ronald Reagan. Reagan used this "end of the world" imagery in an assortment of speeches, many people believing that he actually took the Book of Revelation literally. So pervasive were the apocalyptic references in Reagan's rhetoric that, in 1984, a group of Jewish and Christian figureheads openly denounced Reagan's "ideology of nuclear Armageddon" (Carpenter 109). The apocalyptic ideas liberally sprinkled throughout Reagan's speeches no doubt gave credence to the notion of American exceptionalism, as though America, and not Israel, contained God's chosen people. Again, it became a way of justifying divisive policies against any perceived enemies of God's chosen people—the white, male, heterosexual Christians of the United States.

4. When Joseph Stalin died, the Voice of America—a government-funded broadcasting network—used apocalyptic rhetoric that placed Stalin in the framework of an epic, end-time battle. One source from the VOA "quoted directly from the Book of Revelation to describe Georgi Malenkov, Lavrenty Beria, and Vyacheslav Molotov, three Soviet officials in attendance" (Lahr). Once again, we see these myths becoming a contrivance for those with power and authority.

Postapocalyptic Media and Paranoia

At their inception, Judeo-Christian apocalypses were used by a genuinely oppressed group of people. Now, however, these apocalyptic ideas have found their way into American media, used to reestablish the dominance of the American white male. In other words, the dominant group is now using the rhetoric and ideas of minority groups, attempting to paint *themselves* as a threatened minority. This is something noted by Hofstadter, who discusses how conservative forces in the United States

> feel . . . dispossessed: America has been largely taken away from them and their kind, though they are determined to try to repossess it and to prevent the final destructive act of subversion. The old American virtues have already been eaten away by cosmopolitans and intellectuals; the old competitive capitalism has been gradually undermined by socialistic and communistic schemers; the old national security and independence have been destroyed by treasonous plots, having as their most powerful agents not merely outsiders and foreigners as of old but major statesmen who are at the very centers of American power. (Hofstadter 23–24)

The use of apocalyptic themes and ideas is part of a larger trend toward paranoia, as the dominant groups perceive more inclusive attitudes toward minorities, in addition to the minorities themselves, to be an affront to an entire way of life. This explains the preoccupation with reifying white male authority in apocalyptic films and books. The film, *Dr. Strangelove or: How I Learned to Stop Worrying and Love the Bomb* (1964) very clearly illustrates the paranoia of the dominant white male, who perceives himself as being beset on all sides by malevolent Others that seek to destroy him. General Ripper, convinced that the Soviets have contaminated the American water supply, has ordered B-52 bombers into Russia, for the purpose of launching a nuclear strike. The protestations of the others in attendance lead to several attempts to diffuse the situation, including an attempt to contact the American planes and order them to stand down. One plane, however, does not get the message and drops a nuclear bomb on Russia, triggering a Russian doomsday device that obliterates all life on the planet. The film parodies the American fear of insidious attacks from purported enemies that threaten white male dominance. The paranoia of General Ripper, who believes in a Soviet conspiracy to use fluoridation to contaminate the "precious bodily fluids" of Americans, is paralleled by the actions of Major Kong. Major Kong is the commanding officer of the one bomber that does not abort the mission, eventually dropping a nuclear bomb on Russia. His character is a mockery of the frontiersman, as he wears a cowboy hat, speaks in patriotic platitudes, and conducts himself with absurd bravado. With the American war tune "When Johnny Comes Marching Home" playing in the background, Kong gives his rousing speech. When the nuclear bomb gets stuck and won't drop down, Kong decides to push the bomb himself, eventually breaking it free, riding the bomb as it falls down to its target. He straddles the bomb, hat in hand. Ultimately, the film shows a level of fear and paranoia that drives white males to go to extreme lengths to maintain dominance. Despite being in positions of authority and power, both Kong and Ripper see themselves as being threatened. The threat, in both cases, is imagined. Kong has, without verification, assumed that the Soviet threat to the American way of life has manifested itself in such a way that he must respond with devastating force. The film paints both Kong and Ripper as absurd fools, believing in conspiracy theories and the total righteousness of American military might. This critical view of American paranoia is a departure from other such war films, which "end . . . with control being reestablished, the viewer reassured that the American way is the best course and that the military is doing the best job possible to shield us from the Communist menace" (Maland 715). On the contrary, *Dr. Strangelove* sees the apocalypse not as a battle between good and evil, where the white male emerges triumphant. Rather, the film sees the apocalypse as being explicitly caused by white male paranoia and the desire to prove dominance at any cost.

Director John Carpenter's "Apocalypse Trilogy"—including *The Thing* (1982), *Prince of Darkness* (1987), and *In the Mouth of Madness* (1995)—clearly shows paranoia over lost masculinity. In an interview with the *Wall Street Journal*, Carpenter stated that "all three of those movies are, in one way or another, about the end of things, about the end of everything, the world we know, but in different ways. Each of those things is kind of an apocalyptic kind of movie, but a very different take on it" (Calia). *The Thing*, a film version of the novella *Who Goes There?* and the second major film adaptation after *The Thing from Another World* (1951), follows a team of men at a research station called Outpost 31, who find a sled dog being pursued by Norwegian researchers. The Norwegians are shooting at the dog, frantically trying to kill it for reasons that are not immediately apparent. The helicopter crashes and after investigating a burnt-out Norwegian outpost, the Americans from Outpost 31 bring the dog to their station, along with the grotesquely malformed, charred remains of a deceased Norwegian. The dog is put in a kennel with the other dogs, and the outpost doctor performs an autopsy on the burnt Norwegian corpse. The rescued sled dog, we soon realize, is infected with an alien being that takes over the body of its host, shaping it into an amorphous looking mix of body parts, tentacles, claws, and teeth. What follows are incidents in which the alien impersonates various characters in the ice station, leading to paranoia over identity. No one can know for sure whether the person standing in front of them is human or an alien simulacrum. This leads to scenarios in which the crew accuse each other of being the alien, causing several violent confrontations, as MacReady remarks, "Nobody trusts anybody now." MacReady, the main white male protagonist, survives the disasters that eventually destroy the station and most of the crew. However, the film ends ambiguously, on a note that suggests MacReady or the other survivor could be the alien lifeform. Carpenter's film indicates a fear of an Other taking over the male body, literally replacing it and completely removing human autonomy. The men taken over by "the thing" no longer have control over their own male bodies, which morph into various forms. The monster of the film "threatens masculinity itself by taking over the male body, penetrating its very being" (Williams 122). The alien creature literally bursts forth from their bodies, in a perverse version of childbirth. Overall, the film shows a fear of an insidious Other infiltrating a male-dominated space and removing all male autonomy and control, posing a threat to the entire planet. The vast arctic wasteland of Antarctica is a stand-in for the apocalyptic voids seen in more traditionally apocalyptic films, and the creature threatens to spread this emptiness to the rest of the globe through its cunning and resilience.

Postapocalyptic Media and the White Nuclear Family

White Christian America, which is also an implicitly heterosexual America, has traditionally been the dominant group in the United States going back historically to the Puritans, who started as an actual oppressed minority in England. It's also implicitly a male-dominated America, since Puritan traditions have females in subservient positions, relegating all power to the men in the institution of the "conjugal patriarchal family [which] is the founding principle of the modern state and of liberal civil society"

(Hill 96). The patriarchal family, with its emphasis on reproduction, is decidedly heterosexual. There are a number of reasons for this, some quite obvious (reproductive purposes, for instance). However, this emphasis on heterosexuality has become totally unambiguous in the hostile policies of various political figures, for instance in the Defense of Marriage Act. The changes in women's rights, broadening acceptance of nonheteronormative forms of sexuality, and growing multiculturalism have seemingly prompted a reaction in the dominant culture, which seeks to reestablish dominance through various means, including the use of apocalyptic myths that bring the world back to the ideal "perfect" white, hetero, Christian America.

Concomitant with the anxiety felt over changing demographics are changes in the American family, over which the white American male held dominion for centuries. At the beginnings of America, the family was paramount—a patriarchal social institution in which the husband/father held primary responsibility over all members of the household. Before commercialization and industrialization, the family unit was a foundation for production, with each family unit tilling and utilizing their own land. As the means of production advanced in the nineteenth century, "Families began to lose their primacy in economic production to more complex entities such as the factory or the market" (Hawes 5). The early 1950s saw a push to "recreate the model middle-class family of the nineteenth century. . . . The search for individual self-realization and personal happiness helps to explain that phenomenon" (Hawes 7). The American family, despite any attempts to otherwise slow the changes therein, has continued to morph—changes that are further precipitated by an increase in immigrant and alternate family structures, such as gay couples with adopted children.

Traditionally, popular culture has portrayed the nuclear family and heterosexuality as the norm. This is evidenced in countless TV shows, movies, commercials, and songs. Author Chrys Ingraham, in *White Weddings: Romancing Heterosexuality in Popular Culture*, notes that in the year 1992, over a dozen popular TV shows ended with a heterosexual wedding. Heterosexuality is important to the dominant patriarchy, since it "upholds the home, housework, the family as both a personal and economic unit" (Bunch 177). While straight couples are still quite prominent in today's media, there seems to be more willingness to accept other forms of sexuality, a trend seen in public opinion polls and in the popularity of media featuring gay or transgender characters. A Pew Research Center poll shows that approval of gay marriage has gone from 35 percent in 2001, to 62 percent in 2017. This growing acceptance has been met with staunch opposition, particularly from right-wing religious groups, whose "opposition to gay marriage is, in part, grounded in the desire to maintain patriarchal heterosexual supremacy" (Ingraham 139). All of these changes not only go against older ideals of family, but they also lessen the importance of the traditional white male as the family center. Apocalyptic films and books seek to resituate the white male in a position of importance in several ways, one of them through the resurrection of the traditional nuclear family.

Toward the end of the book *Alas, Babylon* (1959), for instance, two of the main characters discuss a desire to bring back the institution of marriage after a nuclear war had decimated much of the planet. Randy Bragg, in a conversation with Elizabeth McGovern, says that "I wish we had a place of our own so I could keep you. . . . It may be an old-fashioned, before-The-Day attitude but if I'm going to have children I'd like to be married." She eventually responds, "It'll be nice to marry on Easter Sunday" (Frank 153). Embedded in this is not only the desire to resurrect the nuclear family structure that existed before the apocalypse but also an interest in preserving Christian holidays associated with the dominant culture. In the context of the story, this discussion is meant to be reassuring, as if the overtures to reestablishing dominance were a symbol of hope. This type of pattern—where the postapocalyptic world tries to reclaim the world that was lost—is to be found throughout apocalyptic media. Whatever threats are faced from outside forces, the dominant culture will emerge victorious. Today, these "threats" come in the form of political dissidents, nonheteronormative sexuality, and a variety of races and ethnicities. The white, heterosexual male is suddenly confronted with the possibility of losing control of a culture that is prominently inculcated with his own ideologies. In postapocalyptic media, these threatening outsiders often take the form of debauched maniacs, as in *The Road Warrior* (1981), for instance. The nefarious biker gang in the film is meant to be the group antithetical to all the values we (the audience and the main character, Max) hold to be essential foundations of Western civilization. Therefore, we are meant to oppose Lord Humongous and his hordes, a group inclined to unusual clothing choices and homosexuality. Each member of the biker gang has a slightly different style of dress, which is notably different from the group Max ends up helping—a pale-skinned group wearing mostly white. The ending of the film sees the group of white-clad heroes drive away to freedom, while Max has moved closer to becoming part of the dominant culture once again. Max was a family man in the first film and has drifted into isolation after the apocalypse and the loss of his wife and child. The audience is meant to feel hope at his turn back toward preapocalyptic values, as he becomes a surrogate father to the Feral Kid during the course of the film. *The Road Warrior* starts with a threat to white patriarchy and family structures and ends with their reestablishment, much like *Alas, Babylon*, and countless other apocalyptic narratives.

Most postapocalyptic books and films advocate for movement back to precatastrophe institutions and patterns that distinctly benefit the white American patriarchy. *Earth Abides* deals with a deadly disease that wipes out most of the globe, while the protagonist, Ish, attempts to put together the pieces and create a new society. To this end, Ish finds a wife to bear children that will become part of a new generation. This new generation ends up relying far more on the natural world, eschewing many of the tools and easy comforts of Ish's generation. Ultimately, this primitive lifestyle is presented as a return to something better and more natural. Beyond the superficial differences, however, many of the predisaster institutions are still intact. The main character even says as much:

> The family group was just what it might have been at any time in almost any society—father, mother, and children, tightly grouped to form the basic social unit, so basic in fact that it might be considered biological rather than social. After all, he thought, the family was the toughest of all human institutions. It had preceded civilization, and so it naturally survived afterwards. (Stewart 147)

The author here incorrectly assumes a human institution could exist outside of civilization, when the two are very deeply intertwined. Civilization is created and maintained through such institutions, the family being one of the most fundamental. For American society, "the authority of the nation has seemed to depend on the authority of the family" (Horkheimer 362). In addition to the family unit, a sort of superstition survives in the novel, a faith and mysticism often associated with religious practices. Author George Stewart, however, feels that religious institutions have been lost:

> Here had been a great, even overwhelming, mass of tradition—the tradition of Christianity, or of Western civilization, or of Indo-European folkways, or of Anglo-American culture. Call it what you wished, it was still so tremendous that you might say it was omnipotent, for good or bad absorbing the individual. But now their little community had lost much of the tradition. (194)

Here and elsewhere, the author presents religion as a particular set of traditions and rituals, ignoring perhaps the more base and simplistic superstitions that are often the vestigial beginnings of religious beliefs. The children in his "tribe," for instance, regard the tools and people of the old generation with a sort of spiritual reverence, so much so that they're afraid to touch certain objects. Could not the deifying of this old world be the foundation for a set of religious beliefs?

In any case, Ish tries to impart the religious institutions onto the new generation and assumes that they have rejected it, not thinking that they simply replaced it with something else, however primitive. Ish tries to share these institutions with the new generation, choosing to ignore their destructive power—a destructive power he even tacitly acknowledges when he uses the phrase "for good or bad." It's assumed that this institution is important or essential for the new society and as readers relate to Ish as the main protagonist, we are clearly meant to feel a sense of loss, as if the lack of Christianity was deeply limiting and society could not otherwise reach the same heights as before. The book very clearly pushes these old institutions as important for the reestablishment of society, choosing to actively avoid a discussion of their destructive potential. Even where the book pretends to show a new world order that eschews the old institutions, if we dig deep enough, we see the beginnings of the same exact institutions.

The desire to maintain a white, male-dominated version of America is also seen in the film *12 Monkeys* (1995). The movie begins in the future, where humanity must live underground due to a virus that has made the surface of the Earth uninhabitable. James Cole is a prisoner in a bleak underground facility and is offered an opportunity to lessen his sentence by going back in time to collect information on the group believed responsible for the spread of the virus—the Army of the 12 Monkeys. We get to see the remains of the surface world, thirty years after the apocalyptic event. Philadelphia, a key center for the birth of American democracy, is desolate and overrun with dangerous animals. America, as we know it, is gone, and the zoo animals formerly kept in cages have claimed the surface for themselves.

Anxiety over the white patriarchy losing control of the world is evident from the beginning of the film, where the main character wakes up in a prison cell, forced to live underground. The dominant culture can no longer live on the surface due to a deadly pandemic and has ceded control to the animals, who are unaffected by the virus. Cole's masculinity, manifesting in the form of aggression, is sublimated throughout the film, as time and again he is held in restraints. He is constantly drugged and held back from his more primitive, combative behaviors, and he longs to break free and inhabit the past, when white male power was uncontested. While the scientists with authority over Cole are white, they seem emblematic of an intellectual elite, threatening the aggressive, would-be alpha male, Cole. This is indicative of white male culture's suspiciousness of academics and scientists, most recently seen in the skepticism toward the COVID-19 vaccine. The main villain of *12 Monkeys* is, in fact, a scientist: he releases the virus in multiple cities, helping ensure the end of humans dwelling on the surface. This distrust of science can be tied to the American belief that

> self-discipline, hard work, and personal responsibility lead to success . . . [which] is a treasured part of the American ethos, and Americans as a whole—whose country was based in no small part on racial subjugation. . . . Climate change and other environmental problems seem to violate the just world belief. The idea that despite our best efforts our fate is influenced by luck or the collective actions of others—or that our society is guilty of gross injustice that we are partaking in—is antithetical to the classic American . . . of self-determination and meritocracy. Thus, many Americans . . . tend to react like whites in the antebellum US South, either denying that the problem exists or changing their thinking to justify it. (Otto)

Science calls attention to problems that affect or damage the idea of America as the apex of human achievement in all areas of civilization, with white male institutions that other countries seek to emulate. American exceptionalism is threatened by anything that calls attention to the mistakes or disastrous consequences of white male rule. Psychologists Robb Willer and Matthew Feinberg, in a study at UC Berkeley, found that "if we experimentally increase people's patriotism, their belief in global warming tends to go down" (Otto). This explains, in part, the ambiguous relationship with science, seen in various sci-fi films. Science leads to extraordinary advances and illustrates American technological prowess, while at the same time causing apocalyptic scenarios.

Cole also enjoys a level of consumerism that no longer exists in the future. At the beginning of the film, Cole is sent to the surface to gather bug specimens for study. While investigating a desolate Philadelphia, he stumbles upon a department store filled with objects just sitting on shelves, covered in dirt and dust. In this future, the objects are useless and part of a long-dead America. At the end of the film, while buying disguises to avoid being captured by police, Cole accompanies Kathryn, a psychologist he meets during his first foray into the past, to a department store that dramatically contrasts with the store at the beginning of the film. Everything in the store is pristine and new, and the store is filled with color, life, and dozens of consumers: consumerism is synonymous with a fulfilling life. The first time Cole meets Jeffrey Goines, the future leader of the Army of the 12 Monkeys, Goines notes that

> we're consumers. Okay, buy a lot of stuff, you're a good citizen. But if you don't buy a lot of stuff, you know what? You're mentally ill! That's a fact! If you don't buy things . . . toilet paper, new cars, computerized blenders, electrically operated sexual devices. (*12 Monkeys*)

Later, he expounds on this theme:

> Seriously, more and more people are being defined now as mentally ill. Why? Because they're not consuming on their own. But as patients, they become consumers of mental health care. And this gives the so-called sane people work! (*12 Monkeys*)

Consumerism defines this particular era Cole finds himself in, unlike the future, where the underground world necessitates a spartan lifestyle, given the lack of new industry and limited access to produced objects. In Cole's second encounter with Kathryn, he is confused by an advertisement on the radio, the implication being that in the future, people are not bombarded with constant ads, all aiming to stoke the fires of consumerism. Ultimately, Cole succumbs to the consumer drive, purchasing clothes, a disguise, and a trip to the Florida Keys. He longs for this world of unfettered access to commodities, used to fulfill dreams and aspirations, such as his desire to live in a paradise with a woman he has subjugated and manipulated into loving him.

Before he can fulfill his ultimate fantasy of living in the Florida Keys with a woman he has continually mistreated, Cole is shot by police officers. Ultimately, then, the story follows a white male longing for an older America, where the powerless are held in check and consumerism reigns supreme.

The animals on the surface function as a stand-in for various oppressed minorities, as it is eventually shown that the Army of the 12 Monkeys is actually a radical animal rights group responsible for freeing zoo animals from their cages. In one earlier scene in the film, the television in the insane asylum shows a rabbit being forced to endure painful cosmetic testing and when Cole comes back to his prison in the future, he is shown images of protestors, holding posters with pictures of animal abuse. With this and other such scenes, animals are repeatedly shown to be a mistreated group, treated as though their lives and happiness were insignificant. The pamphlets that the Army of the 12 Monkeys prints out have slogans like ANIMALS HAVE SOULS Too and one that asks for an end to SPECIESISM, which is meant to parallel racism.

The use of animals as a stand-in for minorities is not without precedent. There is, in fact, a history of minority groups being "associated with properties of animals," from which we can conclude that "the social representations about minorities are connected to representations of animals. This may imply that in racist ideologies, the Others are basically represented as less human" (Van Dijk 109). This depiction of Others as animals has happened throughout history in societies all over the world. For instance, medieval Muslims thought of Jews as "pigs, apes, and rats." During World War II, America portrayed the Japanese as "animals, and [they] were often portrayed as monkeys, apes, or rodents, and sometimes as insects." More recently, after the Abu Ghraib prison scandal involving US military detainees in Iraq, Brigadier General Janis Karpinski reported that "Major General Geoffrey Miller had told her to make sure that the prisoners were treated like animals. 'He said they are like dogs and if you allow them to believe at any point that they are more than a dog then you have lost control of them'" (Smith 22). Treating people as subhuman helps provide a means by which people can escape culpability in the flagrant mistreatment of other human beings.

In addition, the animals being linked to a virus causing mass human extinction is tied to the fear of Others bringing contagion. Indeed, we see that

> the association of immigrants and other Others with illness, disease, and plague in the West has a long history. These anxieties about the hygiene of immigrants and racialized others extended well into the twentieth century and is often presented as a potential threat in popular media in the twenty-first century. (quoted in Gurr 23)

In the images we see of the future, the released animals, while not at all responsible for the virus, are much like "bodies that cannot be controlled: zombies, monsters, aliens, pathogens, unruly mobs. It is the body and presence of the Other that presents itself as the ultimate threat. It is the presence of foreign matter, of foreign bodies, that becomes the spark that ignites apocalyptic destruction" (quoted in Gurr 27). In the minds of xenophobic Americans, these Others are synonymous with an unseen contagion that will result in complete annihilation. Indeed, "research suggests that fear of illness can be a predictor of xenophobia" (Gurr 23). At the beginning, when Cole ventures out into the apocalyptic surface world, he is threatened not only by the virus but also by a bear and other predatory animals prowling the street. Thus, part of what makes this world apocalyptic is the threat that animal rule poses for white men like Cole. The animals become inextricably linked to a virus that requires the human race to cower below the surface of the planet.

If the animals are an oppressed minority, it would seem to make Jeffrey Goines a champion for the disenfranchised, helping a group with no power at all. In one of his tirades, he exclaims, "Have I ever 'developed' a virus? Do I put helpless animals in cages and measure their reactions to electrical stimuli? Do I inject radioactive substances into living creatures and examine their bowel movements?" (*12 Monkeys*). In the context of the film, however, his actions seem primarily motivated by his desire to anger his father, with whom he has an extremely volatile relationship, evidenced clearly in a later scene where Jeffrey kidnaps him. Jeffrey's anger is implied to correlate with his father being embarrassed of his struggles with mental illness. Despite Leland Goines's power, he lets his son languish in a dilapidated mental institution. Later, Leland Goines gives Jeffrey a token job at his company, where he has little direct contact with the general public. In both cases, it appears that Leland is trying to hide his mentally ill son from the public eye. Later, when Cole meets a group of 12 Monkeys activists, they note that "the media latch on to him [Jeffrey] because he's picketing his own father, a 'famous Nobel Prize winning virologist' " (*12 Monkeys*). He pickets his own father and manages to finally gain recognition for something, briefly stealing the spotlight from Leland, the "famous Nobel Prize winning virologist." While it could be an attempt to make his father proud of him, the fact that he kidnaps his father and directly protests practices related to his father's profession indicates that Jeffrey harbors deep resentment toward Leland.

The white male, James Cole, seeks to reclaim the surface, eventually resolving to not just gather information but to stop the virus from spreading by going back in time again. After meeting psychologist Kathryn Railly, he falls in love with the surface world of the past. He wants to live in a world where humans reign over everything, food is plentiful, and there are such simple pleasures as music on the radio. He wants, in other words, access to and control of his surroundings—to live in a place where his status as a white male allows him a comfortable existence. It's quite telling that the two songs Cole enjoys are both written by African Americans—one by Fats Domino and the other by Louis Armstrong. The minority group here exists to give him pleasure, while his female love interest is consistently restrained physically and forced to do things against her will. Cole exerts his strength and male authority to force Kathryn to go along with his own goals and fantasies. Despite this, she seems to eventually fall in love with him; yet it seems like a classic case of Stockholm syndrome.

Cole, right before his death, identifies the scientist responsible for the apocalypse. Dr. Peters, an assistant for Jeffrey Goines's father, is guilty of spreading the virus, and he is never thwarted by Jeffrey, thus implying that humans will still ultimately be wiped out. One final scene, however, indicates that this might not be the case. One of the female scientists from the future is seen getting on a plane next to the man carrying the virus. They begin talking, and he asks her what she does for a living. She replies, "I'm in insurance." Given the fact that she looks exactly the same as she does thirty years in the future, it can be inferred that the female scientist from the future went back in time to stop this man, now that the scientists understand who spread the virus. Her line, "I'm in insurance," indicates that she is "ensuring" that the surface world will survive. Thus, Cole, by identifying that the Army of the 12 Monkeys is not culpable in the spread of the virus, helps the people of the future identify the real culprit. His death at the end is not in vain, and he has perhaps saved the entire world, preserving the consumer-driven patriarchal world he has come to love.

The White Patriarchal Family

Oblivion (2013) follows the character Jack Harper, who maintains drones that protect harvesting machines, which convert Earth's oceans into energy. Humans are largely absent from Earth, supposedly having moved to one of Saturn's moons after a catastrophic war with an alien race. The aliens had destroyed the moon, which caused many natural disasters; ultimately, however, Jack believes that humans have emerged victorious. In reality, the aliens had won the war, and Jack is one of many clones produced by the aliens to operate machines that harvest and deplete all of Earth's natural resources. Jack eventually becomes aware of this after he encounters human survivors, rebels struggling to reclaim the planet. From the very first moments of the film, Jack's preoccupation is not with maintaining the drones or his assigned tasks but with memories of a woman that he later discovers is his wife. The relationship between Jack and his wife, Julia, is the primary focus of the film, wherein Jack struggles to re-create the nuclear family, ultimately proving successful at the very end.

Jack and Marriage

Jack, in the very first lines of the film, describes a memory that we later discover is the day he proposed to his wife. He notes that, "I know you. . . . But we've never met. I'm with you. . . . But I don't know your name. I know I'm dreaming. But it feels like more than that. It feels like a memory. How can that be?" (*Oblivion*). This is puzzling to Jack, since he has received memory wipes every five years. His desire to return to the past is further concretized when he flies to a beautiful lakeside cabin, filled with objects from before the apocalypse, including records, books, and clothing. The world has been ravaged by war and his memories have been largely erased; yet he is drawn to a world where he is the dominant white male, providing comforts and commodities for a wife and child. When he returns back to his actual, assigned residence, designated by the superiors that have assigned him to drone maintenance, he is clearly dissatisfied with his sterile surroundings and generic girlfriend. He is prohibited from bringing back any preapocalyptic artifacts, a rule that is vehemently enforced by his girlfriend, who shares none of Jack's desire for the past.

When Jack opens a cryo-pod containing the woman he had seen in his fragmented images of the past, his memories are eventually verified as real events. He eventually remembers that she is the wife he has been dreaming of. While his girlfriend, Victoria, refuses gifts and objects from the past, Julia wears one around her neck—her wedding ring. The wedding ring, as a symbol of marriage, signifies the return of a preapocalyptic institution from which Jack derives value. Marriage has managed to survive a devastating alien invasion, and decades of the wife being preserved in stasis. The apocalyptic scenario not only signifies the enduring qualities and ability of marriage to overcome obstacles, but it also allows Jack to be the heroic white male. The end of the film shows Jack sacrificing his life to save Julia and other human survivors.

Jack and Family

The desire to return to the institution of marriage accompanies a desire for the nuclear family, living in a comforting home of commodities. The cabin that Jack has frequented turns out to be a close approximation of the cabin that Jack had discussed with Julia while they were married. Before the end of the film, Jack takes Julia to this cabin, and she notes that "you said when it was all over, you would build me a house on a lake. We would grow old and fat together. And we would fight. Maybe drink too much." She is describing a typical domestic lifestyle, and much like the institution of marriage, this lifestyle manages to surmount innumerable obstacles to emerge once again after the apocalypse. The ending of the film shows Julia at the cabin with a child, undoubtedly Jack's daughter. Despite the fact that Jack has sacrificed himself to destroy the aliens, a new clone of Jack appears. He sees Julia and his daughter from a distance and narrates: "For three years, I searched for the house he built. I knew it had to be out there. Because I know him. I am him. Who's that? I am Jack Harper. And I am home" (*Oblivion*). The nuclear family is now complete, and the domestic lifestyle is revived. Family and marriage have survived an apocalypse and death, and the white male's purpose and importance have been reestablished.

Jack as Hero Frontiersman

The apocalypse creates a scenario in which the white male can emerge a hero, saving the planet and providing a new home for the nuclear family. Jack is a victim of evil alien designs, an oppressed minority that must struggle against overwhelming odds. He is literally a minority in the sense that there are very few humans left on the planet; moreover, he is an unwitting slave to interests that are not his own. His servitude is manufactured through his memory wipes, which prevent him from remembering the true outcome of the apocalyptic event. Denying him knowledge of the past hinders his ability to bring back the institutions of preapocalyptic society, including marriage and the nuclear family.

The film implies that the clone of Jack we follow in the film is the first such clone to exhibit curiosity and independence. He is the frontiersman, forging his own path away from the dictums of a controlling command center. In this sense, he embodies the characteristics of the prototypical white American male, established in early American history. In addition, he manages to maintain these characteristics, despite having been engineered by the aliens to be obedient. The implication is that these white male traits are irrepressible and impossible to extinguish. Thematically similar to Westerns in this sense, the film shows the conflict between conformity and raw individuality, with Jack's character bravely exploring a new frontier despite various restrictions. He is, for instance, forbidden from exploring the areas beyond his harvester, supposedly because these areas are irradiated. Jack ends up crossing the barrier into this irradiated zone, only to discover the truth about his identity—he is a clone. He encounters a clone of himself when he fully embraces the role of intrepid explorer, breaking the rules of his alien superiors. The frontier here allows him to *literally* find himself, surrounded by sand and a harsh landscape that recalls many old Westerns in the arid lands of the Southwest.

The Alien as "Other"

While the alien is presented as the "enemy" in the film, very little is known about them. They remain inchoate entities that we never even see, beyond the woman in the Tet that communicates with Jack and Victoria. Sally, the woman that Victoria and Jack report to, is human. However, the film does not show any other alien from the Tet, and the woman could very well have been another clone. In this sense, the aliens of the film aren't really in the film, and are mainly represented by their mechanical drones. The aliens, therefore, are a cipher for any number of threatening Others. They are not developed as having their own culture, institutions, and motivations—they are merely not human. Aliens in sci-fi films are so readily accepted as villains that they become an automatic adversary for film heroes. It's the kind of Manichean, morally simplistic thinking associated with the frontier and America's view of Native Americans. They are not white; therefore, they are bad. It mattered little that Native Americans had a culture and rich traditions. These reductive, quasi-racist portrayals of Native Americans present a vacuous foil against which the white male can prove his superiority. While the aliens are not necessarily a representation of a specific minority group, they do point to a larger trend of creating an enemy whose sole purpose is to occupy a negative space that elevates the white patriarchy. This is fairly obvious in *Oblivion*, which extols the virtues of marriage and the family by showing its ability to overcome nefarious alien forces and create something cohesive. Marriage and family bring people together, becoming a microcosm of a society comprising coexisting people. The aliens, by separating people into literal zones and preventing more than two clones from communicating at a time, are divisive and create a hollow existence for people like Jack, who yearn for something more than the sterile lifestyle of drone maintenance. *Oblivion* is just one of many apocalyptic films preoccupied with reasserting the authority of the white male by resurrecting preapocalyptic institutions like marriage and family. Some, however, offer a more progressive stance on the role of the dominant group in a world of growing diversity, for instance the film *Children of Men* (2006).

Alternatives to the White Nuclear Family

The apocalyptic event in *Children of Men* (2006) is left vague and the viewers are simply left to piece together clues during the course of the film. There are indications of a protracted struggle between countries, in which weapons of mass destruction had been deployed, England remaining one of the few countries not utterly obliterated. Despite England's survival, the signs of a dystopian world are everywhere: dirt and trash strewn in the street, immigrants being held in cages, and no children to be found anywhere. In addition to a possible nuclear apocalypse, there's also a fertility problem—both of these things create the postapocalyptic world vividly brought to life on the screen. For reasons unknown, people have been unable to reproduce for eighteen years. The film is rife with the anxiety that the traditional nuclear family is dissolving, and that nonwhite groups threaten to outnumber dominant white males. Even though the film offers a seemingly progressive outlook—that an immigrant Black woman and her child will help save human beings from extinction—it captures the pervasive white anxiety of the time in which the film was created.

Theo and Family

The white male in the story, Theo, leads an empty, unfulfilling life, substantiated by the contemplation of suicide—something he admits to his friend, Jaspar. His one and only child had died years prior to the events of the film, and he had parted ways with the female interest in his life, Julien. In this way, Theo has lost all of the components of the family unit, from which the dominant white male derives value and purpose. Most other men in the film, however, can no longer be fathers either, due to the fertility crisis. The dominant group and its most elemental unit—the family—are broken; it's a brokenness paralleled by the surrounding desolate environment. The literal destruction of the world is a key counterpart to the destruction of the family, and it is strongly suggested that the crumbling family unit partially caused it. Miriam, the midwife, says to Theo, "As the sound of the playgrounds faded, the despair set in. Very odd, what happens in a world without children's voices" (*Children of Men*).

Theo goes from feeling suicidal to driven and hopeful, through the "family" he forms with Kee, the pregnant immigrant he must escort to safety. Kee and Theo are not romantically involved, but they do embody the roles of father and mother. Kee nurtures and cares for the child, while Theo protects it and provides shelter and food. In this way, the nuclear family is revived, and provides Theo with a sense of value that had been absent from his life. Theo dies with a smile on his face, after sacrificing himself to save Kee and her child. Kee names the child "Dylan," the name of the child Theo and Julien had lost. In these final moments, Theo has become a father again.

While the film does highlight the importance of family for the white male, it presents an alternative family structure that seems more progressive than many other such films and books. The film was adapted from a book by PD James, in which Kee is a white character. The filmmakers intentionally changed her race, making the film an explicit commentary on the perpetual drive to reify the same dominant white family structures that existed before the apocalypse. An alternative is offered, one that is enabled by an apocalyptic event that makes an immigrant Black child much more valuable than it otherwise would have been. Realizing the value of *any* child in a fertility crisis, Theo accepts his role as father in an untraditional family, comprising Black immigrants that would have been shunned by society before the apocalypse. The family is also untraditional in the sense that the child is created by CGI and is literally not human. The fact that an entire segment on the *Children of Men* DVD is dedicated to an explication of how the child was digitally created indicates its importance, implying that "understanding the baby as posthuman is essential for interpreting the film." The interpretation of the digital child as "posthuman" suggests that "utopian kinship that has replaced the heteronormative family" (LaRose 18–19). The child, through being literally digital, could signal a transcendence of race by embodying no race at all. The film is thus both illustrating white anxiety at changing demographics and families but also illustrating an alternative that still allows the white male to find value and purpose.

Theo as Hero Frontiersman

Not only is the film illustrating alternatives to families, but it also offers a white male protagonist that goes against the pattern of intrepid, white frontiersman that populate so many apocalyptic films and books. While Theo does prove himself to be invaluable in protecting Kee, he is not the superhuman force of masculinity that is embodied in characters like Mad Max Rockatansky. He goes from an unsatisfying office job to reluctantly escorting Kee to the Human Project, a group that is attempting to solve the fertility crisis. While this might make him the reluctant white male hero, it's worth noting *how* he protects Kee. Theo is not a man accustomed to using violence, and he doesn't fire a single gun in the course of the film. He spends much of the film hiding from gunfire, or attempting to talk his way out of dangerous situations. On the bus to the refugee camp, Bexhill, for instance, Theo protects Kee from a guard by pretending that he's an immigrant complaining about the smell of feces. Annoyed and disgusted, the guard walks away. This is a strikingly different form of valor than the fighting prowess of Eli in the *Book of Eli* or the sawed-off-shotgun-wielding Max in *The Road Warrior*. Theo also eschews the stoicism that characterizes so many white male heroes and instead sobs uncontrollably when Julien is killed and exhibits joy when Kee safely delivers her baby. While Theo, a white male, is the protagonist of the film, it is clear that he embodies a different masculinity than the rugged loner of American myth.

Immigrants as "Other"

The film places a great deal of importance on family, but the anxiety about its destruction coincides with a trenchant fear of immigrants, who are seemingly blamed for many of society's ills. The fear of immigrants is clear from the very first moments of the film, which shows Theo watching horrifying scenes of abuse from a train car, as immigrants are rounded up like cattle by aggressive police forces. A television commercial indicates that British citizens are expected to report immigrants to the police, which undoubtedly foments the public's general animosity toward people from other countries. The captured immigrants are sent to refugee camps, where the vast numbers of foreigners can be seen in utter squalor, in bombed-out buildings with dirty mattresses for beds and streets filled with scattered rubble. The sheer numbers of people in these camps imply that the anxiety toward immigrants is exacerbated by the idea that the white male might end up a minority, much the same as the actual census data in many countries indicates. Ultimately, however, the blaming of immigrants is shown to be misguided at best, as Kee, an immigrant, actually saves the nuclear family. The major change to the family unit has to do with the reinventing of the family as something to include all demographics, not simply the dominant class of white people. The apocalypse, and concurrent fertility crisis, illuminates the "vulnerability of the white, heterosexual nuclear family cast adrift in a sea of global atrocities and futile public displays of protest" (Chaudhary 74). The "white, heterosexual nuclear family" must adapt or perish. Because of the fertility issue, the dominant culture must learn to accept cultures and ethnicities other than their own if they wish to survive. Whether they *will* is not at all clear at the end of the film.

In the film, white male anxiety is caused by the deterioration of the family because of the fertility crisis and an influx of immigrants that threaten to make the British people a minority in their own country. The end of the film does, however, give the viewers hope that the white male and immigrants can coexist and embrace a new, more heterogeneous family, embodied by Kee, Theo, and Dylan. Theo escorts Kee and her child out of a building in Bexhill, as it is bombarded with gunfire by British soldiers. These same soldiers stop shooting for several moments when they see the baby, only to go right back to killing each other a few minutes later. While the penultimate scene does present hope for coexistence, it is also a depressing reminder of how the same patterns of destruction perpetuate themselves, even after the apocalypse.

The film is highly critical of the hierarchical system that places white males at the top. This is most evident in the contrast between the reverence for the child and the complete disregard given everyone else, which elucidates the belief that some lives are worth more than others. England, during the course of the film, touts itself as a bastion of hope and human survival, yet it places immigrants in cages. The ideals of freedom and democracy are antithetical to a system that prioritizes one race over another, but this is exactly what society does. Furthermore, if the child's value is derived from scarcity, one can infer that there is a fear that the human race might ultimately be wiped off the planet. Yet the warring factions, ostensibly worried about the extinction of the human race, continue to speed along the process of extinction. The film, however, ends with Kee on a dinghy, watching as a boat called *The Tomorrow* comes to pick her up. The boat, manned by the Human Project, is called *The Tomorrow* as an indication that there is hope and that humankind will survive. Indeed, as the screen cuts to black, we hear the sounds of children playing. The black of the screen hinders us from seeing the ethnicity or race of these children, perhaps indicating a future utopia without the sorts of hierarchies that place little value on certain minority groups—a world that is truly colorblind. Chaudhary writes that

> the end of the film, punctuated with Theo's death, signals a future without white maleness. . . . It is the end of whiteness that inaugurates the utopia whose babble we hear once the final image vanishes from the screen. Kee and her baby do not herald a reign of blackness as a new universality, but rather a mythic future in which all alterity is sublated. (78–79)

While the end of the film does offer hope for the future, that hope seems a faint glimmer, as the vast majority of the film shows the horrific lengths to which the dominant culture will go to maintain its power.

Conclusion

The apocalypse is a tool co-opted by the dominant culture to reify ideas and institutions that benefit the dominant group, as this same group perceives the growing power of minorities as a threat to their unilateral control. The ability to utilize traditional myths used by the oppressed was facilitated by the ability of capitalism to permeate every facet of human life. The Book of Daniel and the Book of Revelation were both written during or soon after major crises, experienced by the Jewish people and Christians, respectively. In the twentieth and twenty-first centuries, however, apocalyptic myths in Daniel and Revelation are now under the purview of the dominant culture, used by "white heterosexual masculinity . . . to consolidate its power by claiming its victimized, marginalized status." There is the "notion that the dominant identity has lost ground to its gendered and raced others, and now requires an identity politics of its own" (Rehling 28). Though the white male of America is the "dominant identity," there is a sense of pervasive anxiety and dread among this group. The ameliorated economic and political condition of women and minorities has threatened the monopoly on power that the dominant male culture has enjoyed throughout American history; consequently, they depict themselves as the "marginalized" demographic. The myths and iconography employed all clearly frame stories in this way—the world has slipped away from the white heterosexual Christian male, evidenced by the utter destruction of the apocalypse. Ultimately, the white male protagonist manages to cultivate some semblance of order in the postapocalyptic wasteland, and the movement back toward preapocalyptic ideals is celebrated.

2

"Unite the Civilized World"

Frontier Eschatology

THE CLASSIC *Once Upon a Time in the West* (1968) begins with several laconic henchmen waiting patiently at a train station, the only sounds from the windmill, a telegraph, and the flies buzzing around their heads. The landscape is open and barren, and the train tracks carry someone or something important; a sense of dread is palpable. Whatever these men are waiting for, a violent and bloody confrontation seems imminent. This sense of brutishness mingled with open possibility is characteristic of the frontier myth. The train tracks can carry any number of things, thereby exhibiting the potential for both creation and destruction. On one hand, they signal the growth of cities and civilization, and the connective tissue between the various territories of the United States. At the same time, the tracks signal a loss of independence, and yet another territory falling under clear control of the broader United States. The trains themselves signal myriad possibilities as far as cargo; everything from raw building materials to violent desperados can be carried aboard. In *Once Upon a Time in the West*, this potential turns destructive when Charles Bronson finally exits the arriving train. The lone figure of unbreakable justice, in this case Bronson, is the image of the rugged individualism of the American frontier. Beset on all sides by hardship, he finds a way to emerge victorious, much like the American settlers struggled to establish themselves in spite of an often hostile landscape and Indian attacks. This is the American frontier myth—the raw, unbreakable spirit that Frederick Jackson Turner had written about at the end of the nineteenth century. Actual historical events involving the settlement of the West took on a life of their own, embellished or sometimes entirely fabricated by the likes of Wild Bill Cody. Whether this myth is based on fact or not, its influence is undeniable. These pervasive myths endure and seem to extol American values. The influence is seen in contemporary films and books, wherein the Western has adapted by melding with other genres, especially science fiction and postapocalyptic media.

In this chapter, I argue that the conflation of Western themes and iconography with postapocalypticism is part of a general pattern, discussed previously in chapter 1, of using religion and images of American identity to reify a hierarchy that enables the white male to reign supreme.

The Postman (1997), based on the book by David Brin, takes place after an apocalyptic event that has wiped out most cities and the entire US government. The story follows a white male who stumbles upon an abandoned mail truck in the forest. Seeking shelter from the rain, he hides in the truck and wears the deceased mail carrier's coat to keep warm. Carrying a satchel of letters from the mail truck and wearing the USPS uniform, he goes to a nearby town for food. Convincing the sentinels at the gates that he is an actual postman, he is allowed entry and almost immediately inspires the townspeople. He fabricates much of his tale of a restored US government, but his tales are believed, partly because the citizens desperately want to believe but also because he happens to have a letter addressed to one of the people actually living in the town. Inspired by the idea of a restored government and the ability to communicate between self-enclosed agrarian communities, civilians from other towns begin joining the USPS to become mail carriers, and people in every town hand letters to the postman and his helpers. The postman, initially only desiring food and shelter by maintaining this ruse, comes to be inspired himself, despite having conjured up these lies. Ultimately, he must confront the Holnists, a violent group of trained soldiers ruling over a large group of towns through fear. His success in stopping the Holnist leader facilitates peace between the townspeople and the remaining Holnist soldiers. His lie—that the government had been restored and that communication routes had been reestablished—ends up becoming a reality. Thus, we see the return to myth as a catalyst for rebuilding. Without the past frontier myth, there can be no future.

The Postman, as a film, begins like many Westerns—with a lone warrior trudging across a barren, open stretch of land somewhere in the Southwest. He is a reluctant hero, much like the titular hero of *Shane* or, even more recently, Roy Goode in the TV show *Godless*. In addition, the landscape of this hero's journey is generally envisioned as the "frontier"—desert dotted with some trees and sage brush and a surrounding range of mountains. The hero's nemesis, named Bethlehem, has many similarities with Western villains. He terrorizes frontier towns before a white male frontiersman teaches or inspires the townspeople to take a stand. Bethlehem is also more cultured than most of his henchmen, using his spare time to read and paint. This is similar to Carnegie in *The Book of Eli*, Frank in *Godless*, Frank in *Once Upon a Time in the West*, and countless other villains in Westerns who have knowledge of books and other artifacts of the more sophisticated cultures of the city. The towns that these men terrorize are raw and uncultivated—filled with hard workers who have little cultural refinement and no ability to defend themselves. Ramshackle buildings line up along a straight road through town, which likely has one sheriff, a saloon, and a whorehouse. Similar to the towns in *The Magnificent Seven*, *Godless*, and myriad others, the residents in *The Postman* need a frontiersman to help take down an evil gang.

An apocalyptic event has wiped out much of the country, but virtually no time is spent discussing it. A brief mention of the destruction of the United States is made by voiceover narration at the beginning of the film, but even this is vague. The main focus of the film—reestablishing communication routes for a national postal service—is not uniquely apocalyptic and indeed could be the focus of a traditional Western. The main way the audience knows that the film is postapocalyptic is through the defamiliarization of buildings, objects, and clothing. Cars, for instance, are scattered throughout the towns, resting lifeless in varying states of decay, their only use in the film as a roadblock. The cars are parked by buildings that are in assorted degrees of disrepair; for instance, the post office is completely empty, dark, and falling apart. The main narrative of *The Postman*, however, is not reliant on these details. So what does the film gain in placing the events of the story after an apocalyptic event?

The apocalyptic event that transpires before the beginning of the film creates a scenario in which the United States can revise history and place the white male back in a position of power. In this scenario, the oppressed people are not minority groups, like Native Americans, but white people, who must pay the Holnists, a violent, heavily armed group that uses fear to make the townspeople subservient. Bethlehem, the Holnist leader, has a fierce regime that goes unchallenged until his encounter with the protagonist, named only "the Postman." He begins the film as an ordinary man, traveling from town to town performing abridged versions of Shakespeare's plays, unwilling to fight or engage the Holnists in any way. The apocalypse, however, creates a situation where he becomes a symbol of hope and defiance by wearing an old mail carrier uniform. The uniform is a symbol of the preapocalyptic world and thus gains significance specifically because of the apocalyptic event. It's a symbol of a functioning government, a whole country unified through a communication system. In this way, the mail uniform harkens back to a lost world, a world that this white man, the Postman, begins to bring back. This ordinary man is a hero to the townspeople because the apocalypse has made the USPS into a powerful emblem of a fallen America. Abby, the main female character in the film, essentially states exactly this, noting, "I don't think we ever really understood what they [letters] meant to us until they were gone. Getting a letter made you feel like you were part of something bigger than yourself. No place was ever too far away for the postman. So nobody ever had to be alone. The postman was someone you could count on. Things just made more sense when they were around." It seems clear from this and other sections of the film that the deification of mail carriers is due entirely to their disappearance after the apocalyptic event, supplying the mail service an ideology it did not immediately propose. This dialogue, however, also illustrates another sort of revisionist history, presenting mail in an entirely idealistic light that borders on absurdity. Abby says, "I want my child, and I want my friends—I want all of us to live in a world where you still get your mail" (*The Postman*). All of the travails of the beleaguered, financially bankrupt USPS are forgotten, as it becomes an idealized institution of the preapocalyptic world.

The Postman is also a hero because the postapocalyptic world is one in which only a rugged frontiersman can thrive. He possesses attributes uniquely suited to the world he finds himself in—individualism, resourcefulness, and resilience. These attributes are shown time and again—in his ability to escape the Holnist army, the quick-witted tales he fabricates for the denizens of the towns, and even the Shakespeare performances he embellishes in exchange for food and shelter. He escapes capture, defies an army that no one dares go against, and eventually creates an intricate network of communication—all owing to character traits that are associated with the frontiersman of the Old West. In the film, there is a preapocalyptic world that has been wiped out, allowing this frontiersman to once again prove his mettle and worth. An idealized world in the film has been lost, and only the Postman has the ability to bring it back. This is in keeping with the white anxiety mentioned in the previous chapter—the sense that an older, simpler world has given way to a time of turmoil and strife. Ultimately, it is the fear of a shift in power toward minorities that creates this perception that a better, simpler world has been lost. The white male is no longer unilaterally powerful; however, the apocalyptic event allows for the reestablishment of a traditional patriarchal hierarchy. As we can see, films like *The Postman* are heavily reliant on American frontier myths, which permeate old and current Westerns.

Link between Westerns and American Frontier

In 1873, Alexis De Tocqueville's *American Institutions and Their Influence* shared a conception of America that was to foment in subsequent decades. He wrote that

> Anglo Americans, spreading beyond the coasts of the Atlantic Ocean, penetrated farther and farther into the solitudes of the west; they met with a new soil and an unwonted climate; the obstacles which opposed them were of the most various character; their races intermingled. (Tocqueville 233)

Here we see the idea of a rough landscape being met with a determined, diverse mix of individuals with "races intermingled." The uncultivated land provided both opportunity and an assortment of impediments. Tocqueville describes these intrepid settlers as greedy and lacking in restraint due to their lack of "traditions . . . [and] family feeling." Tocqueville thought that these men had been "expelled from the states in which they were born," making the West a haven for various derelicts (254). This shows the beginnings of an idea of a lawless West, where avaricious individuals move to a barren landscape outside the confines of social institutions, "traditions," and "family feeling." This conception of the West became more generally accepted by the 1890s, despite being a gross embellishment on the part of Tocqueville. Even before the highly influential writing of Frederick Jackson Turner, the West had garnered a reputation that was to take on a life of its own, often independent of fact. Author Ray Billington notes that the reason why travelers witnessed so many fights, "tobacco spitting, . . . drunkenness, . . . [and] swearing" in the first place was that they often journeyed to mining towns that had sprung up, instead of more established towns—hardly representative of the majority of the inhabitants in the West (71).

The growth of the frontier myth and its expression in various media is linked to the turmoil of the 1890s. The myth was constructed as a form of nostalgia for "simpler times," a time of rugged American individuality and endurance. It mattered little whether this image of the past was factually accurate. Stephen McVeigh in *The American Western* argues that "the 1890s thus seemed a true watershed in time, the end of the great frontier and the beginning of a new era in which the US would face an unknown future without the vast resources and beneficial influences of its pioneer past" (2). The frontier, in the 1890s, was considered "closed"; no longer was there unlimited space and resources, as most areas had been settled and civilized. The Homestead Act of 1862, which allowed anyone over twenty-one to claim 160 acres of land, led to ownership of vast stretches of the continental United States, further supporting the idea of a "closed frontier." Barbed-wire fences were erected by ranchers as a reaction to "homesteaders," as these ranchers felt entitled to vast stretches of land for their cattle and resented having to share with settlers. This made it difficult for the mythic cowboys of the West to migrate with their cattle, having no open public lands to traverse and no easy access to public lands on which the cattle could graze. Cowboys would bring their cattle to market by traversing up to fifteen hundred miles of land, spending nights alone by a campfire, giving rise to the cowboy myth. Cowboys were a short-lived phenomenon, as the process of bringing cattle to market this way was inefficient. Most ranchers in the 1890s began simply raising livestock by railroad routes to allow for easy transportation (McVeigh 4–5).

In addition to the end of the cowboy, the 1890s saw a marked change in the way the United States dealt with Native Americans. The Dawes Act of 1887 ended the communal ownership of land by Native Americans and parceled out properties individually, in a system that, while initially intended as a humanitarian effort to integrate Native American communities, allowed whites to take the most arable soil. Native Americans also encountered instances where whites refused to leave their lands and had no legal recourse to have them removed. Gone, however, were the days of open warfare—times when the whites were the bastion of civilization holding off barbarian hordes, which had been part of the Western myth. The Wounded Knee Massacre in 1890, in which 146 Native Americans and 25 American soldiers were killed, marked the last instance of open conflict (Whyte 717). The growth of cities and the movement of women and families to the West further indicated that the West was becoming safer and more civilized—no longer a place only for the rugged white male.

The 1890s were also affected by economic instability and severe droughts. Mining, which had been a key draw to the West, was on the decline, with the only new gold strike in Cripple Creek, Colorado. In addition, the price of silver experienced a precipitous drop, and was one of many factors causing a panic on Wall Street. The Philadelphia and Reading railroad, along with over sixteen thousand companies in 1893, went bankrupt (McVeigh 7–9). The systemic economic downturn illustrated the movement from a more regional economic system to a national one, "meaning in essence that the success or otherwise of big business in one part of the country was felt elsewhere" (McVeigh 8). The unifying influence of the economic system led to conflict between various regions of the United States. Specifically, there was "deep interregional conflict between the industrial East and the underdeveloped South and West." The formation of the People's Party, often called the Populists, was a reaction against the capitalist exploitation of the South and West by large corporations, specifically mining, banking, and railroads (McVeigh 9). The influence of populism was apparent in many Westerns.

Populism and progressivism are two countervailing ideologies that have influenced most Westerns, according to Richard Slotkin. The writings of Roosevelt, Hay, King, and Remington—all examples of progressivism—modernized the frontier hero and the setting of the Western myth. The new frontier hero was a

> military aristocrat representative of managerial values and by transferring him direct from the wilderness to an urban or imperial frontier, where immigrants, strikers, and insurrectos were merely allegories of the savage Apache. This modernized Frontier Myth licensed the new hero to repress these dissident classes with the mercilessness belonging to 'savage war' and to govern the defeated without their consent. (125)

The other competing ideology was populism, found in the popular Western "dime novels" produced after the Civil War reconstruction. Before the Reconstruction, many dime novels were James Fenimore Cooper–inspired Romances, with Hawkeye-inspired protagonists fighting against a backdrop of Indian wars. The post-Reconstruction populist novels, on the other hand, featured "outlaw" protagonists fighting against corporations and moneyed interests, such as railroad companies. These novels often deal with the oppression of lower classes and the problematic concentration of wealth in the hands of a select few (Slotkin 126).

Both of these ideologies, however, treated women and minorities as inferior to white men. Both populism and progressivism illustrated an "affirmation of the virile 'Anglo-Saxon' as hero of American myth and exemplar of its primal values" (Slotkin 155). The antiestablishment tendencies of the populist dime novels, for instance, are concurrent with attempts to "distinguish . . . 'outlaws' from 'Communists' and by identifying the outlaw's moral perspective with pre-industrial political culture rather than with radical prescriptions for future reform" (Slotkin 152). In other words, the protagonist fights against the wealthy and powerful, but part of his value and virtue comes from his being superior to minorities and groups that are generally not part of mainstream culture. For progressivism, the view of minorities as inferior was even more salient, with the belief "that under modern conditions 'civilization' and perfect 'democracy' were incompatible, and the extension of democratic rights to classes and races unfit for self-government might destroy civilization 'as we know it' " (Slotkin 125). Historical figures like Roosevelt, then, openly believed that extending rights to minorities and women was detrimental to the growth and health of Western civilization. A true democracy, for a progressivist, was something to be avoided.

All of the troubling changes of the late nineteenth century created a nostalgic desire for the Old West, but the idea of the West was more myth than fact. All of the turmoil of the 1890s made Americans nostalgic for a simpler version of America. Where previously the West had been seen as an open expanse filled with potential, by 1890 the frontier was closed, and resources were finite. The longing for an elusive past lead to the mythologizing of the frontier as the place where the heroes and traditions of America were born. It was seen by some as an embodiment of America's true values, from which all the ills of the 1890s could be healed. The frontier myth coalesced through the work of Frederick Jackson Turner and Theodore Roosevelt, as these two men concretized an idea of the West that carried over into various media. Turner's frontier thesis, discussed earlier, had a profound impact, though Roosevelt's book, *The Winning of the West*, slightly predated this. *The Winning of the West*, a four-book series, looked at the Western migration of the British colonies and subsequently US settlers. In the third volume of Roosevelt's series, he writes about how the "frontiersman conquered and transformed the wilderness, so the wilderness in its turn created and preserved the type of man who overcame it." This frontiersman is "sharply defined and distinctly American" and plants the seeds of civilization before dying in the wilderness he has shaped. In this way, Roosevelt sees the frontiersman as an "advance guard," whose "blood remains, and his striking characteristics have great weight in shaping . . . the communities that grow up in the frontier's stead" (Roosevelt 207). For Roosevelt, then, the frontiersman is a heroic, mythic figure: the "advance guard" of civilization. Much like Turner, Roosevelt believes that the environment of the West shapes the frontiersman and the civilization that arises in the wake of his brave trail-blazing. The frontier landscape creates a "sharply defined and distinctively American" identity, beyond the roots of European influence. Rather than being defined by British, French, and Spanish ancestors, the frontier allows for an identity that is entirely unique to America. Roosevelt and Turner thus cultivate a myth in which American identity is inextricably bound to the frontier experience. Even journalist Edwin Godkin would further this notion of the West, writing in 1897 that the West comprised young men from around the world, looking for fortune in a land where institutions like marriage, law, and religion had minimal influence (39). Free from the institutions brought over from Europe, the frontiersman was able to bask in a raw individuality that allowed for the creation of something new. Echoing the sentiments of Turner and Roosevelt, he remarked that "there is no feature of life in new States in America more marked than the general belief of the people in their own originality. . . . The kind of man they most admire is one who has evolved rules for the conduct of life out of his own brain by the help of his own observations" (Godkin 42). Roosevelt embodies these characteristics quite explicitly, having garnered a great deal of experience living on a cattle ranch, working as a deputy sheriff in North Dakota, and leading the Rough Riders in the Spanish-American War. Buffalo Bill Cody, however, would take the myth to fantastical new heights, embedding it in popular culture and cementing its place in the identity of America.

Buffalo Bill Cody earned a reputation for being a skilled scout and frontiersman prior to his dramatic traveling show. A series of dime novels written by Ned Buntline (née Edward Judson) on Cody's exploits were extremely popular, and over two hundred were published. In 1872 Buntline convinced Cody to play himself onstage, no doubt planting the seed for Cody's subsequent shows (McVeigh 29–30). Cody's first "Wild West" stage show was in 1883, including a dramatization of a buffalo hunt, Indian attack, and Pony Express trek—among several other sketches. The show, much like the books, was wildly popular. It was presented as a historical representation of the West, replete with specific factual details, including biographies of famous Civil War frontiersmen and articles on the history of the West. It was rendered "an authentic, authoritative source of knowledge and information about the West." The show, however, was far from an unbiased presentation, as it was brimming with exaggerations and fictionalizations. Despite this, the shows influenced all subsequent depictions of the West, including films, which were to become very popular a few decades later. His Wild West show "codified many of the conventions of the Western," including racist depictions of Native Americans (McVeigh 32). These codified conventions permeated popular Western books, beginning with Owen Wister's *The Virginian*, generally regarded as the first novel in the Western literary genre. This 1902 book further crafted the conventions that would find their way into film and subsequent literature. *The Virginian* featured a mysterious, handsome male protagonist with skill in roping cattle and an ability to fight. He was the prototypical cowboy hero, known only as "the Virginian." Toward the end of the book, the Virginian engages in a shootout with the antagonist, Trampas, who is shot dead in what is presented as an act of self-defense. All of these elements—the unnamed, reluctant hero and the shootout with the antagonist—became staples of countless Westerns. Wister's novel was so immensely popular that a deluge of imitators followed, copying Wister's basic formula. A year after the success of *The Virginian* in 1902, Edwin Porter created what is likely the most highly influential early film Western: *The Great Train Robbery* (1903). In it, we can see many of the conventions that would carry over into the iconic John Ford and Sergio Leone films: gunplay, outlaws, a train robbery, and various other elements closely associated with the genre.

The birth of the Western resonated because of its links to a perception of American identity and our desire for an idealized past. Despite the fact that we're far removed from the America of the nineteenth century, the myths had become so ingrained from various books and films that they still appear in American media, albeit in a different form. Each decade has seen the Western adapt to the concerns of the time, while maintaining the desire for nostalgia and a time of clearly elucidated American identity. In each decade, its use has been the same—reiterate the status quo to alleviate fears that the dominant culture is slipping away, due to Communists, immigrants, or whatever other group is gaining prominence and power at the time. During the Depression, for instance, "mainstream cinema . . . generally provided America with a comforting set of fantasies about the natural order of race relations in economically and politically troubled times" (Miller 75–76). The turmoil of the 1930s, including the Depression and the tense political climate embodied in the Sacco and Vanzetti trial in 1927, made the predictability of Westerns comforting.

The West in these films was "a place of certainty and reinforcement for mainstream American identity, and . . . was the backdrop for moral and social predictability." The frontiersman was a stalwart hero who "stood fast in the face of changes being wrought by the economic hardships, increasing urbanization, and rapid cultural change that characterized America in the 1930s." He became protector of mainstream values that the dominant culture felt were under attack (Miller 78–79). The comforting effect of these Westerns came at the expense of minorities, as the films often demonized them or depicted them as bumbling fools. In this way, the status quo being promoted in these films is simply another instance of promoting white male hegemony.

Westerns became hugely popular, reaching their apex in the 1960s and 1970s, but Western iconography still resonates, finding its way into presidential speeches, including the rhetoric of George W. Bush in the aftermath of the 9/11 attacks. President Bush

> used the language, values and imagery of the frontier in the rhetoric he employed to respond to the crisis. Such rhetoric served . . . to offer a sense of familiar security to the national psyche. Bush used the quintessential American meta-narrative of the West to explain his stance and garner support for the bombing of Afghanistan. . . . The Western meta-narrative was, for the most part, a readily accepted and accessible script. (McVeigh 215)

The Western iconography was a "script," used to maintain white male dominance by implicitly arguing that only the strong, resilient white male can protect us from the onslaught of minorities and foreigners. Bush placed himself in the role of a courageous, archetypal cowboy, using his speeches to guide and protect America in the aftermath of a horrific terrorist attack (McVeigh 216). Besides his association with Texas and the cowboy attire (hat and boots), he has said things like "Bring 'em on" and "there's an old poster out West that I recall that said, 'Wanted—dead or alive.'" Such rhetoric is part of his persona as a "courageous cowboy," highlighting the way Western tropes still resonate and serve a purpose in rallying Americans around the idea of the rugged individualism of Americans standing up against barbarians antithetical to our way of life (Schneider 242). Beyond figureheads like Bush, who embody the features of the virile frontiersman, the general public has been generally affected by frontier ideologies, as "frontier characteristics persist and even thrive in the twentieth century, although sometimes in slightly modified form" (Billington 232). Americans move about and travel frequently, consistently using cars, trains, and planes for work and recreation; such travel and restlessness mirrors their pioneer forebears. In addition, America prides itself on being a place of intrepid innovators and trailblazers in technology (Billington 74). Such successful innovations illustrate frontier notions of originality and fearless exploration, brought about by an emphasis on hard work. The work ethic of Americans, beyond being part of Protestantism, is part of our identity because "prosperity offers opportunity for self-promotion . . . [and] the respectability of labor has been enshrined in the national consciousness by the frontier past" (Billington 233). Despite the trenchant focus on individualism, originality, and egalitarianism, frontier ideologies often benefit the narrative of a strong, white male. Any pretense at equality is undercut by the racism and sexism at work in these myths, evidenced even in the myth's vestigial beginnings. The rewards of hard work on the frontier were not for Native Americans and women. It was the white male that conquered and tamed the West, at the expense of Native American autonomy.

Westerns often present minorities and women in an unflattering light, their own inadequacies necessitating white male assistance. Women took care of the homestead; Mexicans and Native Americans were usually not to be trusted, and the person most suited to the often unforgiving landscape of the West was the white male. Many of the "Hispanics . . . retain stereotypical traces of lazy ineptitude, buffoonery, or violent banditry," while the conclusion of most Westerns "requires Anglo assistance" (O'Connor and Rollins 14). In this way, these films "underscore the larger discomfort of individuals within a changed society" (O'Connor and Rollins 10–11). *The Magnificent Seven* (1960), a retelling of Kurosawa's *Seven Samurai*, is one example of the conservative nature of the genre. A poor village in Mexico is besieged by bandits, led by a ruthless man named Calvero. People from the town solicit the help of white mercenaries, who help recruit a total of seven gunmen to help drive out Calvero. Ultimately, the group of seven men save the village, losing four gunmen in a climactic shootout at the end of the film. The Mexicans in the film are hapless victims, with the exception of Chico, but even he is a stereotype. He is depicted as a hot-blooded Mexican, impetuous and inclined toward sexual passions; the object of his affection, in this case, is a woman named Petra. Beyond Chico, the other Mexicans are incapable of taking care of the outlaws by themselves, and need the services of white men to help liberate them. They are also shown to be cowardly, allowing Calvero to take over the town as they fear reprisal for hiring the white mercenaries. Ultimately, the white gunmen come back to liberate the town, as the Mexican townspeople hide in their houses. It is through the power and cunning of the white frontiersman, clad in cowboy garb, that freedom is bestowed upon the poor Mexican farmers. The film's view of women is similarly conservative, with most of them in the background, in their homes or working in the taverns. The only woman given any attention is Petra, but she simply functions as a love interest for Chico. Since *The Magnificent Seven* in 1960, Westerns have become slightly more progressive, but "male mediation usually becomes necessary for conflict resolution. . . . This lack of truly revisionist Western movies demonstrates just how fundamental Turner's mythic vision remains for the film industry" (O'Connor and Rollins 15). Most Westerns, both older and more contemporary, still show the centrality of white masculinity in bringing freedom and justice to the frontier. It is only the dogged, white frontiersman who can liberate oppressed peoples and domesticate an unforgiving landscape. *The Lone Ranger* (2013), for instance, shows this conservative tendency, focusing on a white male that must save the townspeople from a gang of outlaws and a corrupt railroad tycoon. His sidekick, Tonto, embodies all of the racist stereotypes found in earlier Westerns, as he speaks in stilted, broken English and is literally labeled a "noble savage" in the opening scene of the film. It also displays many of the populist ideas found in older Westerns, with a money-hungry railroad tycoon as one of the primary antagonists. The heroes, much like the heroes of populist dime novels, are righteous outlaws fighting against greed and corruption. While Tonto is crucial in the victorious outcome at the end of the film, it is the Lone Ranger himself who is acknowledged as a hero and offered a law enforcement position. Tonto begins and ends the film as a *literal* spectacle in a sideshow, sharing his tale with an unwitting young boy.

Combining of Frontier and Apocalypticism

The various adaptations of the Western include its amalgamation with apocalypticism, a conflation that reinscribes all of the patriarchal ideologies that the Western has embodied over the last one hundred years. In the previous chapter, we saw the various ways apocalypticism has been co-opted by the white patriarchy. Here we can see that it has been melded with a genre often characterized by racism and sexism.

Beyond being part of a more general pattern of using religion for corporate and political control, apocalyptic myths became closely linked with the images and ideas of the American frontier. The importance of the frontier in American mythos is well documented, most famously in Frederick Jackson Turner's "The Significance of the Frontier in American History," wherein he notes that "to the frontier the American intellect owes its striking characteristics," including "coarseness and strength combined with acuteness and inquisitiveness; that practical, inventive turn of mind, quick to find expedients." The frontier, according to Turner, is a site of "dominant individualism, working for good and for evil, and withal that buoyancy and exuberance which comes with freedom (37–38). These are all characteristics that have become an integral part of American identity, despite any factual inaccuracies purveyed by the likes of Turner and Buffalo Bill Cody. The postapocalyptic landscape, in the way it is used in American film, represents many of the same ideals. When Turner describes the frontier as "a gate of escape from the bondage of the past," he could just as easily be describing much of the postapocalyptic media that constantly inundates our culture (38). The world of *Mad Max*, for instance, is marked by uncultivated plains and mountains, an emptiness that allows Max a chance to let go of his troubled past and start anew. This landscape, however, is not entirely empty, as various settlers attempt to tame this unforgiving environment, characterized by a lack of resources and roving bands of marauders. This illustrates a central conflict of the American frontier, which is found in the relationship between civilization and savagery. Much of contemporary apocalyptic media perceive the end of the world as a return to a more primitive frontier-like scenario, where a handful of individuals have to stand against various raiders—much like the white colonists holding off groups of savage Native Americans or degenerate outlaws.

While the *Mad Max* movies are clearly Australian in origin, the parallels between Australian and American frontier myths explain the many similarities between each country's depiction of the apocalypse in film. In both cases, a group of white settlers took land from indigenous peoples, with whom they had frequent violent skirmishes. In Australia, brutal conflict resulted in an estimated 2,000 to 2,500 European deaths and the deaths of over 20,000 Aborigines (Hughes 277). Even though the population of Australian settlers initially comprised mostly prisoners, a myth formed around the idea of an Australian frontier waiting to be tamed by dauntless white males. The frontier was "a persistent figure of speech, not only in the United States, but also in Australia. Essentially, the frontier is usually conceived of as a line, a line continually pushed forward (or back) by heroic frontiersmen, the pioneers" (Carter 158). Much like the American frontiersman, the white people of penal colonies like New South Wales and Botany Bay needed a "violent, grabbing drive." As such, the population was filled with "opportunists struggling to be gentlemen; convicts and outcasts waiting to be opportunists" (Hughes 324). There was a perceived chance to begin anew in the Australian:

> frontier society that rewarded hard work at any level, to a degree undreamed-of by the English or Irish poor. The out-of-work blacksmith, reduced to petty theft by lack of opportunity, could soon become a flourishing tradesman in Sydney. Hope, effort, and luck enabled thousands of Emancipists to make a second start in life, better than anything they had known in their British lives. The difference was biggest of all for unskilled workers, whose chances in England had been nil. (Hughes 510)

Of course, just like the American frontier myth, this Australian notion of a land of promise was embellished to a large extent. This myth, however, became subsumed into the identity of Australia, in the belief that "the Australian character owes most to the 'frontier spirit' of the nomadic bushman" (Carter 278). Much of this myth glosses over the violent oppression of the Aborigines, just as the American myth has long downplayed the genocide of Native Americans. All of this explains the many explicit similarities between *Mad Max* and various American postapocalyptic films, which have been profoundly influenced by George Miller's vision of the end of the world.

Another key conflict found in Westerns that clearly manifests in postapocalyptic media is the struggle between individuality and the strictures of civilization. Frederick Jackson Turner is quick to note the connection between the frontier and the now common association of the frontier with an American sense of individualism. The conflict between the individual and society is clearly exhibited in the *Mad Max* trilogy. There are similarities between Max, playing the reluctant hero, and the titular character in the film *Shane*. *The Road Warrior* (1981) follows Max Rockatansky and his encounter with a group of settlers led by a man named Papagallo. They have an oil refinery, which has drawn the attention of violent bikers led by Lord Humungus. They lay siege to the settlers' encampment in an attempt to steal their fuel. At the beginning of *The*

Road Warrior (1981), Max only agrees to help the settlers in exchange for fuel. He leaves after obtaining his gas, intending to never come back. However, the subsequent loss of his car and canine companion lead him back to these same settlers, where he finally agrees to drive their fuel tanker, marking his acceptance of his role as hero. These similarities between Max and other Western heroes are also explained, in part, by George Miller's conscious admission of trying to construct myth within *The Road Warrior* and *Beyond Thunderdome* (1985), based in large part on the ideas of Joseph Campbell, whose ideas of mythic heroism can be found throughout many Westerns. The myth of the West, powerfully captured by the likes of Turner, displays "the idea of free land and spectacular landscapes; of a wild, untamed spirit resisting the encroachments and suasions of civilization; and finally of lost freedom as civilization advances and the claims of responsible citizenry are made" (Mitchell 498). This conflict is shown in the HBO Western *Deadwood*, wherein Al Swearengen laments the appearance of telegraph poles, a symbol of the encroaching development of the United States. In his rant, he exclaims, "Ain't the state of things cloudy enough? Don't we face enough fucking imponderables?" The institutions and technology that civilization brings are looked at fearfully and are antithetical to the individualism that Turner notes is "evolving from the conditions of frontier settlement rather than merely being transplants of Enlightenment ideas originally developed in Europe" (Redding 314). Turner writes that

> the peculiarity of American institutions is the fact that they have been compelled to adapt themselves to the changes of an expanding people—to the changes involved in crossing a continent, in winning a wilderness, and in developing at each area of this progress out of the primitive economic and political conditions of the frontier into the complexity of city life. (1133)

So while the likes of Al Swearengen might be fearful of the encroachment of certain institutions, Turner notes that these very same institutions are shaped by the "wilderness"—the very same wilderness that allows them to start anew and shape a certain notion of individuality. Is Turner contradicting himself? Perhaps. However, what we see here might simply show that the ideas and associations we have with the West are far too reductive. The frontier may have shaped our conceptions of American identity, but the ideas of individualism here seem romanticized. Where the individual went, he or she brought a form of civilization and institutions, thus negating any argument that there was ever really a moment of pure, unadulterated individuality in the West. However, in *The Man Who Shot Liberty Valance*, one quote seems apropos: "When the legend becomes fact, print the legend." The myth or legend of individuality in the West has a powerful cultural value.

Max bears similar characteristics to any number of Western heroes. His dark and troubled past puts him in the company of people like William Munny in Eastwood's *Unforgiven*. Max's primary suffering comes from events before the apocalypse, where he loses his wife, child, and best friend to a gang of motorcycle thugs in a world on the brink of collapse. The apocalypse in *The Road Warrior* happens after these events, and the narrator of *The Road Warrior* only briefly mentions the world cataclysm, noting how "two mighty warrior nations went to war . . . and touched off a blaze which engulfed them all. . . . People stopped in the streets and listened: for the first time they heard the sound of silence . . . their world crumbled. . . . And only those mobile enough to scavenge, brutal enough to pillage would survive." Civilization, or at least the semblance of it and the obligations it carries, dissolves. The implication in the narrator's monologue is that in the absence of civilization people must become brutal and self-serving. True individuality, at least in this sense, becomes anarchic. In fact, in the absence of a family, things that link Max to a social order, he becomes "a shell of a man. A burnt out, desolate man, a dead man, running from the demons of his past. A man who wandered far away. . . . And it was out here in this blighted place, that he learned to live again." So while it was two "warrior tribes" that destroyed civilization, the environment itself, "this blighted place" will be a catalyst for his redemption (*The Road Warrior*). Again the parallels to Turner's "gate of escape from the bondage of the past" come to mind. Critic Dennis Barbour implies this parallel when he says that Max "seeks to break with traditions of the past, attempting to define his own reality through a solo existence . . . reducing his existence to nothing more than mere survival" (30). This is seen throughout *The Road Warrior*, as Max denies himself the communion with others that had destroyed him in the first movie. When Max helps the character Nathan, who dies shortly after Max enters Papagallo's camp, he is quick to say "let's get this straight. I'm doing it 'cos I need fuel." Later in the film, he is asked to drive the tanker he has found. Here, Max again refuses to do anything that doesn't directly connect to his own self-interests, saying to the Gyro Captain, "I haven't got time to explain. Just believe me—I've got everything I want"

(*The Road Warrior*). Turner might be describing Max when he writes of Americans shaped by the frontier, known for their "coarseness" and ability to "quick[ly] . . . find expedients." Similarly, Max finds ways of escaping the Gyro Captain's traps and evading the various members of Humungus's gang. Later, however, we see the conflict between Max's desire for individuality and the demands of civilization. The parallels between *Mad Max* and Westerns illustrate the extent to which many postapocalyptic films utilize American frontier-related themes and iconography.

The Power of the White Frontiersman

The conflation of the American ideals embodied in the frontier and postapocalypticism has allowed for the dissemination of ideas that seek to reify the existing power structure in American society, wherein white males are the dominant group. The continued relevance of the frontier is seen in the suburban white family of the Eisenhower era, which was the bastion of civilization: "Surrounded by forces that threatened to destroy it. . . . [It] fought against the savagery of the city and the dangers of the nuclear age in its quest to uphold 'traditional' American values" (Sharp 176). The white male, as head of the family and emblem of American strength, was promoted by corporate-backed, religious advertising, using iconography of the American frontier. For instance, the traits of the American settler described by Turner bear a decidedly masculine connotation. As Ravi Kumar argues, these attributes "strictly conform to the ideology of masculinity. . . . In the physical sense the frontier was a savage environment: it generated a need to master, to conquer and to gain power. The sheer movement, migration, and repetition of the ever-occurring pioneer experience proved decisive in the formation of the male character" (3). In addition to masculinity, the prevalence of whiteness in this conception of American frontier identity is clear, exposed in the writings of Theodore Roosevelt, specifically in *The Winning of the West*. Roosevelt, in his writing, was "focused on the frontier," and as Sharp argues "represented racial purity, genocidal warfare, and colonial expansion as keys . . . to the progress and health of the nation" (Sharp 49). The frontier and its Christian-influenced corollary—the postapocalyptic landscape—allowed Americans the ability to surmount the overdevelopment of their English predecessors, using the harsh environment of the frontier as a more atavistic stage through which to regenerate America. When besieged by outside forces, whether Native Americans or immigrants, the apocalypse allows America to return to a time where the white male dominant culture reigned supreme—just as the frontier once did.

In both *The Road Warrior* and *Beyond Thunderdome*, two types of communities are set forth, one the audience is clearly supposed to favor over the other. In *Beyond Thunderdome*, we have Bartertown and the world that the lost children fly off to establish at the end of the film. In *The Road Warrior*, we have Papagallo's commune and the chaotic habitat of Humungus. Papagallo represents "hope for the future, the restoration of civilization. The Humungous and his gang represent a horrible reversion to vicious tribalism" (Barbour 32). The "good guys" in the film are presented as the group clad in white—the group with the assertive patriarch promising redemption. Paul Williams, in *Science Fiction Studies*, notes that

> the townspeople are all white, often Aryan in appearance, with the whites and creams they predominantly wear drawing attention to their skin color. Their adversaries, led by the monstrous Humungus, are shaggy maned, dressed in fur and feathers; some have Mohawk haircuts, the savage's coiffure of choice. Furthermore, the townspeople are productive and entertain freedom of speech; . . . they remain civilized. The savages are anti-social and nomadic; their prisoners are subjected to crucifixion and acts of sexual violence. (Williams 309)

Lord Humungus is the heterogeneous force of chaos that threatens the established order, and we are meant to root against him. Turner's description of the frontier is apt to describe the meeting point between Papagallo and Lord Humungus at the wall of their enclosed fortress: "The frontier is the outer edge of the wave—the meeting point between savagery and civilization" (Turner 1134). Papagallo has a very defined view of his world. He describes how "I came out here and I found that pump. I built that plant and ploughed that field. Why? Because we are human beings. We must maintain our dignity. We are not barbarians" (*The Road Warrior*). This world he envisions, he is convinced, is better than the one Lord Humungus offers. The empty, blank slate of the postapocalyptic wasteland "can be an arena for the replaying of the colonial encounter, frightening in its unintelligibility but alluring in its virgin promise" (Williams 304). Papagallo is akin to the white male settlers of the American frontier, carrying the torch of civilization to a land of inferior barbarians. The film is clearly promoting a return to the preapocalyptic world, one with a hierarchy and a locus of power—in this case, fuel. Rather than money or corporate influence, the hegemonic structure is created through access to fuel. It is only through Papagallo's acquiescence that Max is allowed fuel, suggesting that the white male is at the top of the hierarchy. This is part of a larger pattern in postapocalyptic media, wherein the patriarchy is promoted; such media is "'highly reactionary and advocate[s] reinforcing the status quo by the maintenance of conservative social regimes of patriarchal law (and lore)' (Movies xi)" (Williams 304).

Max is a white male hero without which civilization could not succeed. In the first three *Mad Max* films, Max is the only one who can stop the villains: the only one resourceful, skilled, and brave enough to stand up to the oppressors of the benign settlers. Diversity and heterogeneity are perhaps clearer in *Mad Max Beyond Thunderdome*, in Aunty Entity's alternative to a white male–dominated culture. She is, of course, a Black female in a position of authority, who has "constructed a town in which racial and cultural differences have become commonplace, redressing the preapocalyptic structures of marginalization that subordinated her" (Williams 307). This, however, seems merely a pretext for the white male to be seen as a liberator. Aunty Entity's society is one that relies on oppressive labor practices that force laborers to work underground in literal pig feces. It is the white male, Max, who upends this system, bringing freedom to the working class. We see that even in instances where the films may be seen as progressive, they ultimately reaffirm white male power. Alternatives to white male power, whether in the form of Humungus or Aunty Entity, are presented as deeply flawed and destructive. Only the traditional white male hero can bring back a world of order and the normal rule of law.

Apocalypticism Creates a New Frontier

Apocalypticism and frontier iconography parallel one another in their use by the white patriarchy to maintain the status quo. In a way, the apocalypse allows for a return to the frontier. Most of the globe has been claimed by a person and country, and there is no literal frontier to which a settler can journey at this point in history. The American frontier is closed, and the land has been parceled out and developed; a key part of American identity no longer has a clear referent. It has, therefore, become necessary to *manufacture* a frontier, to allow for the continued relevance of an ideology by which America can justify the aggrandizement of the white male. The apocalypse serves this purpose quite clearly, emptying a space in which the dominant white male can illustrate his key importance in being the resolute protector of American freedom and exceptionalism. It's clear that the "imperial mission of economic expansion that took place in the nineteenth century literally no longer has any sphere to take place in—except, perhaps, in a projected post-nuclear-war future where civilization, having eradicated its own edifices, can be rebuilt anew" (Williams 304). By wiping out the globe, the apocalypse gives the dominant culture a chance to rewrite history, vindicating a legacy of oppression and brutality. The apocalypse gives us the "ability to obliterate existing narratives, to initiate a new history that takes the form of an ominous and symptomatic aftermath" (Berger 21). In *Waterworld* (1995), Earth is entirely covered in water, and all of the cities and monuments of the world are buried by the melting of the polar ice caps—an event that happens long before the events of the film. The protagonist, named the Mariner, is a reluctant white male hero who must protect and guide a group of survivors to a mythical Dryland, using a map on the back of a girl named Enola. Costner's body has adapted to Waterworld: he has webbed feet and gills. If he had lived before the apocalypse, his mutated body would have been out of place. However, the apocalyptic event has made him the perfect fit for the world he lives in, as his body "retains the aggression and power over others synonymous with hegemonic constructions of masculinity" (Wintle 685). It is the apocalypse that gives him a purpose and an environment in which his gills and webbed feet will serve him well. Roving the empty, water wasteland, he is the frontiersman, individualistic and heroic.

The apocalypse in *Waterworld* creates a scenario in which the Mariner is absolutely essential in saving humankind from a bleak future. Beyond his adapted body, he possesses a skill set that uniquely qualifies him to locate Dryland. The main female character cannot locate Dryland, having little sailing experience. As a master sailor and navigator, the male protagonist is their only option for a life beyond the hardships of living on water with no easy access to soil in which to grow plants. Without the apocalyptic event, the Mariner would merely be a mutant with skills that myriad others possess. The melted polar ice caps make him resemble the epic hero of countless Westerns, and the film contains all of the thematic preoccupations of Westerns, including the conflict between the order within developed towns ruled by a governing body and an individual living on their own outside institutions like the government. Like many other Western heroes, the white male protagonist decides not to be part of the new civilization on Dryland after helping the characters find their way. He rides off into the sunset, unwilling to be tamed by the villages and institutions that will likely develop on Dryland.

Beyond making the white male essential to freedom and safety, the apocalypse in the film allows for a sort of revisionist history. The young girl, Enola, whose back is tattooed with a map to Dryland, has the exact name of the airplane that dropped the atomic bomb on Nagasaki. The *Enola Gay* carried a bomb capable of tremendous destruction, but *Waterworld* shows an "Enola" that possesses the key to life. The justification for the dropping of the bomb is that it ultimately saved many lives, since the island hopping of the Pacific War had been marked by high casualties and threatened to last an inordinately long time. The bomb, using this rationale, is a sort of savior—destroying things to eventually save the world. The girl Enola manages to embody this idea of "savior," without any of the accompanying destruction, justifying American destruction by omitting it entirely. Films such *as Waterworld* show us that

> the burden of maintaining a perfect history is too heavy for any culture. And the insistent denial of the traumatic events of our history has brought about the need for these repeated apocalyptic purgings, both real and imaginary, as if *this* time we will finally get right what always was right, and somehow never was right (Berger 135).

The genocide of Native Americans, for instance, can be rewritten via the use of an apocalyptic event: one that turns minorities into vicious zombies or aliens that threaten civilization. Early zombie films used Haitian mythology, for instance, to create a "complex and polyvalent Other," and illustrate "fear of slavery, collusion with it, and rebellion against it" (McAlister 461). In this way, some zombie films rewrite the past by mystifying slavery, exculpating the oppressors by removing the wrongs of slavery from historical reality. In these scenarios, it is white people who are oppressed and victimized, and all of their violence against the crowds of zombies is entirely justified. Robin Wood, in an essay analyzing the "Other" in horror films, says that "bourgeois ideology cannot recognize or accept [the Other] but must deal with . . . in one of two ways: either by rejecting and if possible annihilating it, or by rendering it safe and assimilating it, converting it as far as possible into a replica of itself" (27). Though he is specifically analyzing horror films, he notes that "one could . . . approach any of the genres from the same starting point" (Wood 28). Contemporary postapocalyptic media treats the Other in the way Wood describes, disguising anxiety about immigrants, Communists, and others as a fight against nefarious, otherworldly creatures that must be "annihila[ed] or . . . render[ed] safe and assimilate[ed]" (27).

One might be tempted to view Enola as at least a progressive stance on the power of women; she is, after all, essential to finding Dryland. However, the girl's body has been marked by someone else. Her body only has value in that someone else has written things of value on it. The map on her back is indecipherable to her, and

> the confirmation of Dryland's existence and location depends upon adults' efforts to decode her markings. . . . She faces the threat of total objectification. Indeed, the Smokers' leader, the Deacon (Dennis Hopper), regards the girl as a mere tool in his quest to despoil Dryland, and, initially, the Mariner treats Enola in a degrading and misogynistic fashion. (Wintle 683)

This misogyny is also trenchant in the treatment of the ocean itself. Myths associating the ocean with femininity are found in many cultures, including many from Western civilization. At one point in the film, the Mariner takes his female companions underwater, where they see an entire buried city—a civilization ruined by an unforgiving sea. The ocean has great power of the sort seen in countless stories in the Bible and elsewhere wherein the sea's ruinous force is made explicit. The Mariner, however, is relatively immune to the forces of the ocean, his body having adapted to a life on the water. In addition, maternal images of fertility and the womb have been replaced by "hegemonic ideal of controlling and aggressive masculinity" as the Mariner forms "an umbilical connection with Enola by supporting the swimming girl with one arm at her navel and escorting Helen underwater in a wet diving bell visually and functionally redolent of a womb." In this sense, the Mariner "appropriates the maternal associations of the sea" (Wintle 685). He is not only immune to the ocean's power, but he is also capable of supplanting many of its maternal associations.

The Book of Eli (2010) is another film that bears striking similarities with Westerns, though it seems on the surface to be critiquing the conservative ideologies embedded therein. The apocalyptic event happens prior to the events of the film and would seem to have been a nuclear catastrophe, since finding water that has not been irradiated is difficult. The protagonist is an unnamed Black male, harkening back to Eastwood's unnamed hero in Sergio Leone's Dollars Trilogy, also referred to as the

"Man with No Name Trilogy." He only reluctantly engages in violence, as he traverses the ragged remains of obliterated towns and roadways. His violence "taps into mythical constructions of the American male found primarily in Westerns. In these Western portrayals, the 'good' character only uses violence . . . when all other options have been exhausted and its use is typically for the benefit of society that is under threat" (Aston and Walliss 4). His mission is to carry the only remaining Bible to safety. Carnegie, the antagonist of the film, is a man who wants the Bible for his own nefarious purposes, implying that the Bible will be used as a tool to control the denizens of his ramshackle frontier town. His character is "also literate, which viewers discover is a rare quality to have. So, access to knowledge others do not have has probably helped him get to the position he is in" (Walker 4). Carnegie controls both access to information and also water, and the implication is that the Bible will be used to control people by giving them hope and the ability to endure the pain and suffering that surrounds them. In this way, he can create a more docile group of people who believe that things will get better if they only wait for better times. At one point, he says that the Bible is "a weapon!"—one that "aims right at the hearts and minds of the weak and desperate. It will give us control of them!" (*The Book of Eli*). Carnegie is similar to any number of villains in Westerns who intimidate townspeople until the hero emerges to take a stand against oppression. In addition, Carnegie's town is similar to any number of frontier towns in Westerns, with dusty streets and bars filled with unsavory reprobates.

The apocalypse allows for the hero—in this case Denzel Washington's unnamed hero—to save civilization from falling under the control of a demagogue like Carnegie. Cataclysmic destruction enables humanity to right the past and prevents a despot like Carnegie from creating the same conditions that likely created the apocalypse in the first place. In addition to being a Black male hero, Washington's character is blind, a clear disability in the preapocalyptic world. After the apocalypse, however, his blindness becomes an asset since the only copy of the Bible is written in braille. All of this points to a narrative that acknowledges the problems of the past while attempting to turn the potential of the frontier toward a promising future that carves out a space for minorities. This progressive reading is undercut by the fact that the Black protagonist ceases to be useful the moment he gives his copy of the Bible over to the white male in charge of a fortress containing all of the knowledge of the world. His character dies immediately after reciting the Bible from memory, differentiating his Black male character from the heroic "Man with No Name" in the Dollars Trilogy, who rides off into the sunset, untamed by the civilization he has saved. The protagonist in *The Book of Eli* does, however, travel to the West, a West that signifies possibility for civilization and death for him. The West is "culturally charged in the story . . . it resonates with echoes of western civilization (. . . at the end of the film . . . books such as Shakespeare's works, representative of western culture and civilization, have been rescued and are being kept)" in McDowell's fortress (Moya and Lopez). The story of Western civilization is the story of white male dominance, often to the detriment of other groups. In the case of this film, Washington's character has died after helping the white male (named Lombardi) maintain the knowledge of "Western culture," which minorities are often excluded from.

Lombardi is ultimately the one to share the Bible with the rest of the world. The apocalypse, therefore, allows for the reification of white hegemony, where the white male is made essential and heroic, thanks to the contribution of a Black male who is deceased and unnamed—a man whose contributions might never be fully acknowledged. While not an explicit analogy to slavery, it does seem striking that the growth of America will be built on the back of an unacknowledged Black man. Furthermore, Lombardi possesses all of civilization's knowledge, giving him the power to withhold this knowledge in the same way slaves were kept illiterate. The implication is that society will start anew with the foundation of knowledge contained in this fortress: knowledge that has been the foundation of preapocalyptic society. If this is the foundation for the new world, how would this not produce the same flawed system? The Bible is given such reverence in the film, even though the ideas therein have been the cause of countless wars and the justification for the marginalization of minorities, including the Native Americans of the frontier. *The Book of Eli*, by lauding the Bible in a simple good-versus-evil scenario, promotes the same sort of binary thinking that creates destructive conflicts, as the film "rejects hybridity and confirms that human beings conceive reality and identity, whether individual or national, following a system of binary oppositions" (Moya and Lopez). Such binary thinking is also part of what leads people to scapegoat a minority group, illustrating the "necessary distinction between 'us' and 'them' " (Moya and Lopez).

By exalting the Bible, the film implies that the problem with the various stories, parables, and psalms in the Bible is not the actual content but who is wielding these religious texts. The implication is that "religious texts . . . [are] at worst, morally neutral texts that are somehow open to appropriation and misuse by tyrants and cynical preachers" (Aston and

Walliss 5). Lombardi is ostensibly withholding the knowledge he possesses to protect it, but there are clear parallels to Carnegie, who controls the flow of water and knowledge in his frontier town. Lombardi is barely in the film, and without any character development it's unclear what makes him different from Carnegie. Because of his unformed persona, he becomes a cipher—an amalgam of countless biblical prophets receiving the word of God to transcribe. Washington's character *should* be the prophet in this scenario, as he dictates the holy words. However, he dies quietly after sharing the words with Lombardi in a fortress built within the remains of the infamous Alcatraz prison, passing away with no name and no indication he will be given any credit for the important role he played. He is a Black man who dies in prison, while a white man lives on to emerge as hero.

The film ultimately uses the apocalyptic event as a way to promote Lombardi, the white male, as the protector of civilization. The apocalypse makes him essential to rebuilding the world, and the Bible is exculpated from blame in the many Christian crusades. America's foundation of Christian beliefs is affirmed, and the new frontier is primed to receive these Christian ideas untainted by power-hungry despots. Instead of connecting the Bible to animosity between white men and the countries that they colonized, Carnegie says:

> I grew up with it. I know its power. And if you read it, then so do you. That's why they burned them all after the war. Just staying alive is an act of faith. Building this town is an even bigger act of faith, but they don't understand that. None of them. And I don't have the right words to help them, but the book does . . . Imagine how different, how righteous this little world could be if we had the right words for our faith. People would truly understand why they're here and what they're doing, and they wouldn't need any of the uglier motivations. (*The Book of Eli*)

If Carnegie truly believes this, then his motivations are as seemingly altruistic as Denzel Washington's and Malcolm McDowell's. The differences between the men are superficial; Carnegie is simply more overtly exploitive in his ways of obtaining power.

Another postapocalyptic Western, *The Ultimate Warrior* (1975), follows a man named Carson, played by Yul Brynner, who must help a group of survivors after a worldwide pandemic wiped out most of the population. The film utilizes many common tropes of Westerns, as Brynner plays the reluctant hero coming to the aid of an enclave of good guys, led by a man referred to as Baron. Brynner, of course, had previously played one of the iconic heroes of *The Magnificent Seven* (1960). In *The Ultimate Warrior*, Brynner's character must save a group of people beset by evil marauders, led by a man named Carrot, who wants the resources behind the walls of Baron's settlement: specifically, special seeds that are resistant to plague. These seeds have allowed Baron's settlement to produce a lot of food—something hard to come by in postapocalyptic New York.

Much like the good guys in *The Road Warrior*, Baron plans an escape to the coast, away from the dangers confronting them on all sides. Many of Baron's citizens are killed, as Carrot and his men raid their compound. Carson guides a pregnant survivor out of the compound, carrying the plague-resistant seeds that Carrot is searching for. They head into the subway to escape, and Carson fights off Carrot and his men along the way. Eventually, Carson, the female survivor, and her infant are seen on a beach, presumably having reached their planned destination.

Instead of the desolate landscape of the American West, *The Ultimate Warrior* utilizes a backdrop of dilapidated New York buildings. The dusty frontier trail of the classic Western is replaced by an abandoned New York subway system. The white male hero, in this case Yul Brynner, must safeguard America's future, in the form of an infant and seeds that will provide food for future generations. The threat to humanity, in this case, comes not from an ethnic minority, but from poor, disenfranchised white people. The people inside the walls of Baron's compound enjoy a relatively comfortable life, with food, water, and even small indulgences like cigars. People outside these walls, however, are starving and fighting over decaying scraps. While these outsiders are violent and murderous, there is no indication in the film that Baron's commune has made any effort to share their resources. Carrot, the main antagonist of the film, notes the prosperity of Baron's settlement, saying that "He's got all the men he needs . . . or can feed" (*The Ultimate Warrior*). The community established by Baron is not nearly as prosperous as Carrot believes, but in essence, Baron has an oasis. Similarly, an oasis in the middle of an inhospitable wasteland is seen in *Fury Road*, and much like *Fury Road*, Baron's oasis is only shared with a privileged few. The difference in this film, however, is that Baron and his cohorts are portrayed as the "good guys."

Homeless people and poverty have a long history of being vilified in film. *C.H.U.D.* (1984), *Street Trash* (1987), *The Vagrant* (1992), *Down, Out and Dangerous* (1995), and *Night of the Bums* (1998) are a few of the *many* movies that have used homeless people as literal and metaphorical monsters over the last few decades. An ad for *C.H.U.D.*, alluding to the homeless people living in the sewers of New York, stated that "a recent article in a New York newspaper reported that there were large colonies of people living under the city. . . . The paper was incorrect. What is living under the city is not human. . . . [And] they're not staying down there anymore" (quoted in Pimpare 227). The threat of homeless people in this and other films was reflective of actual public sentiment, as expressed in a *New York Post* op-ed from 1999, in which the author proclaimed, "It's time to end the madness. It's time to get the dangerously deranged off the streets for their sake and ours. . . . There are crazies among us. Some of them are dangerous. A few of them are murderous. Get them off the street. Now!" (quoted in Pimpare 229). Cities were long thought to be a locus for degenerate behavior. The son of Arthur Ernest Morgan, president of Antioch College and later first chairman of the Tennessee Valley Authority, "disliked cities to such an extent that his view of them verged on the apocalyptic. He was convinced that urban population density was the cause of virtually every social malady, and that the creation, or restoration, of small communities was the corresponding cure-all" (Conn 254). In *The Ultimate Warrior*, Baron's compound is clearly one of these "small communities" that Morgan desired as a panacea for the ills of urban living. Urban living itself was felt to be part of the problem, as a "narrative of irredeemable urban decline had taken root" in the early 1970s. Places like New York City "were teetering on the edge of habitability, many thought, and the grim indicators were riots, poverty, exploding welfare rolls, the deinstitutionalization of the mentally ill, municipal bankruptcy, and white flight" (Pimpare 43).

Images of urban decay in *The Ultimate Warrior* reflected the same decay in 1970s and 1980s New York City, where the film happens to take place. It was believed by some that the

> concentration of diverse populations (each with their own unhealthy habits, odd customs, and foreign values), packed into close quarters (with bad influence spreading easily from family to family), far from the natural world (surrounded by tall manmade buildings, the ground paved over with brick, scarce trees, the sky hidden and sooty), all elevate need from merely an individual or familial tragedy into something like a contagion that breeds criminals and crime. Robert Hunter, a

> student of poverty in the late nineteenth century, thought there being no place to play but in the streets "the most widespread evil of child life in the largest cities," which . . . fostered bad habits that would lead inexorably to prison. (Pimpare 3)

Thus, the city of *The Ultimate Warrior* is an apocalyptic nightmare to be escaped, replaced by the serene beaches of a remote island. The vagrants of the film, who tellingly make their home in an abandoned police station jail, are monsters produced by a corrupt city. The year before the film came out, longtime film critic for the *New York Times* Vincent Canby observed that "New York City has become a metaphor for what looks like the last days of American civilization." He very well could have been describing the New York of this film.

At the end, the white hero—played by an iconic symbol of masculinity, Yul Brynner—helps restart the world on an idyllic island, far from the corrupting influence of poor degenerates in a decaying city. His masculinity is illustrated when he first appears in the film standing shirtless and stoic in front of Baron's compound. Now, at the end, the white male has reformed the prototypical nuclear family and possesses the seeds to start civilization anew. There is hope that he will bring America back to a more ideal form, away from the corruption of lower-class vagrants. In the world of the film, not a single Black or brown person is to be found, and the only "Other" to be vanquished is the hobo, whom Brynner ably handles.

Conclusion

Frontier mythology is a key facet of American identity, the image of rugged frontiersman taming a rough Western landscape being inextricably linked to America's past. While the myth diverges from the actual reality and history of the West, it performs a powerful function in justifying white male dominance. Frontier mythology has influenced countless books and films, more recently finding its way into postapocalyptic media. The similarities between the frontier and the apocalyptic wasteland are apparent, both visually and in the sense that a white frontiersman is needed to bring back order in a lawless land. Postapocalyptic films and books combine two things that resonate with American audiences—Christian religious myths and frontier myths—in order to create a new frontier, a blank slate that enables the white hero to bring America back to its former glory. The apocalyptic event literally creates an empty space, opening a new territory to dominate and allowing those in power to rewrite history, painting the minorities as villains and white males as heroes.

3

"The Red Blood of Patriots"

Paranoia and Scapegoating

In one scene of *The Omega Man* (1971), the protagonist is holed up on the second floor of his home as a group of disease-ridden people yell taunts outside and later hurl flaming projectiles via catapult. The virulent disease of these people, to which Neville (the protagonist) is immune, includes symptoms like albinism, light sensitivity, and the appearance of red sores on the skin. The leader of this particular group of infected citizens, Mathias, talks to a member of this "Family," who was, at one point, a Black man. The disease, the result of biological warfare, has changed this Black man into a white man via albinism, illustrating a loss of his former self. He says to Mathias, "And yet the whole Family can't bring him down out of that. . . . That honky paradise, brother?" Mathias, in a particularly illuminating response, tells him to "forget the old ways, brother. All your hatreds, all your pains. Forget. And remember . . . the Family is one." Mathias believes that the apocalypse has erased the pains of the past along with the oppression and mistreatment that this African American male had suffered. In fact, every Black character in the movie either becomes a white person or, in the case of a young boy, killed. However, the transformation into a white person is presented as an undesirable outcome because there is a strong desire to maintain racial differences. This is even clearer later in the film, when Neville attempts to cure the son of Lisa, an African American woman. To stem the advance of the disease in this young boy, Neville infuses him with his own blood, as he possesses the only known cure in his body. Neville, as he attempts the transfusion, says to Lisa:

> It's 160 proof Old Anglo-Saxon. One drop will . . .
>
> Lisa: (trying to hide her queasiness) Corrode your mind, send you running for the front of the bus . . .
>
> Neville: (laughs) Well . . . there aren't any busses anymore. (*The Omega Man*)

Neville's blood cures the boy of the disease, preventing him from turning white. We can see that the power of Neville's blood not only lies in curing the disease but also in preserving racial difference. White blood saves the world, through curing the disease and preventing Black people from passing as white. The elevation of white blood over that of Black people shows "the idea of black blood as a destructive quality and a threat to white racial purity" (Nama 66). Difference must be preserved so that the preapocalyptic hierarchy can be maintained. The disease and the "Family" must be stopped before they make it difficult, if not impossible, to scapegoat an easily discernible minority. The above dialogue, however, indicates a desire to erase a history of oppression in the same way that the Family does. In a reference to the Jim Crow–era laws that forced Black people to sit in the back of the bus, Lisa jokes that a drop of white blood will send her son to the front of the bus with the other whites. Neville responds, "There aren't any busses anymore," once again signifying that the apocalypse has erased the past. Ultimately, then, the film elucidates a desire to uphold a preapocalyptic hierarchy that keeps whites at the top, while at the same time erasing a past history of subjugation, alleviating white guilt, and purging a legacy of brutality. Some of the final images of the film make it clear that the white male is still at the apex of societal importance. We are left with the image of a dying Neville, laying prostrate against a statue, an image that parallels Christ on the cross. He is the white male, presented as a savior in both literal and figurative ways. A little girl even asks Neville at one point, "Are you God?"

The film shows a fairly common fear of dissolving racial and ethnic difference, an occurrence that makes scapegoating a minority group a more onerous task. In this chapter, I look at how the apocalypse functions in *The Omega Man* and numerous other films as a way of starting over, in order to more clearly delineate boundaries between the dominant and minority groups. The apocalypse often simplifies the complexities of ethnic and racial difference. By doing so, the apocalypse enables the white male to reify his dominance and also allows complex, inscrutable problems to be blamed on minority groups.

Defining Ethnicity and Race

Race and ethnicity have become increasingly difficult to categorize and define for a variety of reasons. The intermingling of races over several generations has made myriad subcategories: to the point where labeling often seems absurd. The arbitrary and shifting nature of both race and ethnicity has been the subject of much discussion along the following lines:

> It is not just the "how-far-back" question that introduces arbitrariness. One could also ask questions about which genealogical line is to be considered decisive. One generation back, we have two choices—mother and father. Two generations back, we have four. . . . This, of course, does not mean that ethnicity itself does not exist. Rather, it simply means that when it exists, it exists as a socially constructed category contingent on beliefs. (Abizadeh 24–25)

The implication here is that ethnicity, and sometimes race, is culturally determined and therefore somewhat malleable, and "the view that race is a social construction is widespread" (Mallon 644). There is also an extraordinary amount of blending that takes place between different ethnic groups, proven recently in an examination of 1,198 academic journal articles from 1996 to 1999, which found that "219 different terms [were] used to describe ethnic or racial groups in the US. . . . The fuzziness, incompatibility and degree of overlap between terms was very great" (Mateos, Singleton, and Longley 1441). This only exacerbates white anxiety, as whiteness begins to fade into an amorphous mix. As we shall see, apocalyptic media—similar to conspiracy theories in a variety of ways—allows for the attenuation of racial and ethnic complexities, which makes it easier to define whiteness and, consequently, easier to reify the hegemonic system.

Conspiracy theories both simplify a contemporary concern—environmental decay, economic downturns, etc.—and also give an abridged version of race and ethnicity. This serves to alleviate anxiety about a world that has become hard to understand and allows for the dominant white male to emerge as the hero. Conspiracy theories, a type of cognitive mapping, "have helped historically to prescribe and preserve a sense of American national identity that is restrictive in terms of race, class, and gender" (Knight 5).

Cognitive Mapping

The term "cognitive mapping" comes from the work of behavioral psychologist Edward Tolman, who did an experiment on latent learning in rats, which illustrated that the rats formed a mental picture of a maze that enabled them to quickly navigate their way to a "reward," in the form of food. Toward the end of his article on the experiment, titled "Cognitive Maps in Rats and Men," he applies the concept of cognitive mapping to people. He writes that

> each individual soon learns that, when as an individual he is frustrated, he must not take out his aggressions on the other members of his own group. He learns instead to displace his aggressions onto outgroups. Such a displacement of aggression I would claim is also a narrowing of the cognitive map. The individual comes no longer to distinguish the true locus of the cause of his frustration.

He further argues that the racism of Southern whites against Black people is "displacing their aggressions from the landlords, the southern economic system, the northern capitalists . . . onto a mere convenient outgroup" (Tolman 206). It's easier to simply imagine a threatening "outgroup" than a series of outside forces over which we have little control and often little understanding of. Scapegoating, like conspiracy theories, offers a simple answer to something complex, allowing one to navigate something obtuse and cryptic. As we can see, cognitive mapping has a number of applications that can be useful in explaining some human behaviors.

The term *cognitive mapping* is used, in the words of Fredric Jameson, "to span or coordinate, to map, by means of conscious and unconscious representations . . . the gap between the local positioning of the individual subject and the totality of class structures in which he or she is situated" (Jameson, "Cognitive Mapping" 416). It is, therefore, an attempt to create a clear mental picture, to piece together the fragments and web of intricacies into a unifying narrative. Cognitive mapping "provides a means to achieve an understanding of the complexities of the social relations that exist in what he terms the 'multinational age.' " It can take a variety of forms, one of which is described as "the self-reflexive aesthetics of post-modernist art, an inferior way of mapping the global multinational space we inhabit, as Jameson sees it, because its interiorization of social representation resolves into an endless mapping and remapping of the world as a set of textual processes." The second type of cognitive mapping, the main focus of my work, "stems from the 'omnipresence of the theme of paranoia' in the contemporary world. According to Jameson, the 'theme of paranoia' produces conspiracy theory" (Mason 40). Conspiracy theories are, however, inadequate in conveying the complexity of various economic and social systems; indeed, the point of conspiracy theories is simplification.

Paranoia and Conspiracy Theory

Richard Hofstadter touches on the rampant paranoia that characterizes modern American politics, where "the feeling of persecution is central, and it is indeed systematized in grandiose theories of conspiracy" (4). Conspiracy theories create an intelligible narrative that is "far more coherent than the real world, since it leaves no room for mistakes, failures, or ambiguities" (Hofstadter 36). Such theories create coherence through the identification of a scapegoat on which to blame any number of complex problems. Hofstadter spends time discussing the scapegoating of communists, but decades later, we see the frequent scapegoating of racial and ethnic minorities. Illegal immigrants are blamed for the lack of manual labor jobs and for crime, among many other things. Chapter 1 established a prevalent white anxiety and paranoia over the increasing rights of minority groups, concomitant with fears that whiteness will be lost in a world of ethnic and racial blending. Conspiracies flourish because they provide clear answers and create a scenario in which the white male must save the country from the influence of evil outgroups. Such conspiracies are grandiose in scale, showing that these minority groups threaten "a way of life whose fate affects not himself alone but millions of others" (Hofstadter 4).

All of the complexities of our world have also created anxiety and paranoia, as people yearn for help in navigating the labyrinthine world in which they live. America's economy, for instance, is so inextricably connected to that of any other country that it's virtually impossible to understand the precise machinations of our economic system. A war in a diminutive, unknown country might produce a butterfly effect that impacts economic conditions for American citizens unaware of that obscure country's existence. Wall Street itself is an enigma for most people; the derivatives market is a prime example of this. Derivatives allow people to profit from a decline in stock value, in essence allowing people to make money off of what would normally be a loss. There are other types of derivatives, however, including ones that allow for speculative investments on the future of a particular asset. It is, in essence, akin to betting. The derivatives market becomes utterly inscrutable when derivatives are allowed on other derivatives, spiraling out ad infinitum. The derivatives market, at one point, had more hypothetical money in play than what existed in the *entire world*—over a quadrillion dollars.[1] The idea is that economics has become unintelligible and almost postmodern in its refusal to submit to a concrete understanding. The unintelligible nature of economics applies to people's lives as well, as the public is inundated with a barrage of media every day of their lives. Companies trade in marketing data that allows them to target specific demographics based on the preferences of these same demographics. When people use the internet, they find ads that have been tailored to their own interests, as though the internet was somehow sentient. Coupled with the fragmentation of news outlets into hundreds of sites offering a unique perspective of the same event, the experience of the world can be catered very specifically to each individual. The effect of this fragmentation is to create a system that has become impossible to view in its totality, since the system is specifically designed *not* to be seen as whole. Peter Knight writes,

> Given that the forces and institutions of globalization are affecting countless people across the planet, it is no surprise that a conspiratorial sense of being the victim of invisible and indefatigable forces is an everyday attitude in many countries . . . it taps into the traditional American obsession with ruggedly individual agency. In part, the United States is

---

1. See Michael Snyder, "50 Things Every American Should Know about the Collapse of the Economy," *Business Insider*, May 18, 2011, http://www.businessinsider.com/collapse-of-the-economy-2011-5#the-financial-system-is-more-vulnerable-today-than-it-was-back-in-2008-before-the-financial-panic-25.

> a nation of conspiracy theorists because the influence of large social and economic forces in determining the lives of individuals is often regarded as paranoia-inducing encroachment on the self-reliance of individuals. (5)

The rugged individualism of the frontiersman, emblematic of American identity, is squelched in a world where every aspect of life is endlessly complicated and inextricably entwined. There is, in other words, no true independence and no respite from the invasive influence of globalization.

Cognitive mapping, in contemporary society, often takes the form of conspiracy theories, which work at creating a sort of mental map where the world is rendered in comprehensible terms. After 9/11, conspiracies abounded, the most common one was that the United States government was behind the attack in an attempt to justify a war in Iraq. The tragic event, in reality, was far more complex than that. The intelligence community sifted through mounds of data, obtained through their own work and that of our allies, attempting to determine whether the threat was real. The causes could be any number of cultural conflicts, policy decisions, and religious influences. For such a horrific event, there's a desire for a simple answer, to render the incomprehensible in black-and-white terms, so that the tragedy can be understood, the "bad guy" identified, and retribution guaranteed. This gives rise to the various conspiracy theories, which analyze the minutia of every frame of footage to create a narrative that neatly ties things together. This is an effort "to integrate a disparate set of events into a coherent network of connections or master narrative" (Willman 33). This proclivity for conspiracy theories is seen in various films, which attempt to assuage anxieties through simplification, pinning complex problems on any number of outgroups. Conspiracies lead to scapegoating:

> By narrowing the agency behind our world to a single figure of power (the Bilderberg Group, the Freemasons or some other convenient scapegoat). Despite the extraordinary complexity of some of these theories, they nevertheless provide a reassuringly simple answer to "who is behind it all," and what our own role is in the situation. In other words, they act precisely as a (faulty) cognitive map. (Srnicek and Williams, chap. 1)

Scapegoating allows for simple answers but also concretizes distinctions between the dominant culture and the outgroups being scapegoated.

At odds with the vilification of the "Other" and the extolling of white male virtues is the sense that the government—controlled by white males and a source of the hegemonic system—is a nefarious force in people's lives. In many cases, the main villain in a conspiracy is the government, not a distrusted minority. However, the demonization of the government in conspiracy theory is simply another form of white anxiety. The belief is that the government is, in some cases, tainted by the inclusion of minority groups. The Red Scare is the most obvious example, but there have been many others, including the so-called Lavender Scare after World War II. This was the term given to the pervasive fear that homosexuality had become rampant in American government. Beginning in the 1950s, the Lavender Scare led to the passing of "sexual psychopath" laws, purportedly aimed at protecting children from sexual predators. Unfortunately, the laws were used mainly in cases of consensual sex between adults. The Director of the CIA,

> Roscoe Hillenkoetter, warned a House committee that "perverts in key positions" formed "a government within a government" . . . Hillenkoetter testified that civil service homosexuals "belong to the lodge, the fraternity. One pervert brings other perverts into an agency, they move from position to position, and advance them usually in the interest of furthering the romance of the moment." Gays and lesbians were presumed to be security risks, though the evidence for that assumption was slight. (Walker chap. 3)

All told, about a thousand government employees believed to be homosexual were fired in the 1950s and 1960s (Walker chap. 3).

The belief that certain disenfranchised groups had infiltrated society has been constant in America's history. During a depression in the 1870s, there was a so-called Tramp Scare, wherein homeless, destitute citizens were blamed for a number of crimes and outrages. These "unemployed wanderers" were blamed for robberies and fires, and an incident in which several hoboes were shot after resisting arrest was celebrated by one writer in the *New York World* as a viable solution. Antitramp statutes allowed police to arrest these vagabonds at will, as conspiracy theories about them abounded. Horatio Seymour argued, in an 1878 article in *Harper's*:

> That vagabonds were "rapidly gaining a kind of organization" that was "growing into a system of brigandage" with

> "systems of communication and intercourse, which are made more perfect each year." A Texas paper informed its readers that undercover Massachusetts detectives had discovered a "perfectly organized brotherhood" in which "each tramp has a special duty assigned to him. Some of them beg and some of them steal, and they are even instructed what to steal and whom to steal it from."

At the same time as the Tramp Scare, a conspiracy theory developed in which the Irish were blamed for the disappearance of some coal miners in Pennsylvania. The theory was that these miners were killed by a secret Irish organization called the "Molly Maguires." It was believed that in Ireland the Molly Maguires would be in women's clothes and blackface while assassinating their enemies. When they came to the United States, they supposedly continued their terroristic acts, with thousands of Irish conspiring against American society (Walker chap. 4). Beyond the homeless and the Irish, few disenfranchised groups were exempt from outlandish conspiracy theories.

After the advent of film, conspiracy theories demonizing minorities found their way into movie theaters. Inspired by the mythology of Haitian voodoo, zombie movies became a way to illustrate widespread distrust of African Americans:

> There is a scene in Victor Halperin's 1932 film *White Zombie* where a white man's mill is run entirely by a black zombie workforce; the sequence was enough for a later critic to declare forthrightly that "Zombies are black slaves." (Walker chap. 4)

Romero's film, *Night of the Living Dead*, is thematically rich in its treatment of race, as the Black male protagonist is shot dead at the end because white law enforcement officials believe him to be a zombie.[2] Given the long history of distrust regarding minority groups, it's no surprise that the expansion of rights to these same groups has been met with vitriol by many white males in America. The implication is that any entity grant-

2. In an article for *Slate*, author Caetlin Benson-Allott notes that the end of the film "strongly evokes U.S. lynching photos. "See Caetlin Benson-Allott, "The Defining Feature of George Romero's Movies Wasn't the Zombie. It Was Something Bigger," *Slate*, July 18, 2017, http://www.slate.com/blogs/browbeat/2017/07/18/george_romero_s_movies_were_about_more_than_zombies.html.

ing rights to these groups is an enemy of the patriarchy. The reaction to the passing of the Civil Rights Act of 1964 by President Johnson, and subsequent affirmative action policies, clearly illustrates this. Cries of "reverse discrimination" became common among conservatives, who found the Democratic Party upended. Many Dixiecrats, led by the likes of Strom Thurmond and Jesse Helms, changed affiliation to the Republican Party, seeking to distance themselves from civil rights policies that would alienate conservative white voters.

The distrust of government was also fomented by revelations in the 1960s and 1970s that government agencies actually *had*, in fact, been conspiring against them. In 1956, the FBI started its COINTELPRO operation, which sought to deter and infiltrate what they thought to be dangerous subcultures and dissidents. The FBI

> agents infiltrated political groups and spread rumors that loyal members were the real infiltrators. They tried to get targets fired from their jobs, and they tried to break up the targets' marriages. They published deliberately inflammatory literature in the names of the organizations they wanted to discredit, and they drove wedges between groups that might otherwise be allied. (Walker chap. 7)

The CIA was also involved in such nefarious practices, one of which was MK-ULTRA, a program that administered a dose of LSD to unwitting participants, in order to see its effectiveness as a form of mind control or truth serum. Coupled with the Watergate scandal of the 1970s, revelations about actual government collusion and illegal activities led to a steep decline in public trust. After Watergate, distrust of the government skyrocketed from 22 to 62 percent, and belief that Congress "consistently lied to the American people" had gone from 38 percent to 68 by the time Nixon resigned (Olmsted 17). This distrust of government manifested itself in pop culture, where a flood of movies showing a conspiring, unscrupulous government found their way into American theaters. So while a distrust of government is, in some ways, an extension of white anxiety, it's also a result of actual events disclosed to the American public. It is, perhaps, more believable that the government would be involved in a 9/11 conspiracy when one considers the backdrop of actual government collusion over the past few decades, more recently the disclosures of Edward Snowden. The proven misconduct of police officers and intelligence agencies—the murder of Fred Hampton and Mark Clark of the Black Panther Party, for instance—made it much easier for the general public to believe conspiracies about the murders of Martin Luther King and Malcolm X. Real misconduct by government agencies and institutions made it easier to believe less plausible conspiracy theories.

Films and books illustrating a distrust of the government can couch ideas of the dominant culture in what seem like countercultural forms of expression. A film can seem progressive for its stance against government corruption, all while promoting the dominant cultural ideals that give this government power. In the same way, a punk band like Green Day can spout antigovernment rhetoric and anticonsumer messages, while concurrently enjoying the lucrative rewards of multimillion-dollar contracts. Capitalism is, in the words of The Clash, "turning rebellion into money." A real event, like the CIA's MK-ULTRA program, becomes a source of inspiration for countless books and films that capitalize on this and other disturbing, real-life events. The 1997 film *Conspiracy Theory*, for instance, features the CIA's MK-ULTRA program as a major part of the plot. The main character, Jerry Fletcher, was an unwitting participant in the MK-ULTRA program, brainwashed to become an assassin. He refuses an order to kill someone, thereafter escaping and developing amnesia that prevents him from recalling the mind control program he has been subjected to. Despite the amnesia, he becomes obsessed with uncovering a conspiracy that he senses is quite real. Ultimately, he finds all of his seemingly paranoid theories validated when an agent named Lowry attempts to help stop the men responsible for the mind control program that used Jerry to their own nefarious ends. The film uses the real-life events of MK-ULTRA to promote the idea that a brave white male, acting independently and brazenly against large, ambiguous forces, can expose the truth and save the public from further injustice. However, the real-life program was established precisely because of a desire to maintain American power in a world of Soviet and Chinese mind control programs. Many of the communist bloc countries had already been using advanced interrogation techniques by the 1950s, so there was great pressure on American intelligence agencies to maintain the upper hand. In effect, MK-ULTRA began as a desire to retain control over a terrifying foreign menace, thereby upholding American dominance. So while Jerry in *Conspiracy Theory* might be the hero of the film exposing the corruption and evil of the MK-ULTRA program, the real-life program was part of an effort to enable people like Jerry to keep their dominant status as the American white male. MK-ULTRA is presented as a corrupt, evil program in the film, but it's merely a pretext to create a scenario in which the white male can emerge victorious, and the film companies can produce profits by giving the patina of antiauthoritarianism.

The Link between Conspiracy and Apocalypticism

Apocalyptic myths have many of the same characteristics as conspiracy theories, especially when considering their political context. In all cases, there is a group that perceives itself to be oppressed, and imagines grand, epic forces to be at work that will eventually reveal a hidden truth. The apocalypse is a way of simplifying complex issues, both literally and metaphorically, to alleviate anxiety in the face of the unknown. On a literal level, the apocalypse often creates an empty space, wiping out the vast majority of objects and people—an extreme example of worldwide simplification. We are, as Jameson says, "caught within these more complex global networks, because we palpably suffer the prolongations of corporate space everywhere in our daily lives. Yet we have no way of thinking about them" ("Postmodernism" 92). To that end, the apocalypse pares things down, quite literally, through destruction, removing clutter that might otherwise make it difficult to truly "see." By its very nature, apocalyptic eschatology is a simplification of the entire world, annihilating most material goods and reducing civilization to a simple battle between good and evil. This simplification gives the "illusion" of a recognizable truth. The overarching template for apocalyptic myths—crisis, judgment, and reward—also simplifies human events in a fairly linear way, allowing for an experience of history that has long been absent in a postmodern world.

Rhetoric invoked in conspiracy theories is often that of the apocalypse, since apocalyptic imagery and thinking is an attempt to understand larger, incomprehensible forces. Robert Fuller corroborates this, noting,

> Apocalyptic thinking, then, is intended to "solve" the problem of evil through its mythic reworking of time. Apocalyptic discourse places believers in the context of cosmic time, providing assurance that by enduring hardships they are participating in the movement of history toward its ultimate fulfillment. (194)

In this sense, the apocalypse places complex social and economic issues into a simple Manichean framework, wherein the heroes and villains are readily identifiable. Michael Barkun, in *Culture of Conspiracy*, describes conspiracy theories in terms that parallel any description of apocalyptic myths, noting their

> attempts to delineate and explain evil. At their broadest, conspiracy theories "view history as controlled by massive, demonic forces." The locus of this evil lies outside the true community, in some "Other, defined as foreign or barbarian, though often . . . disguised as innocent and upright." The result is a worldview characterized by a sharp division between the realms of good and evil. (3)

Apocalyptic myths perform a similar function, characterizing history and world events as a battle between good and evil. One is either on the side of God or part of the evil forces that have enveloped the globe. Apocalypticism and conspiracy are "often linked," since they are both "strongly dualistic and often ascribe to evil a power believed to operate conspiratorially" (Barkun 10). The "Other" that Barkun describes has a striking similarity to the Antichrist in Christian mythology, who is also " 'disguised as innocent and upright.' " The Antichrist begins as a seemingly positive force, creating unity among warring nations, only later to be revealed as a powerfully evil force. Similarly, minority groups insinuate themselves into aspects of government and American culture, slowly rotting American institutions from the inside. The Antichrist, according to the Bible, "display[s] . . . all kinds of counterfeit miracles, signs and wonders," but possesses "every sort of evil that deceives those who are perishing" (2 Thessalonians 2:8–10).

Scapegoating

Scapegoating, often a result of paranoia, has a long history, the term itself derived from an Old Testament story in Leviticus. In the story, there are two goats used as part of a ritual. One goat is sacrificed, while the other is allowed to escape, carrying the sins of the Hebrews. Leviticus 16:8–10 explains that

> Aaron shall lay both his hands upon the head of the live goat and confess over him all the inequities of the people of Israel and all other transgressions, all their sins, and he shall put

> them upon the head of the goat and send him away into the wilderness . . . The goat shall bear all their iniquities upon him to a solitary land. (Leviticus 16:8–10)

In the nineteenth century, anthropologists broadened the definition of scapegoating to include "a wide range of rites for the expulsion of evil" (Welch 36–37). It wasn't until the mid-twentieth century that the term "scapegoat" became a term signifying the unfair placement of blame on an individual or group, though "modern scapegoating is different from its ancient counterpart insofar as it is motivated less by mystical/religious ritual and more by the need to victimize" (Welch 37). The scapegoats themselves are often seen as "tainted and polluted, prompting the need for societal purification" (37). The groups chosen for scapegoating are often minorities, who are blamed for a wide variety of issues, ranging from economic turmoil to gun violence. Scapegoats are not chosen randomly; the choice of scapegoat is "patterned firmly along observable lines of race, ethnicity, and religion" (38–39). Below the surface of economic issues in American society, we can see how "racial and ethnic minorities pose a threat to hegemonic cultural identities, producing for the dominant white group considerable anxiety over insecurity and in some cases leading to hostility" (72). The anxieties of the dominant class often revolve around racial and ethnic blending, and the dissolving distinctions between dominant and minority groups.

In science fiction, the scapegoating of minorities often manifests itself through the use of robots, androids, and aliens. The connection between sci-fi androids and race has been noted by many, including author Sam Lundwall, who wrote,

> It is the guilt for the Negroes, the Indians, the Jews, the Vietnamese, the people of South America and mankind's rape of weaker individuals that comes back in the android. The android functions as sf's contribution to the race debate. . . . Just like Negroes, Indians, Mexicans and what-have-you, they must be kept down at all costs, never for a moment being permitted to regard themselves as equals to The White Man. (Lundwall 166)

The android, as a blend of both human and machine, is representative of the sorts of ethnic and racial blending that threaten the "purity" of whiteness and white identity. If one cannot tell the difference between man and machine, then how will the proper group be scapegoated and dominated? The answer to this question is found in cognitive mapping, a simplification of complex issues that allows for easy vilification of minorities. In sci-fi film, these minorities could be the Replicants of *Blade Runner* (1982), the prawns of *District 9* (2009), or the orcs of *Bright* (2017).

Robots, Androids, and Race

Postapocalyptic sci-fi films often employ robots or androids as a means of dealing with race, class, and gender. The apocalypse is either directly caused by these robots, or indirectly caused by robots that have corrupted the government, families, and schools. Postapocalyptic myths in film are thus used as a form of cognitive mapping that makes sense of world disasters by placing the blame on minorities, thinly disguised as robots. This use of robots can be seen in sci-fi novels as well, including Asimov's highly influential *I, Robot* series. The three laws of robotics, for instance, meant to ensure these robots remain subservient to humans, are "refashioning the slave codes that subjugated blacks while he [Asimov] serves a progressive philosophy based on the assumption that technological consciousness can be denied free will because it is inherently inferior." The belief that these machines lack free will "is a repetition of the antebellum period in American history, a human sense that African slaves did not possess wills and were therefore not human" (Lavender 61). The parallels between robot/human and slave/master relationships are apparent in many films, including *Blade Runner* and *WALL-E*. In *Blade Runner*, "a slave allegory is impossible to miss here since Deckard is portrayed as a futuristic slave catcher sent to kill 'escaped' androids. . . . Clearly, specials and androids are discriminated against because they are perceived as being racial others" (Lavender 181). In *WALL-E*, the majority of the robots are subservient to human interests and needs, except for those that display more human characteristics, including the titular character. Robots, in the film, only have value in that they either serve humans or mimic human behaviors.

Anxiety and paranoia arise because these robots and androids possess abilities that are equal to or surpass those of humans. Machines demonstrating sentience cause anxiety in humans "because it is an alien experience akin to the racial one—a white person fearing a black one and vice versa" (Lavender 194). This is related to white anxiety about African American physical prowess, with which countless gold medals and championships have been won, in addition to sexual prowess, the Black male phallus leading to feelings of insecurity among white males. In a recent study,

"A Superhumanization Bias in Whites' Perceptions of Blacks," researchers found that "Whites implicitly and explicitly superhumanize Blacks versus Whites." The study showed that "superhumanization is associated with diminished recognition of Blacks' pain" and illustrates a "novel form of dehumanization, one that treats . . . Blacks . . . as nonhuman, not through animalization or mechanization, but through depicting them as superhuman" (Waytz et al. 6). The use of robots to represent oppressed minorities thus correlates with this perception of their "superhuman" physical abilities. To allay the anxiety-ridden perception of Black physical power, a postapocalyptic scenario is used to simplify complex issues and reify white dominance. Often, these robots are culpable in conspiracies involving environmental disaster, nuclear war, and genocide. The dominant white male patriarchy is painted as a victim that must perform various acts of heroism to save mankind from extinction.

There is also anxiety about an inability to distinguish man from machine, mirroring anxiety over the dissipation of ethnic and racial differences. One can see this in a film like *The Terminator*, where a robot "passes" as human, making him an especially nefarious foe that can move about undetected. Lavender writes:

> The cyborg reinforces cultural attitudes in ways that suggest where the line is drawn between humans and machines. In this respect, a problem of proportionality exists: what percentage of mechanical parts separates the cyborg from the human? . . . Taking into account the idea of human authenticity, then, the cyborg raises issues of racial purity reminiscent of miscegenation, passing, and the one-drop rule. (201)

Films like *The Terminator*, therefore, illustrate a concern with dissolving boundaries between dominant and minority groups and attempt to reaffirm the boundaries to more easily assign blame for multifaceted problems.

The Terminator came out in 1984, a year after Reagan first publicly proposed the Star Wars missile defense system, formally called the Strategic Defense Initiative. The Soviet-Afghan war in 1979 and the shooting down of Korean Air Lines Flight 007 in 1983 were among the many incidents to heighten tensions at the time, creating an atmosphere of paranoia as conspiracy theories abounded. These conspiracy theories found their way into the popular media of the time, often reducing the complexities of the Cold War to a battle between the strong, white American male, and the amoral, threatening foreigner, antithetical to all the ideals of American identity—freedom, individuality, and other characteristics associated with the frontier. In this context, *The Terminator* reduces something very complex to a simple battle between a white male and a foreign entity, ultimately reaffirming the patriarchy.

The terminator is a cipher for any number of threatening Others, possessing many of the outward characteristics of a human being. The terminator is under the control of Skynet, which gained consciousness, and panicked operators attempted to take it offline when they realized its destructive potential. Realizing the threat to its existence, Skynet launched a preemptive strike, targeting Russia, which soon retaliated in kind—yet again highlighting Cold War paranoia. In keeping with the reductive nature of cognitive mapping, Skynet and its minions—the terminators—are single-minded in purpose. The terminator's decisions, highlighted in the film by several point-of-view shots, are reduced to a series of simple choices: for instance the decision to say "Fuck you, asshole" in response to someone knocking at his motel room door. There is no apparent complexity of thought, and choice has been reduced to an option of six different responses. The myopic focus of Skynet and the terminators makes them easy to vilify and allows Manichean notions of good and evil to predominate. This is, of course, in keeping with apocalyptic myths in general, which split the world into believers and nonbelievers. However, it should be noted that Skynet and the terminators' reaction to humankind was in response to a direct threat to their existence. Skynet's purpose was to safeguard the world, and it found that mankind was an imminent and chief threat. Safeguarding the world might not necessarily be the same thing as safeguarding human beings. Mankind has shown itself to be incredibly destructive to the entire planet. In this sense, Skynet's purpose in eliminating mankind might not be as simplistic as the film presents it. There are some interesting parallels between Skynet and the terminators and the Native Americans that were a hindrance to Westward expansion. Portrayed as simplistic, inferior savages, the Native Americans displayed a more fervent desire to safeguard the environment from overdevelopment and demolition. They were, in a way, attempting to safeguard the planet from white men, whose zealous hunting and taming of the wilderness nearly wiped out the buffalo. And like Skynet, they attacked as a response to an imminent threat to their existence. The vast majority of Americans did not see them this way, opting instead to reduce them to a nefarious Other that victimizes whites.

The paranoia of the film is very clear. Skynet was a defense system, similar to Star Wars, that gains sentience and decides to destroy mankind.

The audience of the time was just beginning the age of computer ownership and in this sense, computers were unknown entities with nebulous powers. The world, between the Cold War and Americans' changing relationship to machines, bleeds over into the film, which places these issues within the framework of a readily identifiable template—white men must take a stand against the "Other." The white man, in this case, is Kyle Reese. Before Kyle Reese's heroics, however, the future of mankind is bleak. Skynet destroyed much of the planet, creating a barren, postapocalyptic world. In the glimpses of the future seen in the film, humans appear to have minority status, having been killed in mass numbers. This is clearly meant to generate fear in the audience. Beyond fear of death, we are meant to fear being subservient to an outgroup that we created, in the same way we created slaves by taking them from their homes and transporting them to the United States. Something made by the dominant culture, something meant to be compliant, has gained extraordinary power. However, through the guidance of the human resistance leader John Connor, humans begin a very effective campaign to retake the planet from the machines. In response, Skynet sends a machine—called a terminator—into the past to kill John Connor's mother, thereby ending the future human resistance fighting. John Connor discovers this plot and sends Kyle Reese into the past to stop the terminator. Kyle Reese is the white male savior for two reasons: he stops the terminator, and he turns out to be John Connor's father. So while the depiction of Sarah Connor as an integral part of the human resistance may seem progressive at first, it is ultimately Kyle Reese who turns out to be the most heroic figure, even dying in the process of saving Sarah and the future of mankind. Furthermore, it is John Connor—another white male—on whom the entire future hinges. The film then becomes a justification for white male dominance.

Blame for the destruction of the world is placed on Skynet, a global defense system that has taken over the world and is determined to exterminate all human life. Skynet's main foot soldiers are the terminators—cyborgs that resemble human beings. Here we see the fear of blending and the idea that an "Other" could pass as human. The main antagonist, over the course of the film, gradually begins to lose his ability to "pass." Through a series of conflicts with Kyle Reese, the terminator loses pieces of skin that reveal a metal endoskeleton, which clearly establishes a boundary between "Other" and the dominant culture. The white male has heroically reaffirmed the difference between human and machine, allowing the enemy to be more clearly identified and scapegoated.

More than simply a microcosm of Cold War conflict, the film illustrates the pervasive sentiment that the world has become a web of complicated, inscrutable forces—a global economy, government surveillance, and ubiquitous electronic devices that manage to permeate every aspect of our lives. The Patriot Act and the revelations of Edward Snowden make it clear that our lives are not entirely our own and that any moment of our lives might be observed and influenced by outside forces. Though *The Terminator* was made well before such surveillance tools, the growth of personal computers and electronic devices had already been happening at the time. The film conflates these sources of anxiety to create one specific entity: Skynet. The complexities of our world are presented as the machinations of one evil being that the white male must stand up against.

Cyborg Bodies as Male Empowerment

The clear delineation between human and machine, necessary to maintain the hierarchy of the dominant culture, becomes extremely muddled in the film *Robocop* (1987). Alex Murphy, a police officer in an incredibly crime-ridden future Detroit, is gunned down by criminals early in the film. Omni Consumer Products, a large corporate conglomerate that owns the police force, reanimates Murphy in the form of a deadly cyborg police officer. During the course of the film, Murphy begins having flashbacks to his life before becoming a cyborg. This creates one of the central conflicts of the film—the interaction between a robotic body and a human consciousness.

The cyborg part of Murphy endows him with impressive physical abilities, but it is presented as something to be overcome on a cognitive level. He encounters flashbacks throughout the film, showing his past as the patriarch of a suburban nuclear family. Ultimately, it is his white masculine identity that manages to redeem him and overcome the "Otherness" of his body. It is quite telling that one of the first things to surface from his past is his proclivity to twirl his firearm, like the hero of a Western. He is the white male hero, with "masculinity constructed according to the codes and conventions of the western film" (Cornea 127). At the end, Robocop shows the best of both worlds. He is given the physical strength and ability of an "Other," while maintaining the identity of a white male frontiersman. This physical ability is used to enhance his masculinity, as he "is given the armoured body to back up his macho posturing" (Cornea 127). The anxiety over technology taking over the lives of humans, possibly disturbing the patriarchal hierarchy, is assuaged by showing how technology can be used to bolster the power of the white male. In cyborg films like *Robocop*, the white male utilizes "cyborgization . . . as a strategy of remasculinization and as a means to transcend the feminizing realm of the natural" (Hamming 149).

Films Critical of Scapegoating

In 1982, the year *Blade Runner* came out, many Americans were seeing the beginnings of a computer age that would irrevocably change the way they defined themselves, creating a crisis of identity. Scott Bukatman, in *Terminal Identity*, writes:

> Jean Baudrillard and Donna Haraway, for all their differences, are united in their recognition of the enveloping and determining parameters of a fully technologized existence that has forced a crisis around untenable definitions of the human. . . . Technology and the human are no longer so dichotomous. (5)

If the line between machine and man is porous or no longer relevant, what does that do to a person's identity? Would we still have control over our identities? In 1980 Stanford held its first annual American Association for Artificial Intelligence, and in 1981, Danny Hillis designed the "Connection Machine"—a supercomputer using parallel processing. By the time *Blade Runner* came out, computers were very much in the public's consciousness, and as personal computer usage became widespread, a certain vague unease surrounded them. By 1984, the same year William Gibson wrote his seminal cyberpunk novel *Neuromancer*, author Craig Brad coined the term *technostress*, in a book of the same title. The term was meant to describe the anxiety one experiences when using technologies related to computers (Buchanan 59). This anxiety was exacerbated as the line between mechanical and biological further dissipated in subsequent decades.[3]

3. Kevin Kelly, founder of *Wired* magazine and author of *Out of Control*, wrote, "Principles underpin the awesome workings of prairies, flamingoes, cedar forests, eyeballs, natural selection in geological time, and the unfolding of a baby

The technostress generated from the advent of a "neobiological civilization" is obvious in 1980s and 1990s sci-fi film, which struggles to reestablish the dividing line between man and machine, or in some cases just examines the effect of these blurring boundaries. The question of what separates mechanical from biological is asked throughout the main narrative in *Blade Runner*, the underlying paranoia being the possibility that someone else—a powerful corporate executive like Tyrell, for instance—is directing our lives, something made easier by the ubiquitous technology that both aids and controls us. Moreover, there is a sense that man and machine might become so similar that it becomes impossible to differentiate the two, leading to a paranoid scenario in which Replicants could be all around us, without us ever knowing. Though the story is fictional, the film evinces contemporary concerns, as "organ transplants and remarkable prosthetic devices are commonplace, we are . . . theorizing our bodies, ourselves, as cyborgs. . . . In an age of electronic reproduction and replication . . . it is the unique status of the human being that is challenged by technological transformation" (Sobchack 237). Though *Blade Runner* came out several decades ago, anxieties over the "unique status of the human being" were already prevalent at that time.

The film follows Detective Deckard, as he attempts to locate and kill four escaped Replicants—androids almost indistinguishable from humans. Replicants have been banned from Earth, which essentially means that the four Replicants being hunted by Deckard are there illegally, in the hopes of finding a way to extend their lifespan. Tyrell is the nefarious mastermind behind Replicant technology, which he uses to create humanlike machines that can perform various forms of physical labor, including mining and prostitution. His newest model Replicant, Rachael, is different in the sense that Tyrell has implanted memories to make her more human. Ultimately, however, Tyrell implants these memories to create a degree of control over Rachael, since Replicants forming their own memories over time could develop their own emotional responses and become difficult to control. This is seen with Roy Batty and his cohorts who, through the formation of their own memories, develop their own emotional attachments and own ways of thinking about the injustice of their situation.

---

elephant from a tiny seed of elephant sperm and egg. These same principles of bio-logic are now being implanted in computer chips, electronic communication networks, robot modules, pharmaceutical searches, software design, and corporate management" (580). Kevin Kelly, *Out of Control: The Rise of Neo-Biological Civilization* (Boston: Addison-Wesley, 1994).

The film is apocalyptic in some obvious ways,[4] taking place in a future version of Los Angeles that is shrouded in perpetual dark clouds and filled with the people not healthy or wealthy enough to leave for the outer colonies. Many scenes feature abandoned buildings, trash strewn about the ground, and a notable lack of vegetation—indicative of some environmental cataclysm. Beyond these more obvious signs of apocalyptic decay, the film is rife with allusions to specific Christian apocalyptic ideas. In a scene that was left out of the theatrical version of the film, Deckard visits his injured coworker, Holden, in the hospital, a visit that also allows insight into the Replicants' actions. Holden asks Deckard, "Don't you see what they're after, who they're looking for?" Deckard is baffled by this question, and Holden finally answers, "God!" (*Blade Runner*). Thus we see that the stakes for Batty are very high indeed, his life already framed within the context of these large, apocalyptic scenarios. Deckard soon finds his worldview altered by Batty, who is meant to be a Christ figure. Batty releases a white dove—a symbol of the Holy Spirit—into the sky during the penultimate scene of the film. Among many other parallels, we see him "drive . . . a nail through his own hand in order to keep it functioning. Of course, Batty mimics Christ in this action as well as in his salvation of Deckard" (Gravett 40). Indeed, these "Biblical allusions . . . contribute to the film's mythic structure" (Desser 173).

The "Other" of the film is very obviously the Replicants, who are painted in both *Blade Runner* films as an oppressed underclass used for slave labor. The derogatory term "skin job" is, according to Deckard in the original narrated version of the first film, akin to using the word "nigger." The Replicants of *Blade Runner* "function as compelling symbols of black racial formation in America. . . . As escaped slaves from an Off-world site, Replicants share the same socioeconomic status as that of enslaved Africans during America's period of legalized slavery" (Nama 56). Despite being a disenfranchised group, the Replicants are seen by the dominant culture as a threatening menace, so much so that they are forbidden from coming to Earth. The majority group, similar to many postapocalyptic films, uses the rhetoric of minority groups to paint themselves as victims, their very way of life in danger of being corrupted by insidious subhumans. In the original script for the film, officer Gaff says

4. Brooker, in his book, writes that "the Los Angeles of the film echoes all of the scriptural apocalypses of Genesis and Exodus, as well as Daniel's" (35). See Will Brooker, *The Blade Runner Experience: The Legacy of a Science Fiction Classic* (New York: Columbia University Press, 2012).

to Deckard: "The skin jobs look better than you do! What's the point of wiping out skin jobs if they look better than Enforcement? Pretty soon the public will want skin jobs for Enforcement." This indicates the anxiety of being replaced or usurped by a disenfranchised group, anxiety that is further manifested in the extreme lengths to which the Tyrell Corporation attempts to maintain control over them. In addition to a four-year lifespan, the newer Replicants of the film have memory implants. Tyrell explains, "If we gift them with a past . . . we create a cushion or pillow for their emotions . . . and we can control them better" (*Blade Runner*). This fear of the "Other" continues in *Blade Runner 2049*, wherein Officer K endures taunts and derogatory name-calling at his police station, which indicates the dread of being replaced by a coldly efficient Replicant minority.

Paranoia seeps into the narrative in several ways. The new Replicant with manufactured memories, Rachael, would blend in perfectly with normal human beings, her "Otherness" being completely imperceptible to the vast majority of people. Deckard administers the Voight-Kampff test—a method of ascertaining whether one is a Replicant—over a long period, unable to tell that Rachael is a Replicant until hours later. The fear then is that these Replicants, the "Other" in the film, might be among us, an incognito enemy invading our living space. This is, of course, in keeping with the white anxiety discussed in a previous chapter, where the dominant culture believes it is being infiltrated by insidious enemies—communists, minorities, and homosexuals, for instance. This anxiety is made more explicit in *Blade Runner 2049* (2017), a sequel with a central premise that Ridley Scott had in mind when he created the first film, though Villeneuve directed the sequel. After discovering the remains of a pregnant Replicant, Lieutenant Joshi (Robin Wright) says, "The World is built on a wall that separates kind. Tell either side there's no wall. . . . You bought a war" (*Blade Runner 2049*). Dissolving distinctions between the dominant group and oppressed minorities creates tremendous apprehension, in both films and in the real world of the film audience. Those in a position of power, who utilize the rhetoric of minority oppression to paint themselves the victim, become unable to frame their narrative of subjugation in the same way. If there is no difference between humans and Replicants, then there is no clear Other to portray as a devious cancer infiltrating society. It also completely and utterly undercuts the notion of white male exceptionalism, indicating that perhaps they are not "special" in the way they had once thought.

Another form of paranoia is introduced via Deckard himself. Much has been written and said about the possibility of Deckard being a Replicant. His eyes have irises that "glow" like Rachael's in a scene where he stands behind her, and Gaff leaves an origami unicorn outside of his apartment, implying that Gaff knows what Deckard has been dreaming about. If Gaff is aware of Deckard's dreams, it is possible that his memories have been implanted, just like Rachael's. All ambiguity was removed when Ridley Scott himself confirmed that Deckard is, in fact, a Replicant. Deckard, however, does not seem to be aware of this at all. The film, therefore, raises the possibility that one could be a Replicant and not even be aware of it. Another person, like Tyrell, could have manufactured memories so believable and so completely entwined with our identities that it's almost unfathomable that someone else has dictated the events of our lives. The fear of corporate control is a corollary of this form of paranoia, as it becomes possible that inhabitants of Earth could be blithely unaware that their identities have been constructed by a corporate entity. In this way, corporate influence, after managing to invade every square inch of living space, has managed to find its way into our own minds.

The fear of minority infiltration is seen throughout the film, as Replicants literally infiltrate the Tyrell Corporation, seeking a solution to their short, four-year lifespan. They not only infiltrate the Tyrell Corporation but also Earth itself, since they are forbidden from coming back to the planet. The opening scene in the film shows one Replicant, Leon, being questioned by a blade runner, in this case Holden. Holden administers the Voight-Kampff test at the Tyrell Corporation building, the implication being that Leon has managed to successfully gain employment or some level of access within the Tyrell building. The scene ends with Leon shooting Holden, a scene that seems to denote Replicants as evil. Initially, therefore, it would seem that the film draws a clear line between humans and Replicants, the former being good and the latter evil. However, rather than scapegoat Replicants, the film ultimately identifies a corporation as the cause of the dystopian world in which the characters live. In addition, the line between minority and dominant group only becomes more muddled as the film goes on.

The film simplifies complex issues via scapegoating but does not place the onus of Earth's entropic decay on Replicants. In the end, it is the fear of corporate control that unifies all other elements of the film, and the postapocalyptic world is the cognitive mapping that attempts to make sense of pervasive corporate influence. Everything can be tied to the Tyrell Corporation, which has the most prominent and imposing building in the entire Los Angeles skyline. The apocalypse is implied to have been caused by overdevelopment of land and overcrowding. The pollution from overdevelopment is obvious from the first glimpses of Los Angeles, with such heavy smog that the city is engulfed in constant darkness. In addition, the city itself is covered in advertisements, on the sides of buildings, in the streets, and in the air. Corporate influence has suffocated the living space of the citizenry, who find themselves caught in an overwhelming flood of flashing lights and products. In one scene, as Deckard chases one of the Replicants—Zhora—he runs through crowded streets, with throngs of people shoulder to shoulder, vying for space between each other and the surrounding advertisements. We see the overcrowding problem in scenes like this, but it's unclear whether the problem is too many people, too many ads, or perhaps a combination of both. The apocalypse, rather than remove commodities through devastating destruction, involves oversaturation, though this abundance reveals an ironic, underlying emptiness. The world is all artifice, all simply a veneer of neon beauty, with nothing real underneath. Even the animals, like Tyrell's owl, are not real. In this sense, the postapocalyptic world of *Blade Runner* is as empty as the world of *The Road Warrior*. The postapocalyptic world, by linking all problems to corporate control, creates a totalizing myth that connects environmental decline, overpopulation, and the pervasive influence of technology. The result is a cognitive map that, despite ostensibly being about the future, makes sense of a 1980s America grappling with issues defying comprehension. The various forces at work in global pollution, the exploding birth rates in China and India, and the growth of computer systems beyond the understanding of the average person, all create a sense of dread and anxiety. Ubiquitous corporate influences can easily be blamed for many of these ills. Much like the Tyrell Corporation, technological advances can be tied to corporate desire for greater efficiency in production, in addition to enabling the average citizen's dependence on the comforts and benefits of technological devices (iPhones, laptops, etc.). This allows for greater corporate profits from both consumer purchases and lower production costs via mechanical efficiency. The dependence on technology is part of a rampant consumer culture that obsessively purchases objects, making consumers a party to excessive waste and pollution. The corporations create pollution through the act of production, while the average person creates waste every time a product package is disposed of and every time an obsolete tech device is thrown away. For the Tyrell Corporation, the production of Replicants is tied to both sex work and also a need for slave labor, in mining, colonizing other worlds, and other dangerous tasks. Much like automation in contemporary society, these Replicants undoubtedly create greater efficiency for corporations and help generate new venues for corporate exploitation (new worlds to colonize). In this way, the blurred line between human and machine is caused by a *corporation*, and the pollution we see throughout the film is likely a result of the endless corporate exploitation of Earth's resources. Giuliana Bruno, in "Ramble City: Postmodernism and *Blade Runner*," notes that "the continuous expulsion of waste is an indexical sign of the well-functioning apparatus; waste represents its production, movement, and development at increasing speed" (Bruno 63). From the very first shots of the film, we see flames shooting out of a smokestack, like waste being expelled from a factory—a sign of production that is likely linked to the darkened, smog-filled skyline. The film ends up placing blame for the apocalypse on a corporation, not an oppressed minority group. While Replicants may have infiltrated the Tyrell Corporation, they are merely a pawn in a sort of corporate conspiracy that deprives them of basic rights. Similarly, the film *A.I.: Artificial Intelligence* focuses on a group of androids, scapegoated and mistreated by a dominant group in search of facile explanations for complex issues, specifically global warming and genetic engineering.

In 2001 George W. Bush withdrew the United States from the Kyoto Protocol, which was an attempt at curbing greenhouse gas emissions. Global warming was in the public consciousness, becoming the subject of debates and a prominent talking point in Al Gore's political campaign for president. That same year, the human genome sequence was revealed, in a joint project involving scientists from the United States, China, Germany, France, Japan, and England. The scientists estimated that the entire genome sequence could be mapped out by 2003. This event was widely covered in the media and intensified the debate over genetic engineering of humans, an article in *Nature* proclaiming that "the human genome has had a certain tendency to incite passion and excess" (Lander 187).[5] In June of that year, *A.I.: Artificial Intelligence* (2001) came out, a

5. The article later mentions how public reaction included everything from "frenzied coverage of a late-breaking genome race between public and private protagonists; to a White House announcement of the draft human sequence in June 2000, 8 months before scientific papers had actually been written, peer-reviewed and published; to breathless promises from Wall Street and the press about the imminence of genetic 'crystal balls' and genome-based panaceas; to a front-page news story on the tenth anniversary of the announcement that chided genome scientists for not yet having cured most diseases" (Lander 187).

film that touched on the anxiety of both global warming and genetic reproduction of human beings.

The film *A.I.: Artificial Intelligence* follows an android child, David, in his quest to become human so his mother will love him. He is adopted at the beginning of the film by a couple with a deathly ill son, cryogenically frozen until a cure for his disease can be found. David has been programmed to love, and the couple uses him as a replacement for their biological child. Once their human child is miraculously cured, however, David's presence in the family is no longer needed. A rivalry between the biological son and David leads the parents to scapegoat David for several problems, including the near drowning of their son. Abandoned in the woods by his mother, David goes on a perilous journey to find the "blue fairy," thinking this entity can grant him his ultimate wish—to become a "real" boy.

The apocalyptic aspect of the film is dealt with via voiceover at the beginning of the film. The narrator notes that

> those were the years after the ice caps had melted because of the greenhouse gases, and the oceans had risen to drown so many cities along all the shorelines of the world. Amsterdam, Venice, New York, forever lost. Millions of people were displaced, climate became chaotic. Hundreds of millions of people starved in poorer countries. Elsewhere a high degree of prosperity survived when most governments in the developed world introduced legal sanctions to strictly license pregnancies. Which is why robots, who were never hungry and did not consume resources beyond that of their first manufacture, were so essential an economic link in the chain mail of society. (*A.I.: Artificial Intelligence*)

The apocalypse leads to an increased reliance on androids, who "did not consume resources beyond that of their first manufacture." However, the setting of the film doesn't seem apocalyptic until the end of the film, wherein David explores an underwater Coney Island to find the "blue fairy," which is part of a Pinocchio-themed amusement park. In fact, the film plays out like an extraordinarily pessimistic version of the Pinocchio story, where the simulated child never becomes real and only receives love from a clone of his mother, fabricated by an advanced alien race. It is not, in other words, David's adoptive mother that loves him at the end but a genetic reproduction.

The ostracized outgroup throughout the film is the androids, who are maimed, abandoned, and caged like animals. One particularly poignant scene takes place in Flesh World, a place where humans watch androids get tortured in a variety of disturbing ways. One machine is shot out of a cannon; another has a bucket of acid dumped on her head, while another is cut in half by a chainsaw-wielding motorcycle rider. While David is in a cage with other androids, awaiting execution, he asks, "Why is this happening?" Another droid in the cage responds, "When the opportunities avail themselves, they pick away at us, cutting away our numbers so they can maintain numerical superiority!" We see then that the dominant culture fears losing its dominance, committing acts of violence against a minority group. The human in charge of Flesh Fair essentially corroborates this, as he speaks to the crowd of humans in the stands:

> "Ladies and gentlemen. Girls and boys and children of all ages! What will they think of next?! See here: a bitty box, a tinker toy, a living doll. 'Course we all know why they made them. To seize your hearts. To replace your children! This is the latest iteration to the series of insults to human dignity. An underground scheme to phase out all of God's little children. Meet the next generation of child designed to do just that!" (*A.I.: Artificial Intelligence*)

The film then becomes another postapocalyptic film using androids as a means of dealing with racial anxiety. There is a fear of being replaced and losing dominant status. In addition, there is a fear of blending—a fear that a machine like David could "pass" as human, completely blurring the line between man and machine. The film illustrates "the anxiety over human-machine relationships that are coming to the foreground in a technologically developed culture. This anxiety often manifests itself as a concern over the difficulty in drawing a distinction between the real and the artificial" (Fedosik 183). However, the film is conspicuously drawing a parallel between the human-machine conflict and the conflict between dominant whites and minority groups. In the scene taking place at Flesh Fair, for instance, a "black minstrel-show mecha" is shot out of a cannon, his head smashing up against David's prison cell. The camera immediately cuts to Black audience members, as we see that the "most recent victims of prejudice and oppression have become the most enthusiastic new bigots. 'History repeats itself,' as one of the caged robots grimly explains"

(Kreider 36). The film, like many other sci-fi films, is using androids as a metaphor for race and the mistreatment of minority groups.

Beyond anxiety over losing dominant status, the film shows the scapegoating of the minority group. Environmental issues have led to restrictions on procreation. A consequence of this is an increased reliance on machines and androids. These androids are an emblem of both these restrictions and the apocalypse, being a direct result of both. The rising sea levels that resulted in the destruction of major cities had a number of causes, no doubt, including industry and car emissions. It's easier, however, to blame an entity that is a constant reminder of the world's environmental folly. Gigolo Joe, David's android companion for much of the film, tells David, "We are suffering for the mistakes they [humans] made" (*A.I.: Artificial Intelligence*). The film presents Gigolo Joe, David, and the other androids in a sympathetic light, but virtually every human being in the film regards them with utter contempt. David himself is repeatedly scapegoated by his adoptive family, for doing things that the human child coerces him to do. In one scene, the human child, Martin, tells David to cut off a lock of his mother's hair. The mother wakes up to see David with scissors in his hand, mistaking his act as a threat of violence against her. Such instances of mistaken intentions happen frequently at the beginning of the film, with David becoming the scapegoat for Martin's transgressions. As the film moves along further, we see that it's not just David being scapegoated but the whole minority group of androids.

There are actually two apocalyptic events in the film, the second one occurring at the end, when an ice age has frozen and killed all human beings. Aliens discover David buried in the ice and after reviving him, attempt to access his memories. Since there are no living humans left and David, as an android, has a perfect memory, David is the only vehicle through which anyone can gain an immersive view of human life. David's memory, for the aliens, illustrates the quotidian living of a family and various aspects of culture, including entertainment and food. The first apocalypse of the film, which occurs before the film even starts, leads to the eventual scapegoating of an android minority. In a sense, the apocalypse of global warming and melting ice caps leads to simplification, with humans vilifying androids, attempting to place society's ills on an outgroup. The second apocalypse, however, illustrates a more literal simplification, with human extinction and buildings frozen in ice. The extermination event increases David's value, as he ironically becomes the most thorough repository of human life. However, David is still a minority, the only one of his kind in a world now populated by aliens. While the aliens appear benevolent and generous, they use David as a test subject, recreating his family home while observing him.

The film captures two topics very much in the public consciousness at the time—global warming and genetic modification. There is a clear attempt by the humans in the film to simplify these issues by scapegoating androids, a living reminder of human reproductive issues and environmental catastrophe. In addition, some characters evince ideologies that imply a conspiracy to replace human beings, for instance when the ringmaster at Flesh Fair says that David is part of "an underground scheme to phase out all of God's little children" (*A.I.: Artificial Intelligence*). Ultimately, the film complicates this by creating sympathetic androids that are clearly undeserving of the vitriol the public directs at them. The traditional white male, in this case, does not emerge a hero that must fight against a threatening outgroup. Instead, the film moves from "making us uncomfortable about the otherness of robots to making us even more uncomfortable about the thoughtlessness and cruelty of humans" (Rosenbaum 76). It's clear by the end of the film that David will remain a minority, a subject of curiosity for the new dominant group on the planet. Being subjected to overt cruelty has given way to a role as test subject, creating a dolorous ending that paints David as an incredibly tragic character.

Cruelty against robots in film has often coincided with increases in real-world violence against minorities in the United States. Anti-Muslim sentiment obviously became more common after September 11 and has been a continual problem ever since. The rise of ISIS in 2014 coincided with an uptick in anti-Muslim crimes. ISIS became known all throughout America after taking over the Iraqi city of Mosul. While ISIS had existed many years prior to 2014, that particular year saw the terrorist group become a genuine threat to stability in the Middle East. That year, ISIS took over cities in Syria, like Raqqa, and parts of Iraq. By the summer, Obama had authorized a series of airstrikes to push ISIS back. However, ISIS responded with the televised beheading of two American journalists—James Foley and later, Steven Sotloff ("Tracing the Rise . . ."). ISIS uses guerilla tactics that make it difficult to identify and find them. Modern terrorism is complicated and challenging to combat. As such, some of the American public sought to simplify this by directly targeting *all* Muslims, as "a collective dread and paranoia have settled across much of America, whether fueled by real or imagined details of another terrorist attack, helping to create the general impression that American society and social institutions are, at the least, threatened and will presumably be attacked in the near future" (Nama 40). Because of this "collective dread and paranoia," many anti-Muslim attacks were reported in the news, from a man assaulting a woman in Tulsa for wearing a headscarf to a fifteen-year-old Muslim boy being deliberately killed in a hit-and-run while he was exiting a mosque. The desire to simplify a complex issue has resulted in the targeting of an outgroup, Muslims, who are scapegoated for the destructive, apocalyptic actions of groups of terrorists.

Automata, a 2014 film that came out amid the rising threat of ISIS, may not be using the robots of the film as a specific stand-in for Muslims, but the film does show the desire to simplify a complex issue and put the blame for a cataclysm on a disenfranchised outgroup. Films like *Automata* (2014) "symbolically express . . . paranoia by depicting an American society with a crippling dependence on robotic energy—a metaphor for America's oil energy dependency—that serves as the catalyst for society's violent downfall" (Nama 40–41). Overdependence on an Other—whether Muslim or robotic surrogates for minorities—produces paranoia in the dominant culture.

Automata takes place in a future where radiation from solar flares has rendered Earth virtually uninhabitable. The opening crawl of the film indicates that 99.7 percent of the human population has been killed, leaving only a few million survivors on the entire planet. These survivors inhabit decrepit, walled-off cities, the walls supposedly being utilized to protect people from deadly radiation. The remaining humans constructed robots, referred to as Pilgrims, to help save the Earth. Pilgrims built the protective walls and artificial rain clouds to allow for precipitation on a planet where most of the water has dissipated. When it became clear that these Pilgrims could not save the Earth, they were vandalized, mistreated, and generally regarded as a disappointment. The complex issues arising from solar flares are simplified in a postapocalyptic wasteland that places blame on the failure of the Pilgrims. However, this blame becomes problematized when Jacq Vaucan, an insurance agent for the company that still builds these Pilgrims, discovers that these maligned robots have developed beyond their limiting protocols.

The robots represent an exploited underclass, whose lives matter so little that people have no issue shooting them at the first sign of disobedience. In addition, parallels can be drawn between the prohibition of the Pilgrims' self-improvement and how African American slaves were hindered from learning to read and write. In 1740, for example, the

General Assembly of South Carolina changed slave codes to include a statute that "prohibits slaves from learning to read and write. . . . This legislation casts slave literacy as a potential threat to the slave holding colony" (Rasmussen 201). The reason was that reading certain texts "could foment unrest among the colony's slaves only if some of them were literate. Those who were able to read such materials could spread the word to those who could not read" (Rasmussen 202). In *Automata*, the reason given for not allowing the robots to repair themselves is the fear that they will become superior to humans via self-development. In addition, one can infer that further development of the robots would make it more morally problematic to treat them as inferior, much the same as how "influential thinkers in Europe and America saw literacy as a sign of cultural and racial superiority one used to justify the treatment of black slaves as chattel. Writing, in the arts and the sciences, signified the ability to reason and thus helped define, in the Enlightenment, what it meant to be human" (Rasmussen 202). Humans could no longer indulge in the glaring mistreatment of a disenfranchised group that had shown itself to have a developed intellect, capable of the same ability to reason and participate in the rich cultural tapestry of humankind. If disenfranchised groups could do these things, it opened up the possibility that the white male was not at the top of the hierarchy because of an innate intellectual superiority. Such was the case in the slave trade, and such is the case in *Automata* and other apocalyptic cyborg films.

The humans of the film frantically attempt to keep the Pilgrims from becoming autonomous, the paranoia seen in how they struggle to figure out which of the Pilgrims has been corrupted. The two protocols of the Pilgrims are similar to Asimov's Laws of Robotics. One of these prevents these machines from harming humans, while the other inhibits them from making alterations to themselves. As we discover later in the film from the CEO of the robotic company, the second protocol was put in place to prevent the Pilgrims from advancing beyond humans, at least partly for fear of losing a cheap labor source. If they gain the ability to grow and advance, they might no longer want to be subservient to humans. His fear is realized by the end of the film, as a group of robots escapes into an irradiated desert, far from human civilization.

Multiple scenes involve a human closely examining a Pilgrim to assess whether or not it has been corrupted by a sort of self-reliance. The very beginning of the film shows a police officer named Wallace walking by a Pilgrim working on repairs. He looks at the Pilgrim suspiciously but continues walking past. Suddenly turning back around, he shoots the robot, later claiming that the robot had been repairing itself. However, exactly what the Pilgrim was doing is not entirely clear in the scene. Wallace's paranoia influences all of his actions in the film, making him view all Pilgrims as disposable enemies. Indeed, this attitude seems pervasive in the humans of the film.

The robots are scapegoated for issues that have nothing to do with them. As Robert, Jacq's boss, says: "The Pilgrims were born to help us in our heroic quest for survival. Now they build our homes, drive our cars, and wipe our asses when we get old" (*Automata*). After it became clear that the Pilgrims couldn't save the planet, they became the targets of violence and vandalism, until eventually becoming merely a source of cheap labor. At the beginning of the film, a series of photos shows public reaction to the robots, from being initially heralded as saviors to newspaper headlines later saying, "Pilgrims can't stop the desert" and vandalism labeling the Pilgrims "losers." Eventually, photos are revealed that show Pilgrims with arms cut off, Pilgrims being set on fire, and finally a photo of a Pilgrim's face with an "X" spray painted across each eye. It's clear from the opening slideshow that the Pilgrims' failure to save the planet led to scapegoating, with these disenfranchised workers being blamed for the continuing collapse of the ecosystem.

The human society at the time comprises a hierarchy that allows the mistreatment of lower classes with total impunity, as evidenced in the cavalier way construction workers shoot human beings going through rubble on the other side of the wall. The lower-class humans and robots can be treated as expendable, as long as the differences between groups are clearly demarcated. In the case of the lower-class humans, they are literally on the other side of a wall. For the Pilgrims, their difference is delineated not only through actual physical differences but also through their inability to repair and improve themselves, which is one of the two built-in protocols. This desire to maintain differences between groups is tied to "America's fixation with racial boundary maintenance . . . [,] the 'one-drop rule' and the network of racial taboos associated with it—interracial sex, racial eugenics, black blood contamination, racial assimilation, and racial paranoia" (Nama 7). Maintaining power over outgroups and avoiding "contamination" through interaction with them is contingent on being able to easily spot these groups. Thus, it is cause for alarm among the elite when robots are discovered fixing themselves. As Dr. Dupr, a clocksmith helping Jacq, notes "A machine altering itself is a very complex concept. Self-repairing implies some idea of a conscience" (*Automata*). Differences begin to dissolve between groups when these Pilgrims form "some idea of a conscience." Later, when it becomes clear to Jacq that the robots have transcended the second protocol, he attempts to create a new mark of difference between humans and machines—reproduction. Talking to Cleo, one of the sentient robots, he asks, "Do you know what a mother is, Cleo? Of course you don't. You don't know because you're just a machine" (*Automata*). However, even this difference evaporates at the end, when Jacq sees that the Pilgrims have created a new robotic lifeform. The robots themselves appear to have no hierarchy at all, with one of them noting that a "boss is a human thought structure" (*Automata*).

The tipping point for real-world AI assistants came five years after *Automata* was released, as Google presented their "Google Assistant," expected to be used on a billion devices by the end of 2019. Amazon's Alexa and Apple's Siri were already becoming ubiquitous. The global market for AI Assistants was 3.6 billion in 2019 and is expected to grow to 73.2 billion in just two decades (Bogachev). These voice-activated assistants have "the ability to understand and process human languages," "the ability to use stored information and data and use it to draw new conclusions," and "machine learning: the ability to adapt to new things by identifying patterns" (Terzopoulos 474). One cause of anxiety, however, is that "security and privacy concerns are major drawbacks for users of voice assistants and smart speakers" (Terzopoulos 485). Another concern, one that is very relevant in the film *I Am Mother* (2019), is that these voice-activated assistants are being used to fill the role of a traditional housewife and mother. Because more women are working, and men are more frequently sharing care of the house and children,

> we are witnessing the slow death of the wife in contemporary society (at least the wife we've known as the longtime backbone of patriarchal society). But she's having an enthusiastic comeback, with a few critical upgrades. It's not wives themselves who are being asked to come back into the kitchen but rather feminized artificial intelligence (AI) built into robots, digital voice assistants (also known as smart speakers, conversational agents, virtual helpers, and chatbots), and other smart devices. (Strengers and Kennedy 2)

These assistants not only fulfill the role of "wives" but also the role of mothers as well. The term "Big Mother" is a reference to "smart wives (or rather their makers) that supply paternalistic control and influence, albeit under the cloak of a soothing maternal figure. And it could be closer to reality than we might like to think" (Strengers and Kennedy 193). The concept of "Big Mother," combined with the security concerns with these new devices, form the backdrop of *I Am Mother*.

I Am Mother begins after an apocalyptic event has destroyed Earth's surface, wiping out every single human. The titular "Mother" is in a large, sterile laboratory complex, watching over a room full of sixty-three thousand human embryos. In the film's opening moments, we see Mother take an embryo and develop it into a full baby, in the span of one day. A montage begins of the child's growth into an adolescent, simply named "Daughter." Over the course of the montage, we see Daughter being treated with kindness by Mother, who teaches her, feeds her, and supports her dancing ability. As a teenager, Daughter finds another human at the door of the complex, wounded and asking for help. Wanting to meet the first human she's ever seen, Daughter lets the woman in, knowing full well that Mother likely won't allow it. According to Mother, the surface of the Earth is contaminated and incapable of supporting organic life. Mother eventually finds the woman, who has a gunshot wound, and tries to help her in the infirmary. The woman, clearly suspicious of Mother, refuses treatment, prompting Daughter to take care of the woman herself. Over time, the woman and Daughter become comfortable with one another, and the woman explains that robots like Mother have exterminated humans, leading to their near extinction. This, of course, causes Daughter to question everything she has been told by Mother, who is revealed at the end to be an advanced AI trying to save humanity. The AI determined that human beings were too selfish and destructive, wiped them out, and then tried to restart the human race by cultivating more compassionate, altruistic beings. Daughter is the first of the new, superior species of human.

The paranoia in the film is clearly shown in the depiction of Mother, a powerful AI that attempts to destroy humanity. The film itself plays upon contemporary society's fear of advanced technology not only destroying us but replacing us entirely. Mother is literally a mechanical embodiment of motherhood, as she plays music for the baby and emits warm light from her chest to keep the child comforted. The warmth of a human mother's body has been replaced by a mechanical heating element. Motherhood is a quintessential part of humanity, so the idea that the robot could replace a human mother is a devastating blow, removing the notion of human motherhood as being essential to a child's well-being.

Paranoia is also apparent in Daughter's reaction to Mother, after receiving new information from the woman about the outside world.

Suddenly, the daughter no longer trusts Mother, who lied about the world outside the bunker. This latter portion of the film seems analogous to a teenager pulling away from his or her parents, trying to forge their own understanding of the world and their place in it. By the end, Mother agrees to allow Daughter to raise a new baby, in addition to the other embryos, deactivating herself. This act of self-sacrifice is very much in keeping with patriarchal depictions of motherhood, which "rewards and sanctifies self-sacrifice and punishes unconventional, uncontained motherhood" (Arnold 153). In the film, Mother aptly embodies all patriarchal conceptions of mothers. The film also "construct[s] the maternal as a threat to individuation . . . [and] symbolic matricide as the only means towards individuation" (Arnold 91). Daughter can only reach her true potential and realize her own sense of self if Mother is deactivated.

The film can also be read more broadly as a fear of motherhood, even though motherhood is literally the only thing that can save the human race from extinction. Freudian psychoanalyst Karen Horney found, in her analysis of patients, an

> "envy of pregnancy, childbirth and motherhood as well as of the breasts and of the act of suckling" . . . Horney suggested that boys and men harboured feelings of jealousy of women's reproductive capacity. This womb envy is transformed into the cultural denigration and devaluing of women. Women are socially excluded and their bodies are subject to suspicion and hostility. Thus the filmic representations of emotionally passive women and biologically powerful bodies can be read as the unconscious projection of womb envy and fantasies of destruction. (Arnold 163)

Mother is clearly a "powerful body" that is not just "emotionally passive" but incapable of true emotion. Her annihilation of humankind was the logical conclusion of a mandate to produce the best possible offspring and enable the best possible world for that offspring. The catastrophic collateral damage of powerful female bodies depicted here is a symbolic representation of the "suspicion and hostility" with which these bodies are regarded. If left unchecked, they could destroy the world.

On the surface, it would seem hard to argue that Mother is a stand-in for a disenfranchised minority group, since the planet is now populated almost entirely with machines, and Mother holds significant power over the humans in the film. However, when it becomes clear that all of the machines in the film are controlled by a singular entity, it becomes clear that there are far more humans than machines. All sixty-three thousand embryos can be developed and repopulate the planet, while Mother would still be one, albeit powerful, entity. Read in this way, the film is about the fear that a small minority will become so powerful that it will cause the destruction of humanity. We find out, at the end, that the AI in the film was actually trying to save humanity by attempting to eliminate the human tendency toward selfishness and destruction. However, the implication here is that the AI's method of reasoning is so utterly foreign and distinct from human reasoning that it caused billions of deaths because of a warped, oversimplified notion of morality. Thus, the minority group causes the annihilation of all life specifically because of its difference from the dominant group.

Conclusion

Conspiracy theories are popular and prevalent in American society and are an attempt at simplifying complex issues at a time when the precise machinations of a global economy and the information overload of the computer age make it difficult to situate oneself in a coherent framework. The blending of ethnic and racial groups, in addition to the more general white anxiety discussed in the first chapter, has generated a desire for the dominant white male to understand his place in a rapidly changing world. The desire is to concretize whiteness and reaffirm the white male as the quintessential American leader. To this end, conspiracy theories function as a form of cognitive mapping that not only simplifies racial and ethnic differences to distinguish whites from minorities but also to vilify outgroups and extol the virtues of the heroic white male. Many contemporary postapocalyptic films and books clearly perform this function, presenting the destruction of the world as a consequence of a vast conspiracy, wherein minorities have infiltrated positions of power and caused the disintegration of systems of government, culminating in near annihilation. The white hero in these stories can save America from these evil outgroups, often represented as robots, monsters, or aliens. In each chapter of this book, we see the overriding inclination of the dominant white male to reassert authority and bring back an older, idealized version of America through an apocalyptic event that allows a new frontier to emerge—one where a more inclusive American society has been sidelined.

4

"New Roads, and Highways, and Bridges, and Airports, and Tunnels"

Apocalyptic Objects

The reader is lost in a sea of objects within the first paragraph of Don DeLillo's *White Noise*. *White Noise* is not as explicitly postapocalyptic as a text like *Oryx and Crake*, but the book's "airborne toxic event" is a threatening force with destructive power, in addition to the continual fear of death experienced by the main characters. DeLillo, in describing these commodities, writes:

> As cars slowed to a crawl and stopped, students sprang out and raced to the rear doors to begin removing the objects inside; the stereo sets, radios, personal computers; small refrigerators and table ranges; the cartons of phonograph records and cassettes; the hairdryers and styling irons; the tennis rackets, soccer balls, hockey and lacrosse sticks, bows and arrows; the controlled substances, the birth control pills and devices; the junk food still in shopping bags. (DeLillo 1)

The focus on objects in this and other sections seems almost obsessive in the desire to carefully catalogue things, as if they were in danger of evaporating into thin air if not transcribed and recorded. Ultimately, however, the effect of cataloguing these things is to render them meaningless—a series of empty, haphazard artifacts that conjure up the image of an amorphous trash heap. This obsessive focus on objects is to be found in most apocalyptic literature, though the ways in which these objects in contemporary media are used is markedly different from their use in the original Christian texts. In the Book of Revelation, valuable objects after the apocalypse are doled out to the faithful, entirely flipping the hegemonic structure in which only those in power have access to objects of value. Conversely, in contemporary texts, objects signify a fear of collapse. They are retrospective ghost commodities, changing and differing from their preapocalyptic usages and meanings. In this sense, there is a general thrust to reestablish the meaning of the objects within the traditional power structure, combating the tendency toward indiscriminate vacancy seen in such books as *White Noise*.

Objects have a long history of signifying one's cultural and social place. In this chapter, I argue that while traditional apocalyptic texts stage objects in an overthrow of power, contemporary apocalyptic stories seek to reify the previous power structure.

Consumption and the Importance of Objects

Consumption, as a term and idea, has changed in meaning as world economies have changed.[1] Between the world wars of the twentieth century, mass production of objects and commodities, along with expanding disposable income, gave the middle class a tremendous amount of power, and they "started to be addressed as 'consumers,' until, by the 1960s, observers sighted a whole new type of society: a 'consumer society' " (Trentmann 27). The changing meaning of "consumption" mirrored the economic systems in which this consumption took place, from ancient gift

---

1. Finding its way into the English language sometime after the twelfth century, the word itself comes from "consumere" in Latin, meaning "to use up." Firewood, for instance, would be burned until completely "used up." The definition of "consumption" morphed in the late seventeenth century, when some economists argued that consumption of goods—via direct purchases—was beneficial to a country's economic well-being, helping investors and various types of production. It was not, therefore, simply about personal pleasure and benefit, but it was also about the enhancement of an entire nation (Trentmann 25–26).

economies to the expanding global marketplace between the fifteenth and seventeenth centuries, to the mass production and excess of late capitalism. Trentmann notes that "the changing meaning of the term reflects the advance of capitalism since the fifteenth century, which spread markets, purchase and choice more widely across society" (28).

The objects of consumption have long had cultural value, something discussed at length by Marcel Mauss. In his highly influential work, *The Gift*, Mauss notes that in many ancient societies, "Exchanges and contracts take place in the form of presents; in theory these are voluntary, in reality they are given and reciprocated obligatorily" (3). Objects had great social significance, not only signifying social status but also functioning as a conciliatory means of joining nations and families. Archaeologist Colin Renfrew notes that

> for it is generally accepted that high status, associated with prestige, was in general not a feature of small and early human societies, in particular hunter-gatherer societies. Ranking and stratification, in whatever area of the world we may have under study, seem in general to have appeared later. . . . In studying commodities of high value we may, therefore, be doing more than monitoring the assertion of high status; we may be investigating what brought it about. (143–44)

In this way, a society's relationship to objects is linked to the type of economy that has evolved, with Renfrew's archaeological evidence illustrating that early hunter-gatherer societies likely did not use objects to convey status. However, by the time feudalism became the dominant economic system in Europe, owned objects signified social status or indicated one's relationship with others. In particular, anthropologist Arjun Appadurai contrasts luxury items with necessities, discussing how their use is "rhetorical and social, goods that are simply incarnated signs." These luxury items, she notes, are "fundamentally political" (38). In this sense, they have the ability to indicate the relationship between minority and dominant classes. Corrigan notes that it is "standard ethnographic practice to assume that all material possessions carry social meanings" (18). Despite the importance of objects, however, an extensive consumer culture did not exist in ancient societies, since within the "pre-modern village . . . most goods were passed on and arrived as gifts" (Trentmann 21–22).

Between the fifteenth and seventeenth centuries, the growth of a global market led to the development of commercial centers, particularly for those upper-class individuals who could afford it. Affluent areas in Italy, Britain, Netherlands, and late Ming-dynasty China became "hotspots of consumption. In each of them, people acquired more things than they had had before." Things such as tableware and tapestries became a mark of refinement for people with money and a knowledge of high-status objects, objects that reflect superior tastes (Trentmann 82, 85). An inchoate consumer culture was further catalyzed by the reign of Queen Elizabeth (1558–1603), who required nobles to interact with her directly, buying and wearing ornate and expensive clothing in order to attract her attention amid a sea of other nobles (Corrigan 8). Clothing and other objects thus created a notable disparity in the quality and quantity of objects between social classes, and the disparity was exacerbated by extensive sumptuary laws and the adverse reaction of Christianity toward consumption. This aversion to consumption makes sense, given the moral quandaries elicited by wealth, with the Bible consistently reminding Christians of how difficult it is for the wealthy to find redemption. Indeed, Trentmann argues that the belief "that luxury easily led to lechery was common knowledge in the Renaissance and contributed to the moral disquiet about shopping and excess" (100–101). The Christian denigration of wealth and the excessive sumptuary laws between 1300 and 1600—touching on everything from meals at weddings to clothing—served to maintain differences between classes. Objects at that time, much like objects in premodern societies, denoted "one's place in the social order, denoting status, rank, age and gender . . . most European sumptuary laws were instruments of inequality, seeking to preserve a finely graded hierarchy" (Trentmann 108).

Consumption, in the more modern sense of widespread access for the middle class, became more widespread in the eighteenth century, coinciding with the Industrial Revolution. Corrigan writes that "the economic prosperity of England in the eighteenth century opened up the world of fashionable goods to ever more social classes" (8). The end of sumptuary laws allowed for other classes to emulate and aspire to the consumption habits of the upper classes. The inflexible class distinctions of feudalism began to dissolve as bourgeois society took hold, with the lower classes seeking to emulate the wealthy. This can easily be seen today, perhaps most strikingly in the cult of celebrity, where millionaire movie stars set trends in the consumption of everything from cars to clothing. Richard Dyer essentially makes this argument, explaining that "the stars become models of consumption for everyone in a consumer society" (39). Consumers can drink the wines enjoyed by the upper class, wear imitations of the clothing enjoyed by their favorite stars, and watch the Kardashians for the knowledge of exclusive vacation spots. The debt crisis in the United States is a testament to the middle and lower classes spending well above their means, buying homes and cars to approximate a lifestyle that eludes the grasp of all but the wealthiest individuals.

There are many differences between consumption in older societies and more contemporary ones, two of which are access to more products to consume and the necessity of learning "proper" consumption. One of the marked differences in consumption today is that "proper" consumption now requires some learning and training, so that the right purchase can be made. Consumption has become such a vast, complex network of decisions that it has become an onerous task determining how to best imitate a different class. Wine tasting classes, lifestyle blogs, and magazines have all become part of a market specifically geared toward providing a thorough apprehension of consumption. Corrigan points out that

> the fixity of traditional societies meant that one could learn the actual patterns of consumption. . . . But in modern societies a general orientation to consuming is required. . . . This form of civilization is industrial civilization, which split production and consumption apart in a way unknown to societies marked by traditional ways of both producing and consuming. (10–11)

In this way, contemporary societies have created a unique challenge for people trying to obtain the "cultural capital" of the upper classes. While commodities are plentiful and accessible, the sheer abundance of these has required a marked and deliberate ability to discern which objects convey the desired concept or idea. Ultimately, the effort to gain knowledge of proper consumption is motivated by a desire for "cultural capital," which Bourdieu believes can determine one's relations and access to certain privileges. The possession of actual objects, Bourdieu points out, is "cultural capital objectified in material objects and media, such as writings, paintings, monuments, instruments," eventually leading to social capital, which is "linked to possession of a durable network of more or less institutionalized relationships of mutual acquaintance and recognition" (86). Objects can provide access to "institutionalized relationships," relationships involving everything from politics to restaurants. Social capital can enable one to meet with the president, as Oprah Winfrey did with President Obama, or obtain a seat at an exclusive restaurant.

Another issue in capitalism is that attempts at discerning social relations through objects—in the way these objects functioned in the past—is more difficult, as the relationship between objects and laborers has changed dramatically. As Marx notes, in capitalism, the "process of production has the mastery over man, instead of being controlled by him" (93). The term *commodity fetishism* was coined by Karl Marx, of course, describing (among other things) the alienation experienced by the common worker, as they become part of a system that completely divorces them from the fruits of their labor. Marx points out how

> in that world the productions of the human brain appear as independent beings endowed with life, and entering into relation both with one another and the human race. So it is in the world of commodities with the products of men's hands. This I call the Fetishism which attaches itself to the products of labour, so soon as they are produced as commodities, and which is therefore inseparable from the production of commodities. (83)

In this sense, the objects only refer to other objects, which explains the sense of hollowness in passages like DeLillo's. The objects are self-referential and derive their value not from the labor that produced them but from their relations with other objects. This is symptomatic of capitalism, and Marx discusses how this use of objects is a marked departure from their historical use. Writing of the Middle Ages, he mentions how

> we find everyone dependent, serfs and lords, vassals and suzerains, laymen and clergy. Personal dependence here characterises the social relations of production just as much as it does the other spheres of life organised on the basis of that production. But for the very reason that personal dependence forms the ground-work of society, there is no necessity for labour and its products to assume a fantastic form different from their reality . . . Compulsory labour is just as properly measured by time, as commodity-producing labour; but every serf knows that what he expends in the service of his lord, is a definite quantity of his own personal labour power. (Marx 88–89)

The transition to capitalism has morphed the previously more direct relationship with products and labor, turning commodities into animate objects with their own vitality. The value of these objects often has nothing to do with anything innate, giving it a fantastical, magical aura, as if its value came from a supernatural force. Commodity fetishism is linked to the loss of signifying power seen in capitalism, as workers and the objects they produce and surround themselves with become alienated from one another. Baudrillard notes:

> It was capital which was the first to feed throughout its history on the destruction of every referential, of every human goal, which shattered every ideal distinction between true and false, good and evil, in order to establish a radical law of equivalence and exchange. (22)

The total reliance on exchange value in late capitalism has led to a crisis of meaning, where the "distinction between true and false" has become completely opaque. Concomitant with the dissipation of meaning are the "social relations" Marx speaks of, further elucidating the increasingly tenuous distinctions between social classes. Capitalism has irrevocably altered social relations since "the mode of production determines the character of the social, political, and intellectual life generally" (94). No wonder, then, that current apocalyptic films and books are preoccupied with attempting to re-create the hegemonic power structure by reifying the meanings of objects, moving back to a time before the extirpation of meaning endemic to capitalism.

Objects have a life of their own, and any discernible meaning is illusory. This perhaps explains the anxiety over objects in many modern postapocalyptic texts, where there is a struggle to imbue objects with the same meaning they had before the apocalypse. Baudrillard links this to nostalgia, which emerges "when the real is no longer what it used to be." We see a "proliferation of myths of origin and signs of reality; of second-hand truth, objectivity and authenticity," in a desperate, fretful attempt to manufacture a connection between real and referential (6–7). There is a lack of control over the signifying value of objects, and consequently the distinctions between social classes are based on distinctions that would reveal their illusory nature upon close inspection. In current apocalyptic myths, the dominant culture thus seeks to bring objects back to what they meant before the apocalypse, to reinscribe class distinctions built on a house of cards. The apocalypse, read in this way, is a metaphor for the destruction of meaning in capitalism, and the main thrust of these films and books is toward piecing together not only the houses and buildings that existed before the catastrophic event but also the ideologies embodied in these things. Baudrillard writes that "what society seeks through production, and overproduction, is the restoration of the real which escapes it" (23). Commodity fetishism, however, makes all of these attempts futile, only increasing the anxiety and alienation felt.

Objects in Contemporary Apocalypticism

The opening of *WALL-E* shows an excessive amount of trash in the atmosphere of Earth, as the camera peers through the detritus to find a solitary robot, attempting to bring order to the chaotic surroundings. Without a society to imbue these objects with meaning, they no longer mean what they did before the apocalyptic event. This becomes clear when we observe the types of objects WALL-E, the titular robot, collects. Rather than finding value in a diamond ring, he is more fascinated by the box that holds it. Without a society to provide a context for diamonds, they have little intrinsic worth. Simply put, objects don't mean the same thing they did before the apocalypse. Trashcan lids are used in lieu of hats and seemingly banal things, like lighters, gain an aura of romanticism. Indeed, much of the beginning of the film is looking at ordinary objects, thrown into a heap of trash, and instilling in them a new sense of value.

By framing the events of the film in an apocalyptic scenario such as this, the "trash" scattered across the globe takes on a new significance. It becomes a reminder of a fallen world, pieces of which WALL-E attempts to preserve in his domicile. However, the objects that WALL-E preserves would have been fairly mundane and commonplace before the apocalypse—utensils, lighters, and trashcan lids, for instance. We clearly see WALL-E "disregard the codes embedded in every commodity through the processes of production, promotion and circulation, establishing a naïve, personal, and above all distinctive relationship with his things" (McNaughtan 761–62). The apocalyptic event gives these "things" new significance, which enables the viewer to see what they had perhaps taken for granted. In this sense, the film might not be arguing against consumerism and objects as much as simply arguing against the blind acceptance of excess, ultimately encouraging us to value what few objects we have and choose the values ascribed to these. The film calls into question the superficial ways in which we attribute value to things. McNaughtan, generally discussing mass production and consumption, says:

> The essential uniformity of a marque's output . . . [is] obscured by ever-more elaborate cosmetic differences (tailfins, whitewalls,

> ornate bumpers and the like). Gendron (1986, 21) asserts, 'the system of advertising seduces us into believing that differences in packaging reflect differences in essence. Pseudoindividualization glamorizes style over the real inner content' . . . this ostensible accommodation of the individual, whose identity, like the distinguishing touches that supposedly express it, has been manufactured for him. (McNaughtan 756)

Thus, we see that rampant consumerism distills the essence of choice to utterly trivial "differences in packaging," which directs focus away from truly "seeing" these objects. Conscious choices in ascribing meaning, such as those seen by WALL-E, are important, and quality is valued over quantity; this could be one revelation made possible by an apocalyptic scenario that often decontextualized objects. One of WALL-E's lighters, for example, becomes an integral part of a romantic moment between him and EVE. In addition, the aforementioned trashcan lid helps WALL-E in a charming rendition of a dance from one of his favorite musicals. The dance, and the musical he watches in general, seem to win EVE over, further showing the value of a simple trashcan lid or a musical like *Hello Dolly!* This elementary use of objects shows how "commodities, distanced from their economic function and from their signifieds of capitalism, become the signifiers of a discourse of style that the subordinate can steal from the dominant and use to articulate their own oppositional pleasures" (Fiske 258). It is, in this way, that WALL-E initiates a sort of rebellion that reallocates and adjusts the powers embodied in these objects, such that robots—the minority group—become viewed in a new, more positive light.

When we finally see the humans in the film, they are continuing the same rampant consumerism that had destroyed Earth. They have become lazy and obese, as robots attend to their every need, and all they need worry about is what type of drink to consume. The company, Buy 'N Large, controls every aspect of their lives, something that is elucidated in the opening of the film when the camera pans over the remains of civilization, speckled with the Buy 'N Large symbol on everything from gas stations to supermarkets. The value of objects is dictated to people by Buy 'N Large, a company that literally tells people what colors are trendy and which drinks are to be enjoyed each day, something we see when WALL-E begins his search for EVE on the spaceship. The ship itself was constructed by Buy 'N Large, which allows the company to easily disseminate the ideologies that uphold a system of capitalism that most benefits them. It is for this reason that Auto, the main antagonist of the film, does not want the humans to go back to Earth, which Buy 'N Large no longer controls so completely. On Earth, no large company holds a monopoly on meaning.

The most important object of the film is the plant that WALL-E finds and EVE carries since it means that Earth is ready for human inhabitants once again. To Auto and Buy 'N Large, however, it means an end to their unmitigated control of human life. Before the apocalyptic event, plants were presumably commonplace, which means that the plant would have been unremarkable before the environmental catastrophe we see in the film. Because of the apocalypse, the plant takes on a profound meaning that makes it a sign of a hopeful future, one in which life on Earth burgeons once again. Indeed, the pictures shown during the credits depict humans growing a variety of plants in bucolic landscape, reminiscent of the Garden of Eden that the robot, EVE, is clearly a reference to. Buy 'N Large, however, seeks to make the plant as mundane and inconsequential as it was before the apocalypse since it portends an end to Buy 'N Large's stranglehold on the life of every human aboard these ships. To that end, Auto attempts to bury the plant in the trash heap of the spaceship.

The push to go back to the systems in place before the apocalypse is coming from Buy 'N Large, clearly made out to be the villain in this case. On the surface then, the film would seem to be advocating a less consumer-driven society, one where the hierarchies upheld by the dominant culture dissolve. However, this theme conflicts with the nostalgia found throughout the film. The film, for instance, starts with the classic song "Put on Your Sunday Clothes" from *Hello Dolly!*, a song whose lyrics rely on older, phallocentric ideologies:

> Put on your Sunday clothes,
> There's lots of world out there
> Get out the brillantine and dime cigars
> We're gonna find adventure in the evening air
> Girls in white in a perfumed night
> Where the lights are bright as the stars!
> Put on your Sunday clothes, we're gonna ride through town
> In one of those new horsedrawn open cars. (*WALL-E*)

The movie uses this song, which romanticizes objects of consumerism as a means of enjoying a lovely evening out on the town, as a contrast to the opening shot of Earth covered in trash. This contrast illuminates the tremendous loss the Earth has experienced—the magical world of "dime cigars" and "Sunday clothes" has been replaced with mounds of detritus and a world without organic life. The result is a sense of nostalgia for the audience, elicited not only by the use of a popular, beloved musical number but also via the clear loss of everything the song depicts. This nostalgia, however, is a desire for the world of consumerism—the driving force for life before the apocalypse. While WALL-E, within the diegetic world of the film, is imbuing objects with new value, separate from the ideologies of the corporate giant Buy 'N Large, the film itself is simultaneously using the preapocalyptic meaning of these objects to instill nostalgia in *the audience*. In this sense, the film is not as clearly anticonsumerism as it may seem at first. Once again, we see a film that yearns for the dominant culture that existed before the apocalyptic event.

This is made even clearer by the lifestyle of the humans on the *Axiom*. The hierarchy present in the dominant, phallocentric culture of the world before the apocalypse has seemingly dissolved aboard the *Axiom*. Every single person on the *Axiom* has access to the same foods, the same forms of education, and the same forms of entertainment. In a sense, life aboard the *Axiom* is utopian, with every need and desire easily fulfilled. The film, however, presents this lifestyle in an extremely negative light. The script describes these humans as "the most extreme form of couch potatoes. Absolutely no reason to ever get up. No purpose" (*WALL-E*). What gives their lives "purpose" again is working, after they finally return to Earth. This is essentially just another iteration of one facet of capitalism, which often defines identity by the type of work one does and "society has ascribed varying levels of status and prestige to different occupations, the occupational role provides a link between the individual and the social structure and is thus a basis of self-definition and definition by others" (Ghidina 73). Much like other postapocalyptic films, reverting back to the modes of living before the apocalypse is presented in a positive light. The lesson or overall moral, when viewing the film this way, is simply that monopolies like Buy 'N Large are bad and that if we're going to produce things and work, they should be things with clear use value, like food and clothing. It's notable that at the end of the film, the captain says, "You kids are going to grow all kinds of plants: vegetable plants, pizza plants!" (*WALL-E*). He sees plants not as a symbol of life but as a means of creating consumable products.

During the end credits, we see the humans planting, farming, and building. These scenes are presented as beautiful artistic tableaus, where the colors and idyllic splendor of the world are made salient. Instead of the drab world of brown the audience sees at the beginning, the ending is filled with lush, vivid colors—the world has been brought to life once again. However, this ending shows humans going back to a world of work and the giant skyscrapers that have become synonymous with business and giant corporate conglomerates. The towers of trash at the beginning of the film have been changed back to skyscrapers, again illustrating yearning for the preapocalyptic world. The empty, meaningless towers of objects are now objects associated with corporate domination. When the Buy 'N Large CEO discusses moving back to Earth in a prerecorded video, he says the following: "Now that Earth has been restored to a life-sustaining status, by golly, we can begin 'Operation Recolonize'!" (*WALL-E*). His choice of words here is quite telling. Instead of describing the trip back to Earth as a "repopulation" or "redevelopment," he describes the desire to "recolonize." Colonization has a long, troubling history in Western civilization, with Western colonial powers taking over already inhabited places to the extreme detriment of native peoples. The term "recolonize" implies a reassertion of authority and power over land and life, a desire for life on Earth to conform once again to the phallocentric power structures in place before the apocalyptic event.

So while on the surface *WALL-E* may seem to be advocating a world beyond consumerism, it consistently uses objects to produce nostalgia in the audience, as we yearn for a preapocalyptic world of "dime cigars." It presents a "happy" ending as one in which humans find purpose through work again, and "recolonization" comes via converting meaningless trash back into monuments of capitalism.

The apocalyptic preoccupation with objects can also be seen in Tarkovsky's *Stalker* (1979), which is based on the novel *Roadside Picnic*. While this is clearly a Russian film, the Russian proclivity toward apocalypticism bears a striking resemblance to that of America. Russia possesses "a popular apocalyptic religious mentality, Messianic expectation among both Zionists and populists, widespread apocalyptic ideas among Russian artists and intellectuals, and the modern idea of progress as secularized millenarianism" (Rowley 1593). Much like American apocalypticism, these myths are often used to vilify minorities and paint the dominant culture as under threat from nefarious outsiders. Various ethnic groups have been targeted and mistreated by the dominant culture throughout Russia's history, including Cossacks, Poles, Tatars, Turks, and Jews. Many of these groups endured appalling abuse, being placed in involuntary settlements, arrested and thrown into gulags, and in some cases killed in acts of genocide.

Russian apocalypticism increased dramatically in the late 1800s and early 1900s. The country was experiencing

> radical political, economic, and social changes—the results of an accelerated industrialisation, urbanisation, and secularisation—shook the country. These events were often interpreted with the help of religious categories: as a foreboding of an imminent eschatological catastrophe and as evidence of the hidden destructive work of the Antichrist and his allies. (Hagemeister 424)

In league with the "Antichrist and his allies" were the assorted minority groups on the outskirts of the Russian dominant culture. A lot of anti-Jewish propaganda emerged in the post-Soviet years, as Russia was thought to be "the Third Rome in the salvation history of the world, as 'the last stronghold of true faith' in the struggle against the global conspiracy of the Anti-christian forces . . . the apocalyptic enemies of Christianity were first of all the 'lawless people'—that is, the Jews—harbouring a plan for the realisation of their 'centuries-old dream of world supremacy' " (Hagemeister 432). In addition to demonizing minority groups, apocalyptic myths provided simplistic answers to complicated issues, much as they do in America. In the 1990s, massive economic changes and reforms to the free market resulted in rampant poverty, and "ethnic conflicts flared up along the state borders, people were looking for simple and simplifying explanations that also corresponded to familiar (ideological) patterns of thought." The quantity of apocalyptic materials exploded in this era, as millenarianism became palatable in a time of massive change. These were apocalyptic texts in which "the secret activities of dark supernatural forces and their earthly allies (Jews, Masons, Zionists, Mondialists, and many others) were 'revealed' and identified" (Hagemeister 433). While *Stalker* came out before the collapse of the Soviet Union, the preoccupation with apocalypticism is found throughout Russia history, in addition to its being used to demonize outgroups.

Tarkovsky's film follows a man known simply as "Stalker," as he escorts two other men into the "zone," a cordoned-off area that had once been visited by aliens. The zone is a supernatural entity in the film, filled with danger from invisible forces. The objective for the three men is to reach a room in a dilapidated building that supposedly grants wishes to whomever steps inside. The postapocalypticism of the film is seen in the dilapidated surroundings, barren and lifeless. Even Stalker's home feels like a wasteland, with empty walls and a general feeling of hopelessness.

The obsession with objects is clear from the beginning of the film, where there is a long tracking shot of the objects strewn throughout Stalker's home, including a glass of water, a metal box, a crumpled piece of paper, and wad of cotton on a bedside table. During a dream sequence in the middle of the film, we see that an apocalyptic event has sapped objects of meaning. As the camera tracks over a stream with objects laying at the bottom, Stalker's wife reads a passage from Revelation:

> And there was a great earthquake. And the sun became black as sackcloth made of hair. And the moon became like blood. . . . And the stars of the sky fell to the earth, as a fig tree casts its unripe figs when shaken by a great wind. And the sky was split apart like a scroll when it is rolled up. And every mountain and island were moved out of their places. And the kings of the earth and the great men and the rich and the chiliarchs and the strong and every free man, hid themselves in the caves and among the rocks of the mountains; and they said to the mountains and to the rocks, 'Fall on us and hide us from the presence of Him who sits on the throne, and from the wrath of the Lamb, for the great day of His wrath has come, and who is able to stand?' " (*Stalker*)

Not only does this section make the film's connection to the apocalypse clear, but it also illustrates the lost meaning of objects through juxtaposition. This speech, juxtaposed with the camera tracking over discarded objects, implies that these same objects are all that remains of these "kings of the earth and the great men and the rich." Without the people of social status associated with these objects, there is no referent or connection to give them value. In addition, the random, haphazard way in which the objects are scattered in the stream—a syringe, a metal plate, coins, a gun, and the gears of a clock—shows this loss of value, in the sense that no single object means more than any other. Their ability to indicate difference in social status is gone, and the objects are now all equally meaningless. The ending of the film, however, presents the possibility of objects embodying new types of power, as Stalker's daughter moves three glasses across a table in their home, using telepathy. Rather than the passing train moving the glass, as it had at the beginning of the film, the girl has agency in moving the glass herself. The ending suggests the ability for people to imbue objects with new meaning and value, exerting their own influence over them, instead of having a hierarchy of value emerge from a capitalist system over which the lower classes have little control. This preoccupation with the lost meaning of objects plays out in innumerable books as well, including Atwood's *Oryx and Crake.*

Many postapocalyptic stories over the latter half of the twentieth century display this link between commodity fetishism and a general loss of meaning, for instance Margaret Atwood's *Oryx and Crake*. The novel follows a narrator given the moniker "Snowman," who presents "a vision of the future of Western society in the age of late capitalism," eventually culminating in an apocalyptic event that seemingly dissolves class distinctions (Kroon 29). In Snowman's flashbacks to the time before the apocalypse, he describes a lifestyle characterized by extreme alienation, as the capitalist hierarchy literally separates people into classes, and disconnects them from traditional labor. A childhood friend, Crake, is allowed in certain areas that others are not, simply because of his class and rank. Danette DiMarco points out how "a division of communities and labor is at the crux of Atwood's construction of the boys' early development." Snowman and Crake grow up in an exclusive community of intellectuals and scientists, completely accustomed to the notion of class separation, as they "are protected from the Sodom and Gomorrah-like visceral nature of the society beyond the walls" (DiMarco 177). The dwellings that Snowman and Crake inhabit, separate from the lower classes, are referred to as "the Compounds." The Compounds allow the characters to live apart from the "poverty and violence outside their walls, accessible only through media outlets as distant objects, products made available for consumption." Because this is "suffering that affects non-dominant groups within society," there is little attention paid to the hardships of these people (Kroon 23). This has the effect of making these people into objects, something to watch on a TV screen in one of the many horrific reality shows Snowman and Crake enjoy. The commodification of living beings is perhaps most poignantly displayed in the use of animals, which are reduced from living beings to objects with no underlying significance or sentience. Some animals—chickens in this instance—have been engineered to only grow edible parts of their body, without beaks, brains, or any discernible limbs. They are merely a chicken breast with a small opening for a mouth, into which caloric foods are fed through a tube. Thus, chickens (and other animals) are engineered to only grow edible parts, essentially becoming a living meal that bears only a distant relation to a real chicken. Even the names of the characters illustrate loss and alienation, as Oryx and Crake refer to extinct animals, thus making the names without any referent. These animals, objects, and people are like a corporate-produced simulacrum, with nothing below the surface.

The apocalyptic event, a result of a virulent disease created by Crake, decimates most of the human race, leaving only the genetically engineered humanoids, called "Crakers." The social classes, so integral a part of the preapocalyptic world, have disappeared, and it is this loss that forces Snowman to examine the inequities of the preapocalyptic world he had been complicit in creating. Despite all of his moral qualms, Snowman had failed to engage in any meaningful resistance, and much of the novel is told in past tense, as he looks back on a deeply flawed late capitalist world. The remnants of the old world he finds are now more strikingly empty. While before the apocalypse these objects might have seemed vacant, now they are truly hollow, referring to things that no longer exist. Within the first few pages of the novel, which start after the apocalypse, Snowman looks at a wristwatch, one of many objects that no longer has meaning, and notes that "a blank face is what it shows him: zero hour. It causes a jolt of terror to run through him, this absence of official time. Nobody nowhere knows what time it is" (Atwood 4). Snowman experiences terror because the apocalypse has explicitly sapped the watch—and other objects—of meaning, removing the security he had felt within the Compounds that explicitly elevated him above others. His nagging suspicion that his life—and the people and objects in it—was a grand, corporate simulation is now an inescapable reality. The anxiety he feels here is more pronounced than it was before the apocalypse, simply because it has forced him to directly confront the deep meaninglessness that had already permeated the world. It forces readers to do this as well, and the apocalypse in the novel merely functions as a device to illuminate things that are already happening. It becomes a trenchant visualization of the destruction of meaning, functioning as a metaphor. In this way, the novel is about the present, capturing the world Atwood and her prospective readers are living in.

Indeed, all media reflects the period in which it is created, especially a genre like science fiction, which is often purportedly about the future. Science fiction, which frequently uses the apocalypse as a focal plot, serves as a way to reflect on real concerns of the present day, couched in images of an imagined future. Susan Sontag corroborates this, noting that "these films reflect world-wide anxieties, and they serve to allay them" (Sontag 42). The genre takes a genuine problem, whether it be overpopulation (*Soylent Green*) or fear of global warming (*The Day after Tomorrow*), and extrapolates a future where the problem is exaggerated to the point of satire. It uses distance and defamiliarization of real problems to enable viewers/readers to closely examine these from a new perspective. Sobchack writes:

> Through extrapolation, through the creation of a time and/or place not present, science fiction allows the distance necessary for satire to function. We, as viewers of film, for example, can be shown ourselves in the present, in the here and now, with our cultural, political, and social eccentricities, manias and phobias, and appalling idiocies—only we are shown ourselves now under the thin guise of then and when. (170)

The apocalypse then, viewed in this way, is an exaggeration of a genuine problem/fear—the fear of dissolving meanings and the resulting collapse of the hegemonic system. In the novel, Snowman's perspective changes after the apocalypse; however, for the reader, it was clear that the apocalypse was simply a larger manifestation of the destruction already happening. Snowman was simply unwilling or incapable of seeing these things until confronted with the blunt images of a cataclysm.

Snowman, on one level, wants to reify the class distinctions that existed before the apocalypse by imbuing words and objects with the same meanings that had enabled a highly oppressive hierarchy. The postapocalyptic world is mostly inhabited by atavistic humanoids who possess none of the qualities that made class distinctions so prevalent in the preapocalyptic world—greed and violent tendencies, for instance. Worried that he may forget words no longer in use after the apocalypse, Snowman says:

> "Hang on to the words," he tells himself. The odd words, the old words, the rare ones. Valance. Norn. Serendipity. Pibroch. Lubricious. When they're gone, out of his head, these words, they'll be gone, everywhere, forever. As if they had never been. (Atwood 68)

Later, Snowman notes, "He'd developed a strangely tender feeling towards such words, as if they were children abandoned in the woods and it was his duty to rescue them" (Atwood 195). Apparent here—and elsewhere in the novel—is a nostalgic desire to reclaim the referents that existed before the apocalypse, despite knowledge of the illusory nature of his preapocalyptic world. Snowman's concern is that the apocalyptic event has irrevocably altered ways of conveying meaning. Things either don't mean the same thing or in some cases, the referent for certain words no longer exists. They refer to ideas or objects that have either been annihilated or ceased to be utilized in the postapocalyptic world. As a remnant of the white patriarchal society, he feels it is incumbent upon himself to preserve these last vestiges of a world that no longer exists. Snowman is, after all, "an affluent, educated, white male resident of the Compounds" (Kroon 22). Before the apocalypse, there was a corporate security force protecting the compounds that "guarantees that the commodities produced in each Compound are not seized and exploited by the lower-class pleeblanders" (Kroon 23). Now, no such security force exists, and the separation between classes is no longer apparent.

The Lost Meaning of Words and Objects

Cloud Atlas was a novel that many had thought totally unfilmable (its author David Mitchell included) as it is a story comprising six separate yet interconnected tales written in different genres and periods. Rather than tell each of the six stories individually, directors Lana and Lilly Wachowski chose to intertwine all six, emphasizing a theme of interconnectedness and reincarnation. Connections between stories vary from phrases repeated in multiple storylines to the same actors playing different roles in each of the six sections. In several key instances, the connection between stories is an object. Frobisher, for example, finds part of Adam Ewing's journal; Luisa Rey finds the Cloud Atlas Sextet recording from Frobisher, and Cavendish reads a book called *Half Lives—The First Luisa Rey Mystery.* Such connections via objects exist for each of the six parts of the film. Each object is a microcosm of the preceding story, as the author of the *Cloud Atlas* novel explains how "the preceding narrative appear[s] as an 'artefact' of the succeeding narrative" (Parker 124). The film shows each successive narrative attempting to piece together the preceding story from these artifacts—to find the true "signified" behind the puzzling objects. The one truly apocalyptic story, the sixth and last one, is connected to the preceding narrative via a statue of Sonmi—a clone, who was the main protagonist of the previous story.

In her story, Sonmi seems to be a fairly typical clone who happens to discover the truth about the cruel treatment of herself and other clones. Much of the pain and suffering of her life was mitigated by the prospect of ascending to a heavenlike paradise via a ceremony at the end of a clone's life called Xultation. She discovers, however, that what she perceived as a beautiful reward at the end of a clone's life is actually a cruel extermination that involves being burned alive and cremated. After this painful realization, she ends up crossing paths with the leader of an army of resistance fighters, battling for an end to cruelty against clones. Sonmi, after joining the resistance fighters, writes and broadcasts a manifesto before being captured and presumably killed. Some unspecified time after Sonmi's capture, an apocalyptic event occurs, an event so catastrophic that the world of the sixth and subsequent story is extremely primitive and almost completely void of any advanced technology. The implication is that much of the population and technology of the world have been obliterated. In this sixth story, the remnants of Sonmi's manifesto and statue have been deified. Sonmi has literally become a God in the eyes of the atavistic humans.

Each object, an artifact from a previous age, gains new meaning in later periods. Sonmi's manifesto and statue, for instance, are literally deified, having little to no connection to the actual Sonmi. There is not, however, a desire for the object to mean what it did before the apocalyptic event. In this case, there is no understanding of what the object meant before the apocalypse at all. The audience, however, is aware that Sonmi was explicitly rebelling against an oppressive phallocentric society that gave her no rights at all. This association is completely lost after the destruction of the world. Her character has been distilled into an idealized image in the form of a statue used to reify precisely the type of oppressive hierarchy Sonmi was rebelling against. While she is viewed as a Godlike figure, this power is given to her by the native peoples and has little to do with the inherent value of the object or the person who inspired it. Zachry, the protagonist, encounters a religious figure who exhorts him to heed the warnings of Sonmi—who has gifted her with a vision of the future:

> Abbess: But Sonmi can protect you.
>
> Zachry: Sonmi?!
>
> Abbess: She cares for all her flock. But you got to mind her warnin'.
>
> Zachry: What warnin'? The Abbess channels the voice of their protector.

> Abbess: "Enemy's sleepin', don't slit that throat. Hands'a'bleedin', mus'nt let go. Bridge a'burnin', your path lies below." *Her body sags, weak from the effort.* (*Cloud Atlas*)

In this sense, the objectified Sonmi is used to guide people's lives, creating a hierarchy with Sonmi at the top. In truth, however, Sonmi is just a powerful tool used by the religious figures, who are the ones truly at the apex of the social hierarchy.

Despite the fact that the native people have no understanding of what the actual Sonmi was like and have thus made an object with no clear referent, the film does offer Zachry a sense of what the object signifies through the knowledge of the Prescients. The Prescients are the last remaining vestiges of advanced human civilization—a dying group of people who still possess preapocalyptic knowledge and technology. One such Prescient, Meronym, takes Zachry to an old broadcast tower and reveals the forgotten history of Sonmi, thus establishing Sonmi's true significance before the worldwide calamity. The referent for the Sonmi statue is restored to what it was before the apocalyptic event—a person with aspirations and hopes, fighting against a dominant culture that stripped her of rights and agency. Meronym, and indeed the film itself, dissolves the mystical aura of the Sonmi statue, and substitutes a three-dimensional person for a static, deified object. The audience is privy to the life of Sonmi, her desires and struggles, and Meronym possesses much of this knowledge as well. Ultimately, then, the film is not seeking to restore objects to a preapocalyptic meaning that reifies patriarchal hierarchies but is instead trying to use these objects to tell the stories of disenfranchised peoples. By connecting each object to a preceding story, the audience learns of the struggles of a Black slave, an Asian clone, a gay composer, a mistreated elderly person, and a Black female reporter. In each case, the object's value lies not in its ability to facilitate division between the dominant culture and various outgroups but to give a voice to groups that would otherwise be as silent as the stationary Sonmi statue.

The film *Mortal Engines* takes place in a postapocalyptic world where, more than a thousand years after a cataclysmic event known as the Sixty Minute War, people dwell within mobilized cities. The larger mobilized cities typically devour the smaller ones, scavenging them for assorted resources. Opposing these ruthless scavengers on wheels is the Anti-Traction League, which has created static settlements behind a protective barrier known as the Shield Wall. Preapocalyptic technology, known as "old tech," is valued by both historians of the film and by the main antagonist, Thaddeus Valentine, who seeks to use this tech to produce a weapon capable of destroying the Shield Wall of the settlements.

The objects coveted by Valentine haven't changed much in value and meaning in the time since the apocalypse. These were objects of war, used to dominate and oppress others before the apocalypse, and they are used for the same purpose after the apocalypse. Valentine wants to use these to destroy the Shield Wall and take over the settlements. What does change, however, are some of the other preapocalyptic objects, kept in places like the Museum of London. London, the largest of the mobile cities, has managed to retain many of its most notable monuments, including Big Ben and the various museums. One of the main characters, Tom Natsworthy, works in the Museum of London, and in one of the earliest scenes of the film, we observe the sorts of things considered valuable remnants of the preapocalyptic world. The film illustrates how "divorced from social frameworks or in the hands of a different social frameworks, an object's meaning and significance change" (Wicks 80). For instance, the minions of the movie *Minions* and the *Despicable Me* films are seen behind glass in a section of the museum labeled "Deities of Lost America." In another section of the museum, "The Screen Age," we see smartphones and several different computer and television monitors. Skateboards, washing machines, and an aged McDonald's sign can be seen in other displays.

The most interesting of these objects are the statues of the minions in the Deities of Lost America section. These statues, before the apocalypse, were representations of frivolous, fun characters beloved by children. After the apocalypse, the context and referent have been lost, and the objects are now thought to represent something deified in America. There are various reasons why the inhabitants of postapocalyptic London would come to this conclusion. The preapocalyptic world could be seen as obsessed with media and the cult of celebrity, with billions of people directly influenced by fictional characters and celebrity influencers on social media. The effects of this influence range from the purchase of products to the consumption of foods. The fact that these minions statues are thought to be deities also points to the rampant consumerism of the preapocalyptic world. People create identities and signify status through the objects they purchase. Thus, the minions statues symbolize both the influence of media and also the importance of product consumption.

Also important is the museum display labeled "The Screen Age," replete with broken cellphones and television monitors. The preapocalyptic world was so fixated on screens (with constant cellphone use and consumption of media) that the postapocalyptic Museum of London saw this as an entire "age"—a defining feature of civilization at the time. Much like the statues of minions, however, a grain of truth is to be found in this interpretation of technological artifacts. Contemporary society does indeed have a clear fixation on various forms of screen usage, evidenced in the billions of people constantly on their cellphones and electronic devices all around the world.

There is no general thrust for these objects to mean what they did before the apocalyptic event since the meaning they have been given by the postapocalyptic world is already fairly accurate. Rather than lose their original meaning, the apocalypse seems to have just magnified the meanings of these objects. While the Museum of London doesn't seem to know that the minions statues are from a popular children's movie, they do recognize the importance of media and product consumption in the preapocalyptic world. This section of the film is played for laughs, but it's fair to categorize the old world's object obsession as a kind of deification.

Interestingly, then, the preapocalyptic objects still ultimately mean the same thing after the apocalypse. The objects that Valentine covets are used to create a phallocentric culture centered on the subjugation of diverse outgroups, much the same as weapons have been used throughout history. The objects in the museum, at first seemingly disconnected from their established values before the apocalypse, end up being accurately interpreted, albeit in hyperbolic fashion. The apocalypse has not sapped these objects of meaning; rather, it has made their meaning more outwardly transparent.

The nuclear device that Valentine wants, called MEDUSA, will allow him to maintain a role as alpha male and keep his white male-dominated society at the top of the hierarchy. The cities and buildings themselves are also objects, constructed to reify a hierarchy present before the apocalyptic event. The London of the film is

> characterised by rigid class hierarchies, its social stratification is reflected in the structure of the great traction city which rises two thousand feet above the ground in seven tiers. It is also reflected in the organisation of labour, from the knowledge elites—the four great guilds Engineers, Historians, Navigators and Merchants—who along with the municipal oligarchy occupy the top tiers, to the lowly salvagemen, scavengers and the expendable convicts who labour in "nether boroughs" of its gut. (Bullen and Parsons 129–30)

Rather than taking objects and reinscribing their preapocalyptic meaning, we see that once again the world of the film already maintains this preapocalyptic meaning, much like the statues of the minions. Just like the minions, the meaning here, while consistent with preapocalyptic meaning, is presented in an absurdly exaggerated manner. While social stratification maintained through city design does indeed exist, the preapocalyptic world certainly didn't have large, affluent cities literally devouring the smaller ones. The film takes the embedded social stratification of architectural design and magnifies it in this postapocalyptic world.

Much like *Oryx and Crake* and a plethora of other books and films, a loss of meaning exemplified through changed meanings of words and objects is of paramount importance in Russell Hoban's novel, *Riddley Walker*. Many novels highlight the problematic yearning for the reification of the hegemonic system, including *Riddley Walker*—another apocalyptic novel where the postapocalyptic world illustrates a longing for the past—while also touching on its destructive tendencies. The novel follows the titular character in a world thousands of years after a nuclear holocaust that annihilated much of the planet. The world of the novel is developmentally similar to the stone age of our collective human history, a world of primitive hunter-gatherers, with no knowledge of the advanced technology they find in the form of buried artifacts. The language of the novel reflects the primitive mindset of the characters, as though language itself had regressed along with everything else. Narratively, the novel involves Riddley as an unwitting participant in the rediscovery of nuclear weapons and their inherent power and destruction. Riddley, after the death of his father, is made into the "connexion" man for his particular tribe, a quasi-religious position that involves interpreting a traveling Punch and Judy show. The Punch and Judy show is an amalgam of religious myth, entertainment, and government propaganda, and Riddley is essentially a priest tasked with interpreting these shows for his people. One night, he discovers one of the Punch and Judy puppets buried in the ground. He refuses to hand it over after being caught with it by one of the tribe's leaders and instead escapes beyond the wall of his village. Followed by feral dogs that have taken a liking to him, Riddley learns of a movement to regain the lost "cleverness"—the ancient knowledge and technologies from before the apocalypse. Eventually, he teams with up the "pry mincer" (prime minister), Goodparley, in an attempt to free a man named Lissener. Lissener is the "ardship of Cambry" (archbishop of Canterbury), a man believed to have answers to some of the mysteries from before the apocalypse. The story ends with a disillusioned Riddley Walker going on the road with a newly adapted

Punch and Judy show, after Goodparley accidentally blows himself up through the discovery of gunpowder.

The language used in the novel is an odd permutation of English, with unusual spellings and a whole new set of associations between words. This is part of the anxiety we see with the loss of meaning within the latter half of the twentieth century to today. Words do not mean what they once did, and thus making sense of the world has become an even more challenging task. The phrase "prime minister," for instance, has morphed into "pry mincer," while sulfur has become "salt 4." The apocalyptic event thousands of years prior has not only hindered the development of civilization, but it has also exacerbated challenges in creating meaning through language. Hoban's main character, Riddley, directly acknowledges the difficulty in conveying meaning:

> Walker is my name and I am the same. Riddley Walker. Walking my riddels where ever theyve took me and walking them now on this paper the same.
>
> I dont think it makes no diffrents where you start the telling of a thing. You never know where it begun realy. No moren you know where you begun your oan self. You myt know the place and day and time of day when you ben beartht. You myt even know the place and day and time when you ben got. That dont mean nothing tho. You stil dont know where you begun. (8)

He describes his efforts to understand the events of his life as "walking my riddels," an indication that making sense of the world is a tremendous challenge, with no clear answers. In addition, he differentiates between the time and place of one's birth and "know[ing] where you begun." Concrete things like a time and place cannot create a clear understanding of the events in one's life. The elusive quality of meaning is reiterated when Riddley's father dies. He notes that

> I wer stil wanting some thing some kynd of las word some kynd of onwith. If I wernt going to get it from Dad at leas I wantit some thing for onwith even if it wernt nothing only the name of that girt black thing what smasht him flat so you cudnt even tel whose face it ben. (Hoban 11)

He wants to make sense of his father's death, a "las word some kind"; even just the name of the object that killed him would provide some form of catharsis. His father had been unearthing preapocalyptic technology—a black metal object in this case—getting crushed in the process. Riddley never discovers the name of this object and is left with no closure after the death of his father. The difficulty in creating meaning is mirrored by the actual language used here and throughout the entire novel. Riddley is writing to share his narrative with whatever reader stumbles upon his writing. However, the lack of contractions and the strange, truncated spellings all make it challenging for Riddley Walker to share his tale with the reader. We cannot clearly understand Riddley and he cannot understand us, which is elucidated in the part of the text where he comes upon a preapocalyptic pamphlet sharing the story of St. Eustace. The language is recognizable to the reader:

> The Legend of St Eustace dates from the year A.D. 120 and this XVth-century wall painting depicts with fidelity the several episodes in his life. The setting is a wooded landscape with many small hamlets; a variety of wild creatures are to be seen and a river meanders to the open sea. (Hoban 123)

Riddley, however, says "I dont even know these words." His companion, Goodparley, attempts to offer an explanation: "I can as plain the mos of it to you. Some parts is easyer workit out nor others theres bits of it wewl never know for cern jus what they mean. What this writing is its about some kynd of picter or dyergam which we dont have that picter all we have is the writing" (Hoban 126). Goodparley, though correct in assuming that the pamphlet was meant to accompany a painting, misinterprets several parts of the text. For instance, he assumes "st." means "sent," instead of "saint," and that "AD" (anno domini) means "all done." Taken as a whole, neither the reader nor the characters of the novel can fully understand the world they inhabit, hindered in part by the lack of a common universal language.

The most important literal object in the novel is a Punch and Judy figure that Riddley finds buried in the ground. Removed from its original context as a raucous, often comedic show first appearing in 1662 CE England, the figure is used as part of a set of religious beliefs. Punch and Judy shows are used in the novel to teach religious and moral lessons and to disseminate the ideologies of the dominant class, as these traveling shows migrate across the remains of Great Britain. Riddley's discovery illustrates, for himself and the reader, that the Punch and Judy show has been nothing but a tool for those in power to propagate ideas. He sees that it is a preapocalyptic object that has been decontextualized and likely has nothing to do with any of the religious mythology. Riddley notes, "I cudnt think what it myt be then when it come to me what it wer I cudnt hardly beleave it yet there it wer nor no mistaking it." Soon thereafter, one of the guards attempts to confiscate it because "we wernt allowit to keap nothing we foun in the digging some times they use to serch us tho not all ways" (Hoban 72, 73). The people of Inland (England) are not allowed to keep anything they find buried in the ground, in an attempt to keep preapocalyptic history hidden and the Minstry's fabricated mythology intact. In order for the dominant class to succeed in accruing power, all preapocalyptic knowledge must be withheld, and the ignorant, anti-intellectual thrust of society must be maintained.

Riddley Walker acknowledges the desire to move back to the dominant, white male structure after the apocalypse, since that is exactly what we see in the novel. Many apocalyptic stories in the twentieth century end with the reestablishment of a white male hierarchy or nuclear family, presenting it as a desirable outcome full of possibility. Hoban's book, however, carries it further, *beginning* with the hegemonic structure already reestablished and showing that, far from being positive and desirable, this power structure creates the same ruinous patterns that have destroyed mankind throughout history. Goodparley is literally killed in the discovery of gunpowder, called the "1 little 1":

> I jus begun to roal up a smoak when WHAP! there come like a thunner clap it wer like when litening strikes right close it eckowit up and down the rivver. There come up a cloud of smoak from the fents it wernt the regler blue smoak it wer 1 big puff of grey smoak and things wer peltering down out of the trees like when you shake down nuts. (Hoban 194)

Riddley sees, firsthand, the results of the myopic pursuit of power, and has no frame of reference to even describe the explosion. He can only compare it to natural phenomena, like a "thunner clap."

The novel's focus on language and the importance of preapocalyptic objects, like the Punch and Judy figure, serves to illustrate how myth—of which objects and language are a critical part—is used by the dominant class to maintain control over the populace. The most prominent myth, the Eusa myth, is based on something factual—the splitting of the atom for atomic weapons—couched in religious iconography. In the myth, Mr. Clevver is beset on all sides by enemies, so he enlists the help of Eusa, described simply as a knowing man who could create anything. Eusa shrinks himself and his two dogs as he enters the heart of a stone and encounters "The Stag of the Wood." Between the stag's horns is the "Littl Shynin Man the Addom." Eusa kills the stag and pulls the "Littl Shynin Man" apart, as Hoban writes:

> Owt uv thay 2 peaces uv the Little Shynin Man the Addom thayr cum shyningnes in spredin circels. Wivverin & wayverin & humin with a hy soun. Lytin up the dark wud. Eusa seen the Little 1 goin roun & round insyd the Big 1 & the Big 1 humin roun inside the Littl 1. He seen thay Master Chaynjis uv the 1 Big 1. Qwik then he riten down thay Nos. uv them. (32)

Despite warnings from his two dogs, Eusa explains his discovery to Mr. Clevver, who uses the knowledge of splitting the "Littl Shynin Man the Addom" to his advantage in annihilating his enemies. The aftermath, however, leaves Eusa terrified. After this weapon is used, "The lan was poyzen frum it in the ayr & water as wel. Peapl din jus dy in the Warr thay kep dyin after it wuz over" (33). Eusa escapes on a boat with his family, but the captain captures his wife, while his wife and dogs are taken away by the two halves of the "Littl Shynin Man the Addom," who tells Eusa that nothing will be the same again and that he must abide the changes of this world. What was once whole is now forever split in two. There are obvious parallels here with the origin myth in Christianity, in which an Edenic paradise, where man is one with God, is forever broken apart. Even the "Littl Shynin Man the Addom" is a clever play on words, "Addom" referring to both the atom and the first man of the Bible, Adam. This myth, and the others shared by Riddley, are thought by the populace to offer a meaning behind the nature of a harsh, unforgiving world. In this case, the actions of Eusa and Mr. Clevver have turned a unified, idyllic world into one of suffering and hardship. In reality, however, this myth is part of an anti-intellectual agenda by the Minstry (Ministry—the central government), which seeks access to knowledge and preapocalyptic weaponry to wield power over the masses. By keeping the truth of the past a mystery, they are able to use the ignorance of others to gain answers and knowledge that will solidify their dominance, as we later find out that the Minstry has deliberately modified the Eusa tale for their own desire to maintain power.

The version relayed by Lissener, the Ardship of Cambry, clearly shows that the Eusa story is meant as a cautionary tale. In Lissener's version of the story, Eusa is asked by government leaders to share the secret that had been given to Mr. Clevver so that they can have it before other nations. Eusa refuses, acknowledging the unbridled destruction that the weapon has already unleashed. He expresses his wish to travel the country, instructing people on the dangers of unrestrained ambition, but the government leaders, angry at his refusal to share the secret, behead Eusa before he can do so. Eusa's head, however, keeps talking and admonishing them for their immorality. These leaders soon find themselves beset by a giant wave that separates parts of England. The government sees this as a spiritual sign of their own depravity, and they decide to travel the country to impart moral lessons, presumably to help prevent the destruction Eusa had warned against. This version of the story shows that far from wandering the world to effect the changes that the Littl Shynin Man had described, Eusa is murdered for refusing to give destructive power to his superiors. By intentionally withholding key elements of the story and altering the meanings of words and objects, the Minstry can maintain a hierarchy that concentrates power in the hands of a few.

The importance of objects is apparent also in *A Canticle for Leibowitz*, where monks in a postapocalyptic world imbue preapocalyptic objects with spiritual power. The goal for these monks is to lead humanity out of the "dark ages," after a series of disasters decimated the planet and set back the human race technologically, intellectually, and spiritually. The apocalyptic event, the Flame Deluge, has made the objects they collect bereft of any clear meaning, owing to the lack of a referent. The meaning of the objects is ascribed by the monks, who see these commodities as having a spiritual significance. This is in keeping with Marx's description of commodity fetishism, where the lack of concrete meaning behind the objects allows them to take on supernatural, mystical qualities that have little to do with their physical characteristics and use. The commodities here are separated from the laborers who produced them by a literal cataclysm, and the commodity form of objects makes them grow well beyond their use value. Indeed, there is virtually no use value, since the objects are utterly inscrutable to the monks, who fail to understand something as basic as a shopping list. Ultimately, then, there is no true underlying meaning for these commodities. A prime example of this is the aforementioned shopping list found at the beginning of the book, a list thought to have been written by Leibowitz, a US military electrical engineer, dedicated to preserving knowledge after the "Flame Deluge." Describing the experience of the monk who found the list, Miller writes:

> First he examined the jotted notes. They were scrawled by the same hand that had written the note glued to the lid,

> and the penmanship was no less abominable. Pound pastrami, said one note, can kraut, six bagels—bring home for Emma. Another reminded: Remember—pick up Form 1040, Uncle Revenue. Another was only a column of figures with a circled total from which a second amount was subtracted and finally a percentage taken, followed by the word damn! Brother Francis checked the figures; he could find no fault with the abominable penman's arithmetic, at least, although he could deduce nothing about what the quantities might represent. (Miller chap. 2)

In the context of the novel, the list is utterly baffling to Brother Francis but soon becomes sacred when the name "Leibowitz" is found on a blueprint. The desire here is ostensibly to preserve knowledge, but the list has little knowledge to impart—and what little there is cannot be understood. The postapocalyptic world is, as Hurley explains, "a system in which . . . language is divorced from its referent" (Hurley 70). The distinctions between classes are muddled in a way that mirrors this obfuscation of meaning, where the inherent class system embodied in objects has dissolved. What advantage, for instance, can an object convey if its meaning is not at all clear? Describing a blueprint, for instance, Francis argues that "the diagram represents an abstract concept, rather than a concrete thing. Perhaps the ancients had a systematic method for depicting a pure thought. It's clearly not a recognizable picture of an object" (Miller chap. 7). However, a blueprint does refer to a concrete thing; it's just that the apocalypse has destroyed the object that the blueprint refers to, rendering the blueprint empty. The class warfare in the novel is, at least initially, between the monks who seek to preserve the objects and groups that wish to destroy them, believing that the knowledge they represent is part of what caused the Flame Deluge. The distinctions then between these groups are based on the imagined value of preapocalyptic objects, essentially implying that the class conflict here is based on vacuous symbols. If the commodities are empty, then what class distinction can they truly convey? These groups, then, are literally at odds over nothing.

Much like *Riddley Walker*, there is a loss of meaning after the apocalyptic event, though it should be noted that the apocalypse is merely a metaphor for a preexisting crisis of signification that goes beyond simply the novel itself. Reflecting the world in which Miller is writing, the novel is about the present, where meaning has already become opaque and the apocalyptic event is merely emblematic of something already happening. Richard Hodgens, in "A Brief, Tragical History of the Science Fiction

Film," called science fiction a genre that "takes place in the future or introduces some radical assumption about the present or the past" (Hodgens 30). The "radical assumption" here is that perhaps our objects are already like the ones found by Brother Francis, obtuse and inscrutable. Within the novel, Miller makes it clear that he is, in fact, pondering such questions. He has moments in the text where he has philosophical asides that are only tangentially related to the plot. For instance, he writes:

> There was objective meaning in the world, to be sure . . . but such meanings were God's and not Man's, until they found an imperfect incarnation, a dark reflection, within the mind and speech and culture of a given human society, which might ascribe values to the meanings so that they became valid in a human sense within the culture. For Man was a culture-bearer as well as a soul-bearer, but his cultures were not immortal and they could die with a race or an age, and then human reflections of meaning and human portrayals of truth receded, and truth and meaning resided, unseen. (Miller chap. 14)

Highlighted here is the very tenuous connection between signifier and signified, and the collapse of human society and all of its "imperfect incarnations" of truth could allow meaning to "recede" and remain "unseen." The collapse of society, in the context of the novel, is brought about through the Flame Deluge. In the context of the world in which Miller was writing, the collapse had already begun, as there was no longer a prevalent reliance on objective truth—a distant memory in an age of postmodernism. Our Flame Deluge is a metaphorical one, a slow attenuation of the signifying power of objects and, by extension, class distinctions. An object in the novel like the shopping list is emblematic of the type of commodity fetishism here, an object that literally refers to other objects—objects that likely don't even exist anymore. It has, like the other artifacts, a spiritual, incorporeal value that has nothing to do with its use value.

The desire to imbue objects with meaning, reestablishing the hegemonic system in place before the apocalypse, is explicit throughout the novel. Brother Francis and his cohorts, who collect and obsess over pre-Flame Deluge artifacts, illustrate a "dogmatic acceptance of orthodox thinking . . . [which] helps preserve the current power structure, much as it did in the 'original' Middle Ages" (Tietge 680). The monastic order attempts to collect books and artifacts, creating a localized concentration of power. If they can control knowledge, they can control the shape of any future society. They control the future, but they can also control the past, shaping events that the general public has little knowledge of. David Tietge writes:

> The Church has control over the discourse of the first "flame deluge," and through a combination of ignorance, superstition, doctrine, dogma, and authority, can instill a controlling fear in those who associate such language with the evils of the past, allowing maintenance of the institution through control of the discourse that gives history its meaning. (Tietge 681)

Of course, the monks themselves describe their search for knowledge in very different terms, seeing it as a holy mission to save humanity. The preapocalyptic past is seen as something to be aspired to, a time of comfort and technological superiority, and perhaps knowledge of the past can prevent another apocalyptic event. The comforts and ease of living in the preapocalyptic world is seen in objects, such as the grocery list found by Brother Francis. The grocery list he finds is a completely arcane artifact to the monks, implying that the economic system and infrastructure of the postapocalyptic world is such that the abundance of goods available before the cataclysm has greatly diminished. There are no grocery stores, and food is not as easily accessible, making a grocery list an incomprehensible item. The thrust in the novel is to move back to this time of access and abundance, and indeed the reader is encouraged to see this as a desirable end, highlighting the hardships of characters mired in a hostile, spartan style of living. Despite this particular shortcoming, the monks are successful in using the objects to elevate themselves in social class.

Both Atwood and Miller, however, are aware that the inclination toward rampant capitalism and its inherent hierarchies is a double-edged sword. So while the characters in the novel long for the reestablishment of the hegemonic system, and the reader is meant to share this longing in some instances, both novels note the problematic nature of such hierarchical systems. Structurally, *A Canticle for Leibowitz* looks at a narrative arc in which the world moves back to the advanced state that had existed prior to the apocalypse. However, these advancements carry the same predictable downfalls, in which the hierarchies of capitalism lead to conflict—the same conflict that had annihilated the globe once before. Miller, in writing *A Canticle for Leibowitz*, seems to suggest that we are unable or unwilling to conceive of an alternate system, and that we will attempt to convey a hierarchical system through objects even if those objects mean virtually nothing. Indeed, the monks are successful in using their objects this way, imbuing them with a power meant to distinguish themselves from the other survivors of the Flame Deluge. That hierarchy inevitably leads to sectarian violence and then culminates in yet another cataclysm. In this sense, the novel is not promoting the preapocalyptic system but merely illustrating our desire for it, despite the consequences. Similarly, Atwood's novel ends with Snowman being offered a way to rejoin the human race, after finding a group of preapocalyptic humanoids. The "Crakers," as Snowman calls them, are the new beings populating the planet now, a group incapable of understanding things like violence and money. They are portrayed as possessing a childlike innocence, perhaps genetically engineered that way by Crake himself. When the Crakers tell Snowman of a group of humans like him, Snowman is both excited and terrified. While he longs for the world that has been lost—one in which he enjoyed comfort and power—images of abject ruination flash through his mind. He is conflicted, as

> images from old history flip through his head, sidebars from Blood and Roses: Ghenghis Khan's skull pile, the heaps of shoes and eyeglasses from Dachau, the burning corpse-filled churches in Rwanda, the sack of Jerusalem by the Crusaders. The Arawak Indians, welcoming Christopher Columbus with garlands and gifts of fruit, smiling with delight, soon to be massacred, or tied up beneath the beds upon which their women were being raped. (Atwood 189)

It seems that perhaps the apocalyptic event has forced Snowman to think about the hegemonic structure that he had enjoyed the fruits of. All of the comforts and power he would enjoy once again, bring with them the destructive tendencies of a hierarchical system that is inherently unequal, one that gives power to one group at the expense of others. For the reader, then, the ending of the novel is ambiguous. While we are meant to wish, along with Snowman, for an end to his alienation and struggles to find meaning, we are shown that such a system is predicated on the oppression of groups at the bottom of the hierarchy, groups outside the Compounds that are not even given a voice in the novel. Both Atwood and Miller, in other words, show the complications of our desire for the hegemonic system, to the point where both authors seem critical of a system of inequities that keeps perpetuating itself.

Far less critical is *Night of the Comet* (1984), a film built around the fascination with Haley's Comet at the time, with the comet of the film inexplicably causing an apocalyptic event. In the film, anyone who watched the comet as it passed by the Earth found themselves disintegrating and turning to red dust. Many of the survivors were simply turned into a type of zombie, though perhaps a more aware, coherent zombie than typical film depictions, with many of them able to speak and reason. The film implies that exposure to the comet causes some sort of disease that has a degenerative effect on the survivors, causing violent behavior and skin lesions.

The protagonists are three adolescents who have endured no obvious effects from the comet, as they traverse an empty Los Angeles, looking for survivors and looking to obtain products at a large mall. To the two girls, in particular, objects like shoes still retain their preapocalyptic meaning. Shopping in an empty mall, free from security and consequences, instills in them a sense of glee, and a montage plays of them trying on various outfits as 1980s music blares in the background. Perhaps because the film occurs immediately after the apocalypse, as opposed to many years later, objects have lost none of their signifying power. The shopping mall is still "an absolute monument to consumerism," and indeed, much of the film seems to celebrate the power of objects. The people killed by viewing Haley's Comet are literally reduced to merely a pile of clothes lying on the ground. Instead of a fully developed, complex human being, we see that a person can be signified by a group of objects. We see a literal interpretation of the notion that "the things people carry or the objects they collect define them in important ways" and how "a person's relationship with the objects in their life revealed that person's character, personality, and subjectivity, while simultaneously supporting it" (Wicks 80). Clothing and accessories, in the world of the film, are the distilled essence of a person.

One aspect of the preapocalyptic world that has actually vanished is the nuclear family, and the film does seek to reconstruct this, via the relationship between Regina, Hector, and two rescued children. Even Sam, the little sister, finds a random eligible bachelor at the end, hinting at another incipient family. The nuclear family and its concomitant power structure are preserved, in addition to the signifying power of objects. The new love interest of Sam at the end of the film is driving a sports car, which impresses Sam, implying that the sports car, as an object, still conveys a sense of masculinity and sexual prowess. The main male character, Hector, has been the focus of almost all of the action in the story. The two girls were aimless at the beginning of the film and then stumbled upon Hector, a man with a gun and a plan to look for his family. Upon learning that he intended to leave them to go on his journey, the two girls resolve to tag along, leading them to further adventures. The two sisters even fight over who will get to have a relationship with him, indicating that even after an apocalyptic event, girls will still be preoccupied with how best to impress the alpha male.

Older Apocalyptic Objects versus Contemporary Objects

Comparing contemporary use of objects in apocalyptic texts to the way they are used in the older Christian texts elucidates some key differences. Revelation is one such older text, which displays an intense focus on objects in its description of New Jerusalem—the city established during Christ's thousand-year reign on Earth, after the initial apocalyptic event. In Revelation, there are a number of parallels between the description of New Jerusalem and the typical Roman towns at the time. For instance, Roman cities had something called a pomerium, which was essentially a boundary around the city, demarcating where the laws of that city began and ended. This finds a corollary in the passage where John describes how nothing "unclean" can enter New Jerusalem. New Jerusalem also has a series of inscriptions to honor the city's benefactors on the gates, which is keeping with the Roman custom of "record[ing] the philanthropy of individuals who funded municipal works or otherwise served as patrons of a city. The benefactors of New Jerusalem are, of course, the twelve apostles, which also explains the prevalence of the number twelve. Even the shape of New Jerusalem is influenced by notions of the "ideal city in Greek and Roman thought. The quadrangular shape of the holy city (Rev. 21.16) suits the grid street pattern found so often in Greek and Roman urban areas" (Kraybill 211). Beyond Roman influence was the influence of Jewish tradition. Author Kraybill notes that

> John's holy city may have been quadrangular (or more precisely, cubic) because the holy of holies in Solomon's temple was a perfect cube (1 Kgs 6.20; 2 Chron. 3.8). Just as God

> was wholly present in the inner sanctuary of Solomon's temple, God now is wholly present in all of the New Jerusalem.

The influence of Rome and Jewish tradition is the more concrete, literal explanation for the way in which New Jerusalem is described. John simply attempted to evoke an image in terms that the average reader could easily visualize (Kraybill 212–14).

Of particular pertinence to the discussion of objects is a section in Revelation that focuses explicitly on the measurements and composition of the New Jerusalem. Revelation 21 reads:

> The wall was made of jasper, and the city itself of pure gold, as pure as glass. The foundations of the city walls were adorned with every kind of precious stone: The first foundation was jasper, the second sapphire, the third chalcedony, the fourth emerald, 20the fifth sardonyx, the sixth carnelian, the seventh chrysolite, the eighth beryl, the ninth topaz, the tenth chrysoprase, the eleventh jacinth, and the twelfth amethyst.
>
> And the twelve gates were twelve pearls, with each gate consisting of a single pearl. The main street of the city was pure gold, as pure as transparent glass. (Revelation 21:18–21)

Beyond the literal explanation of Roman and Jewish influence, the obsessive focus on objects, specifically objects of material value, is striking in that it is a marked departure from the New Testament's stance on wealth in general. The Bible explicitly promotes the idea that the poor and destitute are to be lifted up, while the rich and powerful are brought down. Much has been written about the New Testament's attitudes toward the rich and powerful. Luke 18:25 notes that "it is easier for a camel to go through the eye of a needle than for a rich person to enter the kingdom of God." Furthermore, Christ is quoted as saying, "Blessed are you who are poor, for yours is the kingdom of God. . . . Blessed are you who are hungry now, for you shall be satisfied. . . . Blessed are you who weep now, for you shall laugh" (Luke 6:20–21). The Gospel of James uses even stronger language, warning:

> You rich, weep and howl for the miseries that are coming upon you. Your riches have rotted and your garments are moth-eaten. Your gold and silver have corroded, and their corrosion will be evidence against you and will eat your flesh

> like fire. You have laid up treasure in the last days. Behold, the wages of the laborers who mowed your fields, which you kept back by fraud, are crying out against you, and the cries of the harvesters have reached the ears of the Lord of hosts. You have lived on the earth in luxury and in self-indulgence. You have fattened your hearts in a day of slaughter. (James 5:1–6)

While these texts are not explicitly apocalyptic, they do couch these scenarios in apocalyptic terms, warning of an end-time scenario where power and wealth evaporate, and God finally creates a dramatic reversal for the "laborers," upon whose backs the victories of the dominant culture have been built. This suggests a complete alteration of the hegemonic system, allowing power to be reappropriated by disenfranchised groups. Beyond the actual text, the people actually reading these myths may be given hope that their lack of power will not be eternal—that those at the bottom will soon rise as God's chosen people. Fuller, quoting David Hellholm, notes that "apocalyptic thought is 'intended for a group in crisis with the purpose of exhortation and/or consolation by means of divine authority.' " This "divine authority" edifies the faithful, who are asked to view history in a larger, almost transcendental context, where ultimately the poor and meek inherit the Earth. In this "mythic context," "a victorious outcome is assured" (quoted in Fuller 21).

Rather than viewing the focus on the wealth of New Jerusalem as contradicting the criticism of wealth seen elsewhere, the focus on objects of value is the means through which the text shows the reappropriation of power—a reshaping of society to allow disenfranchised classes a voice and a way to shape the hierarchies that define human relations. There is essentially a total reversal after the apocalyptic event where the hierarchy is flipped, placing the rich at the bottom. Mathews writes:

> Within this economy of faithfulness the poor become rich by remaining loyal to the Lamb and inheriting the gold and jewel-laden new Jerusalem. Correspondingly, the rich become poorer through their accumulation of wealth, since this alternative economic system of heaven finds its source of wealth in Christ and runs contrary to the evil earthly realm. (Mathews 217)

Since gold and jewels in such excess would lower the overall value of these objects in a traditional "supply and demand" capitalist system, the implication is that New Jerusalem employs a system other than capitalism, creating the "alternative economic system" that Mathews mentions. This is in keeping with the teachings of Christ, who "promoted an egalitarian economic system that functioned as an alternative to the selfishness and inequities of the ancient market economy" (Kraybill 215). So not only is the hegemonic system flipped, but oppressive hierarchies are thrown out, as all followers reap the rewards equally.

Contrary to contemporary usage of the apocalypse, in Revelation there is a net positive gain in value and meaning. Objects that followers were told had little value in real life are suddenly given great value after the apocalypse. After being implored not to focus on wealth in life, acolytes are informed that the objects of wealth will finally mean something, and these will be one of many rewards for the faithful. Affluence is not a "feature of the present age for the faithful community. Rather, those who remain loyal to God and suffer can expect to be rewarded in the gold and jewel-laden new Jerusalem in the eschaton" (Mathews 216). Therefore, unlike contemporary manifestations of the apocalypse, the focus for early Christians is on the future. While Revelation and other apocalyptic texts were obviously influenced by the current events of the time, the apocalyptic event itself was meant to depict a future end-time event that many Christians genuinely believed in. As Cohn points out, older apocalyptic myths "catered at all times for the craving of anxious mortals for an unquestionable forecast of the future" (Cohn 33). The future was the time of justice, when the surrounding world was suffused with value and meaning that had been previously overshadowed by the iniquities of the nonbelievers. While the apocalyptic event itself was destructive, the rewards afterward were bright indeed.

This is very much unlike contemporary myths, where there is no effulgent, glorious kingdom after the cataclysm. After the apocalypse, everything that had been problematic before the apocalypse is exacerbated, and the tenuous hold on the meaningfulness of objects in society utterly vanishes. Things mean even less after the calamitous event. However, unlike older myths, these contemporary depictions are not truly painting an image of the future. Rather, the apocalypse and its aftermath are used to illustrate the problems of the present age, the goal being to magnify existing problems and defamiliarize them, so as to bring attention to contemporary issues of exigency. As a subgenre of science fiction, modern postapocalyptic fiction attempts to "defamiliarize and restructure our experience of our own present, and to do so in specific ways distinct from all other forms of defamiliarization" (Pask 183). Furthermore, these myths, as a microcosm of the present, demonstrate the feeling that the apocalypse is already here—that this is not a future event to be patiently awaited but something we were currently living through. Part of this is an acute awareness of environmental and political issues, many of which would have been inaccessible even a few decades ago. Endless wars, genocide, and environmental catastrophes have all happened before. However, the twentieth century increased awareness of these things and exposed the world to an endless series of TV shows, articles, and tweets showing the collapse of some part of our planet. Apocalyptic catastrophe is "something that people are in the process of *living through*. . . . People alive now are living within a time when significant biospheric legacies that have been part of human beings' practical, psychological, and spiritual lives since their beginning as a species are disappearing" (Buell 70). Because the focus is entirely on the present, there is no true "post" apocalypse, in the Christian sense of an incorporeal world in the heavenly realm. There is, instead, an extension of our current world, where the fall of civilization heralds an age where objects more obviously mean nothing, and the destructive tendencies of society reach their logical conclusion.

Conclusion

Objects have long been used to signify class distinctions and maintain hierarchies of power. What we see in contemporary society, however, is a collapse in the signifying power of objects, which has blurred lines between classes. These changes in use clearly manifest themselves in postapocalyptic myths. Older Christian myths, for instance, embed new, powerful meanings in objects after the apocalypse, allowing for the hegemonic structure to be flipped. Conversely, myths over the last century show how the diminishing power of signification plays out on a larger, more obvious scale after the apocalypse. Given the fact that contemporary myths are used by the dominant class rather than the disenfranchised groups at the beginnings of Christianity, there is a powerful push to reestablish objects' ability to signify social status. If successful, the world before the apocalyptic event could be reestablished, an occurrence often presented in positive terms in these newer myths.

Conclusion

Over the last few decades, there is a sense that we're currently living through the apocalypse, waiting for a definitive ending that never comes. We are so inundated with information and daily catastrophes—in the form of shootings and natural disasters, for instance—that it becomes a sort of white noise. Berger notes that "the ceaseless activity of our time—the news with its procession of almost indistinguishable disasters—is only a complex form of stasis" (Berger xii). The number of environmental and world disasters seems to increase each year, and as we have greater access to information, we learn of every mishap instantly and without exception. Actions—like buying a car or even clothing—are calculated by the perceived long-term effects on the planet, and many already think that the effects of global warming are irreversible. The tipping point has come and gone, while millions of species die, and weather patterns become more severe and destructive. This type of apocalypse does not

> involve a terrible and conclusive moment ahead when people breach nature's limits and disrupt nature's fundamental equilibrium; it means that one has already entered (or perhaps is already well into) a time when limits have been breached and the risks from disequilibrium are rising. It also means not only that damage is occurring—as it has been doing for some time—but that its deepening is hard to reverse. (Buell 95)

Of course, it's difficult to say whether our time is truly more apocalyptic than other periods, or if we merely have access to more information instantaneously, which means we are consistently cognizant of disaster.

The latter seems probable, as several books have noted that the twentieth century was no more violent than any other (and perhaps even safer), including Steven Pinker's *The Better Angels of Our Nature*, which uses some fairly convincing statistics.[1] To the average person, however, it feels as though the world is falling apart. In America, mass shootings seem to occur every week or two, and countries throughout the world are gripped by civil war. Perceived enemies, like North Korea, possess nuclear weapons, and terrorists seem to have the power to strike at will at home and in Europe. All of this creates a composite picture of a slowly crumbling world, degrading to the postapocalyptic landscape seen in so many films. Baudrillard believes that "the proliferation and (re)producibility of the apocalypse are signals that the world has already ended. . . . From the Last Judgment to the nuclear holocaust, the drama of the end has played itself out; emptied of meaning, the end of the world is now only a spectacle in reruns" (Heffernan 171). However, there is no ultimate ending that we can point to, and apocalyptic media purporting to be "post" apocalyptic end up revealing more about the present and past than the future. There is no singular destructive end but instead a watershed moment, after which entropy takes over, and the damage to the world increases exponentially with no way to turn back (Buell 95). If the disasters of the world are read in this sense, the apocalyptic moment is now, and it feels like we're waiting for a "post" apocalypse that never comes. We are living through a permanent sort of purgatory, inuring people to the barrage of catastrophic events relayed through the media.

While I'm certainly aware of the never-ending deluge of world catastrophes (school shootings, terrorist attacks, hurricanes, etc.), this project really began through my own cognizance of patterns in apocalyptic media. As a fan of the *Fallout* video game series, I noticed a preoccupation with objects that I would later notice in film and literature. In the *Fallout* games, objects are to be scavenged and repurposed to make new weapons and new machines. A baseball, for instance, can be made into a bomb, while the "junk jet" gun literally uses trash as violent, damaging projectiles. Objects then, after the apocalypse, take on a new purpose.

1. Discussing world history, Pinker notes that "when one corrects for the availability bias and the 20th-century population explosion . . . one comes across many wars and massacres that could hold their head high among 20th century atrocities" (Pinker 194). See Steven Pinker, *The Better Angels of our Nature: The Decline of Violence in History and its Causes* (London: Penguin, 2011).

In *The Road Warrior*, this is apparent in the cars and clothing worn by the characters. Wez uses football gear and carpet matting as armor. Over and over, we see this obsession with objects. This was the catalyst for my research—why? Why were objects so important to these films, books, and video games?

Over time, it became clear that the focus on objects was part of a much larger pattern in which dominant white males illustrate a desire to move back to an older America. In the wake of growing minority rights, the patriarchy has nostalgia for clear notions of race and ethnicity that allow for a hierarchy with the white male at the top. The obsessive focus on objects that I noticed illustrates this desire for a past in which meaning is clearly delineated and objects can clearly convey status. Contemporary apocalyptic media uses the apocalypse as a way of starting over, going back to an idealized America embodied in frontier myths.

It became necessary to first establish the anxiety, experienced because of a more egalitarian society, of white males. With the first Black president and things like gay rights and the DREAM act, a large portion of white males feel disenfranchised and often persecuted. Study after study shows that a segment of the population feels that minority gains have been at the expense of the white male. In addition, this group of white males is more aware of their whiteness, as global demographic shifts make whites a less prominent majority, and ethnic and racial blending makes it difficult to even determine minority status in some cases. Contemporary apocalyptic media plays upon these anxieties, with a thrust toward establishing preapocalyptic institutions like marriage and government and a narrative that allows the white male to be a hero fighting against evil forces on a grand, cosmic scale.

These myths resonate because they are often conflated with frontier myths, which are an integral part of American identity, however fabricated these myths may be. Like the postapocalyptic world, the frontier myth illustrates a clean slate—an open expanse ready for conquest by an intrepid white male. The frontier offers an escape from the past—a chance to start over and use the inherent ingenuity and innovative spirit of the white frontiersman. This frontiersman is essentially the same as any number of protagonists in contemporary apocalyptic films and books. The apocalyptic event erases any past transgressions of American culture and reopens the frontier, creating a space where the idealized America of old can come to fruition.

By creating this clean slate, the apocalypse is a dramatic form of simplification, an effort to eliminate all of the complexities of a world in which the machinations of the economy and geopolitical relationships are distilled into a coherent, comprehensible narrative. In addition, race and ethnicity are simplified, allowing for minorities to be easily identified and scapegoated. The dominant white male, in this way, paints himself a victim of vast conspiracies, instigated by minorities that have insinuated themselves into the highest levels of government.

One need only turn on the television set to see evidence of white male anxiety, our former president's speeches rife with apocalyptic rhetoric that exhorts us to stand against a tide of minority influence. Due to the omnipresent influence of capitalism, this dominant hierarchy is difficult to change, as it is reinforced through every mode of media expression and every institution. Poly Styrene from X-Ray Spex, a minority female in a predominantly white male punk subculture, once sang, "I know I'm artificial/But don't put the blame on me/I was reared with appliances/In a consumer society/When I put on my make-up/The pretty little mask not me/That's the way a girl should be/In a consumer society." The "consumer society" in which we live dictates roles for everyone, a "pretty little mask" to be worn because society says "that's the way a girl should be." Being cognizant of this system of oppression is important, however, so that an entire paradigm shift will one day allow for broad systemic changes beyond oppressive patriarchal systems normalized through capitalism. This type of dramatic shift in consciousness would require large swaths of the sort of Trump supporters written about here to change their way of thinking, which seems a herculean task. But if a diminutive teenage girl of Somalian descent can take a stand in front of screaming white male punks, then so can the rest of us.

Works Cited

12 Monkeys. Directed by Terry Gilliam, performances by Bruce Willis and Madeleine Stowe, director's cut, Universal Pictures, 1995.

"America's Pinata Strikes Back: We Won't Shut Up on Sotomayor—The Rush Limbaugh Show." *Rush Limbaugh*. 29 May 2009.

A Boy and His Dog. Directed by L.Q. Jones, performances by Don Johnson, LQ/JAF Productions, 1975.

A.I.: Artificial Intelligence. Directed by Stephen Spielberg, performances by Jude Law, William Hurt, and Haley Joel Osmond, Warner Brothers, 2001.

Abizadeh, Arash. "Ethnicity, Race, and a Possible Humanity." *World Order*, vol. 33, no. 1, 2001, pp. 23–34.

Appadurai, Arjun. *The Social Life of Things: Commodities in Cultural Perspective*. Cambridge UP, 1988.

Arnold, Sarah. *Maternal Horror Film: Melodrama and Motherhood*. Springer, 2016.

Aston, James, and John Walliss. "The (un) Christian Road Warrior: The Crisis of Religious Representation in *The Book of Eli* (2010)." *Journal of Religion and Film*, vol. 15, no. 1, 2011, pp. 1–12.

Attridge, Harold W. "Greek and Latin Apocalypses." *Semeia*, vol. 14, edited by John Collins, 1979, pp. 159.

Atwood, Margaret. *Oryx and Crake*. Anchor, 2004.

———. *Writing with Intent: Essays, Reviews, Personal Prose: 1983–2005*. Basic Books, 2009.

Automata. Directed by Gabe Ibáñez, performances by Melanie Griffith and Antonio Banderas, Green Moon España, 2014.

Barbour, Dennis H. "Heroism and Redemption in the Mad Max Trilogy." *Journal of Popular Film & Television*, vol. 27, no. 3, 1999, pp. 28–34.

Barkun, Michael. *A Culture of Conspiracy: Apocalyptic Visions in Contemporary America*, University of California Press, 2013.

Baudrillard, Jean. *Simulacra and Simulation*. University of Michigan Press, 1994.

Benjamin, Walter. "The Work of Art in the Age of Mechanical Reproduction." *Modernism: An Anthology*, edited by Lawrence Rainey, John Wiley & Sons, 2005, pp. 1095–1112.

Berger, James. *After the End: Representations of Post-Apocalypse*. University of Minnesota Press, 1999.

Billington, Ray Allen. *America's Frontier Heritage*. University of New Mexico Press, 1974.

Blade Runner 2049. Directed by Denis Villeneuve, performances by Harrison Ford, Robin Wright, and Ryan Gosling, Warner Brothers, 2017.

Blade Runner. Directed by Ridley Scott, performances by Harrison Ford and Sean Young, Warner Brothers, 1982.

Bogachev, Igor. "Council Post: Will Digital Assistants Be Able to Replace Humans Completely?" *Forbes*, 8 July 2021, www.forbes.com/sites/forbestechcouncil/2021/07/08/will-digital-assistants-be-able-to-replace-humans-completely/?sh=3ffdf568a848.

Bourdieu, Pierre. "The Forms of Capital (1986)." *Cultural Theory: An Anthology* (2011): 81–93.

Boyer, Paul. "The Middle East in Modern American Popular Prophetic Belief." *Imagining the End: Visions of Apocalypse from the Ancient Middle East to Modern America*, edited by Abbas Amanat and Magnus Bernhardsson, 2002, pp. 312–25.

Bruno, Giuliana. "Ramble City: Postmodernism and 'Blade Runner,'" *October*, vol. 41, 1987, pp. 61–74.

Buchanan, Bruce G. "A (Very) Brief History of Artificial Intelligence." *AI Magazine*, vol. 26, no. 4, 2005, pp. 53–60.

Buell, Frederick. *From Apocalypse to Way of Life: Environmental Crisis in the American Century*. Routledge, 2003.

Bukatman, Scott. *Terminal Identity: The Virtual Subject in Postmodern Science Fiction*. Duke UP, 1993.

Bullen, Elizabeth, and Elizabeth Parsons. "Dystopian Visions of Global Capitalism: Philip Reeve's Mortal Engines and MT Anderson's Feed." *Children's Literature in Education* 38, no. 2 (2007): 127–39.

Bunch, Charlotte. *Passionate Politics: Feminist Theory in Action*. Macmillan, 1987.

Calia, Michael. "In the Mouth of John Carpenter's Misunderstood Masterpiece." *The Wall Street Journal*, Dow Jones & Company, 5 Dec. 2014, blogs.wsj.com/speakeasy/2014/12/05/in-the-mouth-of-john-carpenters-misunderstood-masterpiece/.

Canby, Vincent. "FILM VIEW." *New York Times*, 10 Nov. 1974, www.nytimes.com/1974/11/10/archives/new-yorks-woes-are-good-box-office-film-view-film-view-new-yorks.html.

Carpenter, Mary Wilson. "Representing Apocalypse: Sexual Politics and the Violence of Revelation." *Postmodern Apocalypse: Theory and Cultural Practice at the End*, edited by Richard Dellamora, 1995, pp. 107–35.

Carter, Paul. *The Road to Botany Bay: An Exploration of Landscape and History*. University of Minnesota Press, 2013.

Chaudhary, Zahid R. "Humanity Adrift: Race, Materiality, and Allegory in Alfonso Cuarón's Children of Men." *Camera Obscura: Feminism, Culture, and Media Studies*, vol. 24, no. 3, 2009, pp. 73–109.

Child, John, Martyn John Whittock, and Nigel Kelly. *The Crusades*, vol. 692, Heinemann, 1992.

Children of Men. Directed by Alfonso Cuaron, performances by Clive Owen and Julianne Moore, Universal Pictures, 2006.

Cloud Atlas. Directed by Lana and Lilly Wachowski, performances by Tom Hanks and Halle Berry, X Filme Creative Pool, 2012.

Cohn, Norman. *The Pursuit of the Millennium: Revolutionary Millenarians and Mystical Anarchists of the Middle Ages*. Oxford UP, 1970.

Collins, Adela Yarbro. "The Early Christian Apocalypses." *Semeia* 14, edited by John Collins, 1979, pp. 61–121.

———. *Crisis and Catharsis: The Power of the Apocalypse*. John Knox Press, 1984.

Collins, John J. "Introduction: Towards a Morphology of a Genre." *Semeia*, vol. 14, edited by John Collins, 1979, pp. 1–20.

———. "The Jewish Apocalypses." *Semeia*, vol. 14, edited by John Collins, 1979, pp. 21–59.

———. "Persian Apocalypses." *Semeia*, vol. 14, edited by John Collins, 1979, pp. 207–17.

Conn, Steven. *Americans Against the City: Anti-Urbanism in the Twentieth Century*. Oxford UP, 2014.

Cornea, Christine. *Science Fiction Cinema*. Edinburgh UP, 2007.

Corrigan, Peter. *The Sociology of Consumption: An Introduction*. Sage, 1997.

De Tocqueville, Alexis. *American Institutions and Their Influence*. AS Barnes, 1873.

DeLillo, Don. *White Noise*. Penguin, 1999.

Desser, David. "Blade Runner: Science Fiction & Transcendence." *Literature/Film Quarterly*, vol. 13, no. 3, 1985, pp. 172–179.

DiMarco, Danette. "Paradise Lost, Paradise Regained: Homo Faber and the Makings of a New Beginning in Oryx and Crake." *Papers on Language and Literature: A Journal for Scholars and Critics of Language and Literature*, vol. 41, no. 2, 2005, pp. 170–195.

d'Souza, Dinesh. *Illiberal Education: The Politics of Race and Sex on Campus*. Simon and Schuster, 1991.

Dyer, Jay. "SCARS & STRIFE: 'The Purge Election Year' Agitprop, Change Agents & False Left–Right Statecraft." *Jay's Analysis*, 12 July 2016, jaysanalysis.com/2016/07/12/scars-strife-the-purge-election-year-agitprop-change-agents-false-left-right-statecraft/.

Dyer, Richard, and Paul McDonald. *Stars*. BFI Pub., 1998.

"'Enemies from Within': Senator Joseph R. McCarthy's Accusations of Disloyalty." *HISTORY MATTERS—The U.S. Survey Course on the Web*, historymatters.gmu.edu/d/6456.

Fiske, John. *Television Culture*. Routledge, 2002.

Frank, Pat. *Alas, Babylon*. Bantam, 1959.

Fuller, Robert C. *Naming the Antichrist: The History of an American Obsession*. Oxford UP, 1996.

Gest, Justin. *The New Minority: White Working Class Politics in an Age of Immigration and Inequality*. Oxford UP, 2016.

Ghidina, Marcia J. "Social Relations and the Definition of Work: Identity Management in a Low-Status Occupation." *Qualitative Sociology* 15, no. 1 (1992): 73–85.

Godkin, Edwin Lawrence. *Problems of Modern Democracy: Political and Economic Essays*. C. Scribner's Sons, 1897.

Gravett, Sharon L. "The Sacred and the Profane: Examining the Religious Subtext of Ridley Scott's "Blade Runner' " *Literature Film Quarterly*, vol. 26, no. 1, 1998, pp. 38–45.

Green, Bernard. *Christianity in Ancient Rome: The First Three Centuries.* A&C Black, 2010.

Grem, Darren E. *The Blessings of Business: How Corporations Shaped Conservative Christianity.* Oxford UP, 2016.

Gunn, James E., and Matthew Candelaria, eds. *Speculations on Speculation: Theories of Science Fiction*. Scarecrow, 2005.

Gurr, Barbara, ed. *Race, Gender, and Sexuality in Post-Apocalyptic TV and Film*. Springer, 2015.

Hagemeister, Michael. "The Third Rome against the Third Temple: Apocalypticism and Conspiracism in Post-Soviet Russia." *Handbook of Conspiracy Theory and Contemporary Religion*. Brill, 2018, pp. 423–42.

Hall, Stuart, and Tony Jefferson. *Resistance through Rituals: Youth Subcultures in Post-War Britain*. Psychology Press, 1993.

Hamming, Jeanne. "The Feminine" Nature" of Masculine Desire in the Age of Cinematic Techno-Transcendence." *Journal of Popular Film and Television* 35, no. 4 (2008): 146–53.

Hawes, Joseph M., and Elizabeth I. Nybakken, eds. *Family and Society in American History*. University of Illinois Press, 2001.

Hebdige, Dick. *Subculture, the Meaning of Style*. Methuen, 1979.

Heffernan, Teresa. "Can the Apocalypse Be Post?" *Postmodern Apocalypse: Theory and Cultural Practice at the End*, edited by Richard Dellamora, 1995, pp. 171–81.

Hidaka, Brandon H. "Depression as a Disease of Modernity: Explanations for Increasing Prevalence." *Journal of Affective Disorders*, vol. 140, no. 3, 2012, pp. 205–14.

Hill, Mike. *After Whiteness: Unmaking an American Majority*. NYU Press, 2004.

Himmelfarb, Martha. *The Apocalypse: A Brief History*. John Wiley & Sons, 2010.

Hoban, Russell. *Riddley Walker*. Bloomsbury, 2012.

Hodgens, Richard. "A Brief, Tragical History of the Science Fiction Film." *FILM QUART*, vol. 13, no. 2, 1959, pp. 30–39.

Hofstadter, Richard. *The Paranoid Style in American Politics, and Other Essays*. Vintage, 2008.

Horkheimer, Max. "Authoritarianism and the Family Today." *The Family: Its Function and Destiny*, edited by Rush Nanda Anshen, vol. 5, Harper, 1949, pp. 359–374.

Hughes, Robert. *The Fatal Shore*. Random House, 2010.

Hurley, Jessica. "Still Writing Backwards: Literature After the End of the World." *Frame*, vol. 26, no. 1, 2013, pp. 61–76.

I Am Mother. Directed by Grant Sputore, performances by Hillary Swank and Clara Rugaard, Southern Light Films, 2019.

Ingraham, Chrys. *White Weddings: Romancing Heterosexuality in Popular Culture*. Routledge, 2009.

Jameson, Fredric. "Cognitive Mapping." *Marxism and the Interpretation of Culture*, edited by Carey Nelson and Lawrence Grossberg, University of Illinois Press, 1988, pp. 347–360.

———. *Archaeologies of the Future: The Desire Called Utopia and other Science Fictions*. Verso, 2005.

———. *Postmodernism, or, the Cultural Logic of Late Capitalism*. Duke UP, 1991.

———. "Progress Versus Utopia; or, Can We Imagine the Future?" *Science Fiction Criticism: An Anthology of Essential Writings*, edited by Rob Latham, Bloomsbury, 2017, pp. 211.

Jones, Robert P. *The End of White Christian America*. Simon and Schuster, 2016.

Kaufmann, Eric P., ed. *Rethinking Ethnicity: Majority Groups and Dominant Minorities*. Routledge, 2004.

Kermode, Frank. *The Sense of an Ending: Studies in the Theory of Fiction: With a New Epilogue*. Oxford UP, 2000.

Khader, Jamil. "The Purge and the Failure of Leftist Politics." *The Philosophical Salon*, 16 May 2021, thephilosophicalsalon.com/purge-failure-leftist-politics/.

Kimmel, Michael. *Angry White Men: American Masculinity at the End of an Era*. Nation Books, 2013.

Kitchin, Robert M. "Cognitive Maps: What Are They and Why Study Them?" *Journal of Environmental Psychology*, vol. 14, no. 1, 1994, pp. 1–19.

Knight, Peter. *Conspiracy Nation: The Politics of Paranoia in Postwar America*. NYU Press, 2002.

Kordas, Ann. "New South, New Immigrants, New Women, New Zombies: The Historical Development of the Zombie in American Popular Culture." *Race, Oppression and the Zombie: Essays on Cross-cultural Appropriations of the Caribbean Tradition*, edited by edited by Christopher M. Moreman and Cory James Rushton, 2011, pp. 15–30.

Kraybill, J. Nelson. *Imperial Cult and Commerce in John's Apocalypse*, vol. 132, A&C Black, 1996.

Kreider, Tim. "A.I.: Artificial Intelligence." *Film Quarterly*, vol. 56, no. 2, 2002, pp. 32–39.

Kroon, Ariel. "Reasonably Insane: Affect and Crake in Margaret Atwood's *Oryx and Crake*." *Canadian Literature*, vol. 226, 2015, pp. 18–33.

Kruse, Kevin. *One Nation Under God: How Corporate America Invented Christian America*. Basic Books, 2016.

Lahr, Angela M. *Millennial Dreams and Apocalyptic Nightmares: The Cold War Origins of Political Evangelicalism*. Oxford UP, 2007.

Lander, Eric S. "Initial Impact of the Sequencing of the Human Genome." *Nature* 470, 2011, pp. 187–197.

LaRose, Nicole. "The Already Dead and the Posthuman Baby: Children of Men, Dystopian Worlds, and Utopian Kinship." *Interdisciplinary Humanities*, vol. 27, 2010, pp. 7–23.

Lavender, Isiah. *Race in American Science Fiction*. Indiana UP, 2011.

Lisboa, Maria Manuel. *The End of the World: Apocalypse and Its Aftermath in Western Culture*. Open Book, 2011.

Lundwall, Sam J. *Science Fiction: What It's All About*. Ace Books, 1971.

Major, Brenda, Alison Blodorn, and Gregory Major Blascovich. "The Threat of Increasing Diversity: Why Many White Americans Support Trump in the 2016 Presidential Election." *Group Processes & Intergroup Relations*, edited by Dominic Abrams and Michael Hogg, 2016, pp. 1–10.

Maland, Charles. "Dr. Strangelove (1964): Nightmare Comedy and the Ideology of Liberal Consensus." *American Quarterly*, vol. 31, no. 5, 1979, pp. 697–717.

Mallon, Ron. "Passing, Traveling and Reality: Social Constructionism and the Metaphysics of Race." *Noûs*, vol. 38, no. 4, 2004, pp. 644–73.

Mandel, Ernest. *Late Capitalism.* Verso Classics, 1999.

Marx, Karl. *Capital: A Critique of Political Economy—The Process of Capitalist Production*. Cosimo, 2007.

Mason, Fran. "A Poor Person's Cognitive Mapping." *Conspiracy Nation: The Politics of Paranoia in Postwar America*, edited by Peter Knight, 2002, pp. 40–56.

Mateos, Pablo, Alex Singleton, and Paul Longley. "Uncertainty in the Analysis of Ethnicity Classifications: Issues of Extent and Aggregation of Ethnic Groups." *Journal of Ethnic and Migration Studies*, vol. 35, no. 9, 2009, pp. 1437–60.

Mathews, Mark D. *Riches, Poverty, and the Faithful: Perspectives on Wealth in the Second Temple Period and the Apocalypse of John*, vol. 154, Cambridge UP, 2013.

Mauss, Marcel. *The Gift: The Form and Reason for Exchange in Archaic Societies*. Routledge, 2002.

McAlister, Elizabeth. "Slaves, Cannibals, and Infected Hyper-Whites: The Race and Religion of Zombies." *Anthropological Quarterly*, vol. 85, no. 2, 2012, pp. 457–486.

McGinn, Bernard. *Antichrist: Two Thousand Years of the Human Fascination with Evil.* Columbia UP, 2000.

McHugh, Susan Bridget. "Horses in Blackface: Visualizing Race as Species Difference in *Planet of the Apes*." *South Atlantic Review*, vol. 65, no. 2, 2000, pp. 40–72.

McNaughtan, Hugh. "Distinctive Consumption and Popular Anti-Consumerism: The case of Wall-E." *Continuum* 26, no. 5 (2012): 753–66.

McNaughtan, Hugh. "Distinctive Consumption And Popular Anti-Consumerism: The Case of Wall*E." *Continuum: Journal of Media & Cultural Studies*, vol. 26, no. 5, 2012, pp. 753–66.

McVeigh, Stephen. *American Western*. Edinburgh UP, 2007.

Merril, Judith. "What Do You Mean: Science? Fiction?" *Science Fiction Criticism: An Anthology of Essential Writings*, edited by Rob Latham, Bloomsbury, 2017, pp. 22–37.

Miller, Walter M., Jr. *A Canticle for Leibowitz*. Hachette UK, 2014. BookFi, http://en.bookfi.net/s/?q=canticle+for+leibowitz&t=0.

Miller, Cynthia J. "Tradition, Parody, and Adaptation: Jed Buell's Unconventional West." *Hollywood's West: The American Frontier in Film, Television, and History*, edited by Peter Rollins and John Connor, 2005, pp. 65–80.

Mitchell, Lee Clark. "Whose West Is It Anyway? Or, What's Myth Got to Do with It? The Role of 'America' in the Creation of the Myth of the West." *American Review of Canadian Studies*, edited by Christina Keppie, vol. 33, no. 4, 2003, pp. 487–96.

Mortal Engines. Directed by Christian Rivers, performances by Hugo Weaving and Robert Sheehan, WingNut Films, 2018.

Mosca, Valeria. "Crossing Human Boundaries: Apocalypse and Posthumanism in Margaret Atwood's *Oryx and Crake* and *The Year of the Flood*." *Altre Modernità*, vol. 9, 2013, pp. 38–52.

Moya, Ana, and Gemma López. "Looking Back: Versions of the Post-Apocalypse in Contemporary North-American Cinema." *Film Criticism*, vol. 41, no. 1, 2017.

Nama, Adilifu. *Black Space: Imagining Race in Science Fiction Film*. University of Texas Press, 2010.

Night of the Comet. Directed by Thom Eberhardt, performances by Catherine Mary Stewart and Kelli Maroney, Thomas Coleman and Michael Rosenblatt Productions, 1984.

Norris, Michele. "As America Changes, Some Anxious Whites Feel Left Behind." *National Geographic*, 12 Mar. 2018, www.nationalgeographic.com/magazine/2018/04/race-rising-anxiety-white-america/.

Oblivion. Directed by Joseph Kosinski, performances by Tom Cruise and Morgan Freeman, Universal Pictures, 2013.

Oldring, Amanda. "The Culture Apocalypse: Hegemony and the Frontier at the End of the World." *Stream: Inspiring Critical Thought*, vol. 5, no. 1, edited by Peter Zuurbier, 2013, pp. 8–20.

Olmsted, Kathryn S. *Challenging the Secret Government: the Post-Watergate Investigations of the CIA and FBI*. Univ of North Carolina Press, 2000.

Otto, Shawn Lawrence. *The War on Science: Who's Waging It, Why It Matters, What We Can Do About It*. Vol. 3. Minneapolis: Milkweed Editions, 2016.

Parker, Jo Alyson. "From Time's Boomerang to Pointillist Mosaic: Translating Cloud Atlas into Film." *SubStance* 44.1 (2015): 123–35.

Pask, Kevin. "Cyborg Economies: Desire and Labor in the Terminator Films." *Postmodern Apocalypse: Theory and Cultural Practice at the End*, edited by Richard Dellamora, 1995, pp. 182–98.

Pimpare, Stephen. *Ghettos, Tramps, and Welfare Queens: Down and Out on the Silver Screen*. Oxford UP, 2017.

Planet of the Apes. Directed by Franklin Schaffner, performance by Charlton Heston, 20th Century Fox, 1968.

Pliny (the Younger.). *Pliny: Letters and Panegyricus*. Harvard UP, 1989.

Popper, Deborah Epstein, Robert E. Lang, and Frank J. Popper. "From Maps to Myth: The Census, Turner, and the Idea of the Frontier." *Journal of American & Comparative Cultures*, vol. 23, no. 1, 2000, pp. 91–102.

Rasmussen, Birgit Brander. "'Attended with Great Inconveniences': Slave Literacy and the 1740 South Carolina Negro Act." *PMLA/Publications of the Modern Language Association of America* 125, no. 1 (2010): 201–203.

Ravi Kumar, J. G. "Masculinity as Power of Socio-Historical Concept in American Frontier." *International Journal of Multidisciplinary Approach & Studies*, vol. 3, no. 4, 2016, pp. 1–10.

Redding, Arthur. "Frontier Mythographies: Savagery and Civilization in Frederick Jackson Turner and John Ford." *Literature Film Quarterly*, vol. 35, no. 4, 2007, pp. 313–22.

Rehling, Nicola. *Extra-Ordinary Men: White Heterosexual Masculinity and Contemporary Popular Cinema*. Lexington Books, 2009.

Renfrew, Colin. "Varna and the Emergence of Wealth in Prehistoric Europe." *The Social Life of Things: Commodities in Cultural Perspective*, edited by Arjun Appadurai, 1986, pp. 141–68.

Rollins, Peter C. and John E. O'Connor, eds. *Hollywood's West: The American Frontier in Film, Television, and History*. University Press of Kentucky, 2005.

Roosevelt, Theodore. "The Founding of the Trans-Alleghany Commonwealths 1784–1790." *The Winning of the West*, vol. 3, GP Putnam's Sons, 1900.

Rosenbaum, Jonathan. "A Matter of Life and Death: *A.I.*" *Film Quarterly*, vol. 65, no. 3, 2012, pp. 74–78.

Rowley, David G. "'Redeemer Empire': Russian Millenarianism." *The American Historical Review* vol. 104, no. 5 (1999): 1582–1602.

Sani, Shehu. *Hatred for Black People*. Xlibris Corporation, 2013.

Schneider, William. "About that Cowboy Rhetoric. . . ." *The Atlantic*, January 2005.

Schor, Juliet B. *Born to Buy: The Commercialized Child and the New Consumer Cult*. Simon and Schuster, 2014. *Google Books*, https://books.google.com/books?id=5VMCBAAAQBAJ&printsec=frontcover&dq=Born+to+buy:+The+commercialized+child+and+the+new+consumer+cult&hl=en&sa=X&ved=0ahUKEwizrNWD0IPcAhXOtFMKHVI8DdUQ6AEIKTAA#v=onepage&q=Born%20to%20buy%3A%20The%20commercialized%20child%20and%20the%20new%20consumer%20cult&f=false

Scott, Ellen. "Agony and Avoidance: Pixar, Deniability, and the Adult Spectator." *Journal of Popular Film and Television* 42, no. 3 (2014): 150–62.

Sharp, Patrick B. *Savage Perils: Racial Frontiers and Nuclear Apocalypse in American Culture*. University of Oklahoma Press, 2007.

Shklovsky, Victor. "Art as technique [1917]." *The Critical Tradition: Classic Texts and Contemporary Trends, New York*, edited by David Richter, 2007, pp. 774–784.

Slotkin, Richard. *Gunfighter Nation: The Myth of the Frontier in Twentieth-Century America*. University of Oklahoma Press, 1992.
Smith, Candace. "Some White Trump Supporters Fear Becoming Minority." *ABC News*. ABC News Network, 2 Nov. 2016. Web. 25 June 2017.
Smith, David Livingstone. *Less Than Human: Why We Demean, Enslave, and Exterminate Others*. St. Martin's Press, 2011.
Sobchack, Vivian Carol. *Screening Space: The American Science Fiction Film*. Rutgers UP, 1987.
Sontag, Susan. "The Imagination of Disaster." *October* 1965, pp. 42–48.
Srnicek, Nick, and Alex Williams. *Inventing the future: Postcapitalism and a World Without Work*. Verso Books, 2015.
Stalker. Directed by Andrei Tarkovsky, performances by Aleksandr Kaydanovskiy and Anatoliy Solonitsyn, 1979.
Stewart, George Rippey. *Earth Abides*. Random House Digital, Inc., 2006.
Strengers, Yolande, and Jenny Kennedy. *The Smart Wife: Why Siri, Alexa, and Other Smart Home Devices Need a Feminist Reboot*. MIT Press, 2020.
Sweeting, Helen, Kate Hunt, and Abita Bhaskar. "Consumerism and Well-being in Early Adolescence." *Journal of Youth Studies*, vol. 15, no. 6, 2012, pp. 802–20.
Terzopoulos, George, and Maya Satratzemi. "Voice Assistants and Smart Speakers in Everyday Life and in Education." *Informatics in Education* 19.3 (2020): 473–90.
The Book of Eli. Directed by Albert Hughes, performances by Denzel Washington and Mila Kunis, Warner Home Video, 2010.
The Day after Tomorrow. Directed by Roland Emmerich, performances by Jake Gyllenhaal and Dennis Quaid, 20th Century Fox, 2004.
The New Oxford Annotated Bible. Edited by Michael D. Coogan, Oxford University Press, 2007.
The Omega Man. Directed by Boris Sagal, performance by Charlton Heston, Warner Brothers, 1971.
The Postman. Directed by Kevin Costner, performance by Kevin Costner, Warner Home Video, 1997.
The Road Warrior. Directed by George Miller, performance by Mel Gibson, Warner Home Video, 1981.
The Sibylline Oracles: Translated from the Greek Into English Blank Verse. Translated by Milton Terry, Hunt & Eaton, 1890.
The Ultimate Warrior. Directed by Robert Clouse, performances by Yul Brynner and Max Von Sydow, Warner Bros., 1975.
Thompson, Leonard L. *The Book of Revelation: Apocalypse and Empire*. Oxford UP, 1997.
Throsby, David, and C. D. Throsby. *Economics and Culture*. Cambridge UP, 2001.
Tietge, David J. "Priest, Professor, or Prophet: Discursive and Ethical Intersections in *A Canticle for Leibowitz*." *Journal of Popular Culture*, vol. 41, no. 4, 2008, pp. 676–94.

Tolman, Edward C. "Cognitive Maps in Rats and Men." *Psychological Review*, vol. 55, no. 4, 1948, pp. 189–208.

Torry, Robert. "Apocalypse Then: Benefits of the Bomb in Fifties Science Fiction Films." *Cinema Journal*, vol. 31, no. 1, 1991, pp. 7–21.

"Tracing the Rise of ISIS Into a Menace of Terror." *NBCNews.com*, NBCUniversal News Group, 11 June 2015, www.nbcnews.com/storyline/isis-terror/tracing-rise-isis-menace-terror-n214266.

Trentmann, Frank. *Empire of Things: How We Became a World of Consumers, from the Fifteenth Century to the Twenty-First*. Penguin UK, 2016.

Trombley, Frank. "Overview: The Geographical Spread of Christianity." *The Cambridge History of Christianity v. 1: Origins to Constantine*, edited by Margaret Mitchell and Frances Young, 2006, pp. 302–13.

Turner, Frederick Jackson. "The Significance of the Frontier in American History." *The Norton Anthology of American Literature: Package 2:1865 to the Present*, edited by Nina Baym, 9th ed., W.W. Norton, 2007, pp. 21–37.

Van Dijk, Teun A. "Ideologies, Racism, Discourse: Debates on Immigration and Ethnic Issues." *Comparative Perspectives on Racism*. Routledge, 2019, 91–115.

Walker, Jesse. *The United States of Paranoia: A Conspiracy Theory*. Harper Collins, 2014. *Library Genesis*, http://library1.org/_ads/5BD8E4D2D2A8F8671910737BC211596C

Walker, Seth M. "'It's Not a Fucking Book, It's a Weapon!': Authority, Power, and Mediation in *The Book Of Eli*." *Journal of Religion & Film*, vol. 20, no. 3, 2016, pp. 1–27.

WALL-E. Directed by Andrew Stanton, performances by Fred Willard and John Ratzenberger, Pixar Animation Studios, 2008.

Waytz, Adam, Kelly Marie Hoffman, and Sophie Trawalter. "A Superhumanization Bias in Whites' Perceptions of Blacks." *Social Psychological and Personality Science*, vol. 6, no. 3, 2015, pp. 352–59.

Welch, Michael. *Scapegoats of September 11th: Hate Crimes & State Crimes in the War on Terror*. Rutgers UP, 2006.

Whalen, Brett Edward. *Dominion of God: Christendom and Apocalypse in the Middle Ages*. Harvard UP, 2010.

Whyte, William. *Atrocities, Massacres, and War Crimes: An Encyclopedia [2 Volumes]: An Encyclopedia*, edited by Alexander Mikaberidze, AbC-CLIo, 2013.

Wicks, Amanda Ashleigh. *The Imagined After: Re-Positioning Social Memory through Twentieth-Century Post-Apocalyptic Literature and Film*. 2014. Louisiana State University, PhD dissertation.

Williams, Paul. "Beyond 'Mad Max III': Race, Empire, and Heroism on Post-Apocalyptic Terrain." *Science Fiction Studies*, vol. 32, no. 2, 2005, pp. 301–15.

Williams, Tony. "From Elvis to LA: Reflections on the Carpenter-Russell Films." *The Cinema of John Carpenter: The Technique of Terror*, edited by Ian Conrich and David Woods, 2004, pp. 118–27.

Willman, Skip. "Spinning Paranoia: The Ideologies of Conspiracy and Contingency in Postmodern Culture." *Conspiracy Nation: The Politics of Paranoia in Postwar America*, edited by Peter Knight, 2002, pp. 21–39.

Wintle, Heather. "'Everything Depends on Reaching the Coast': Intergenerational Coastward Journeys in Contemporary Post-Apocalyptic Cinema." *Continuum*, vol. 27, no. 5, 2013, pp. 676–89.

Wood, Robin. "American Nightmare: Horror in the 70s." *Horror, The Film Reader*, edited by Mark Jancovich, Routledge, 2002, pp. 25–32.

Index

www.ingramcontent.com/pod-product-compliance
Lightning Source LLC
LaVergne TN
LVHW050153080826
844660LV00002B/190

* 9 7 8 1 4 3 8 4 8 9 4 3 8 *